continued . . .

"Ramsland tracks killers throughout history. She discusses the social implications behind the killings as well as the forensic challenges and responses to the killers. [She] discusses, with research to back up her positions, the reasons why such killers exist, [and] the forces which contribute to their creation . . . A very informative book . . . A good resource for writers looking to understand the mind-set of serial killers." —ReviewingTheEvidence.com

FURTHER PRAISE FOR THE WORKS OF

Katherine Ramsland

The Unknown Darkness: Profiling the Predators Among Us
Coauthored with Gregg O. McCrary

"This is a must-read for true crime fans. A beautifully written expert analysis of high-profile killers." —Ann Rule

"One of the most intensely readable and gripping accounts of serial murder I have ever read."
—Colin Wilson, author of *Manhunt: A Study in Detection: Tracking Serial Killers*

"Combines engrossing writing with seasoned insight."
—*Publishers Weekly*

"Many of us may think we know quite a lot about FBI profilers, but . . . our knowledge comes almost entirely from fictionalized portrayals in films like *Silence of the Lambs* and television series like *Profiler*. The truth . . . is rather different from fiction . . . [*The Human Predator* is] surprisingly lively and will captivate true crime fans with a yen to know more about profiling and related investigative practices."

—*Booklist*

"A must-read for those who are interested in the investigative and forensic aspects of major murder cases. Ramsland's experience with the techniques of narrative nonfiction helps to set this book apart by taking readers right into the crimes and crime scenes so they can experience a profiler's feelings and perceptions, and also see the actual steps taken to make crucial crime-solving decisions. This is a book to buy."

— *truTV Crime Library*

The Forensic Science of C.S.I.

"Fascinating . . . [A] must for anyone who wonders how the real crime solvers do it."   —Michael Palmer

"With the mind of a true investigator, Ramsland demystifies the world of forensics with authentic and vivid detail."

—John Douglas

Piercing the Darkness: Undercover with Vampires in America Today

"[A] riveting read, a model of engaged journalism."

—*Publishers Weekly*

THE HUMAN PREDATOR

A Historical Chronicle of Serial Murder
and Forensic Investigation

KATHERINE RAMSLAND, PH.D.

BERKLEY BOOKS, NEW YORK

THE BERKLEY PUBLISHING GROUP
Published by the Penguin Group
Penguin Group (USA) Inc.
375 Hudson Street, New York, New York 10014, USA

Penguin Group (Canada), 90 Eglinton Avenue East, Suite 700, Toronto, Ontario M4P 2Y3, Canada
(a division of Pearson Penguin Canada Inc.) • Penguin Books Ltd., 80 Strand, London WC2R 0RL,
England • Penguin Ireland, 25 St. Stephen's Green, Dublin 2, Ireland (a division of Penguin
Books Ltd.) • Penguin Group (Australia), 707 Collins Street, Melbourne, Victoria 3008, Australia
(a division of Pearson Australia Group Pty. Ltd.) • Penguin Books India Pvt. Ltd., 11 Community
Centre, Panchsheel Park, New Delhi—110 017, India • Penguin Group (NZ), 67 Apollo Drive,
Rosedale, Auckland 0632, New Zealand (a division of Pearson New Zealand Ltd.) • Penguin
Books (South Africa), Rosebank Office Park, 181 Jan Smuts Avenue, Parktown North 2193,
South Africa • Penguin China, B7 Jiaming Center, 27 East Third Ring Road North,
Chaoyang District, Beijing 100020, China

Penguin Books Ltd., Registered Offices: 80 Strand, London WC2R 0RL, England

The publisher does not have any control over and does not assume any
responsibility for authors or third-party websites or their content.

THE HUMAN PREDATOR

A Berkley Book / published by arrangement with the author

PUBLISHING HISTORY
Berkley hardover edition / October 2005
Berkley trade paperback edition / March 2007
Berkley premium edition / February 2013

ISBN: 978-0-425-26553-6

BERKLEY®
Berkley Books are published by The Berkley Publishing Group,
a division of Penguin Group (USA) Inc.,
375 Hudson Street, New York, New York 10014.
BERKLEY® is a registered trademark of Penguin Group (USA) Inc.
The "B" design is a trademark of Penguin Group (USA) Inc.

PRINTED IN THE UNITED STATES OF AMERICA

10 9 8 7 6 5 4 3 2 1

Most Berkley Books are available at special quantity discounts for bulk
purchases for sales, promotions, premiums, fund-raising, or educational use.
Special books, or book excerpts, can also be created to fit specific needs.

For details, write: Special Markets, The Berkley Publishing Group,
375 Hudson Street, New York, New York 10014.

This book is dedicated with boundless affection
to my literary agent, John Silbersack.
Not only did we envision it synchronistically
over one of our stimulating lunches,
but since the start of my writing career,
John has been my advocate and good friend.
I owe him a lot.

Contents

Acknowledgments

In many ways, this book has been more a product of my own reclusive work than any before it, and yet it is also the result of years of interaction with many people, as well as opportunities to research and write about individual cases of serial killers. I'm sure I can't name everyone who should be acknowledged, but among those with whom I discussed portions of this book and received productive feedback are:

Kim Lionetti, my former Berkley editor, who's had a continuing "conversation" with me about everything forensic; Marilyn Bardsley, my editor and friend at Crime Library, who has always encouraged me to write about as many serial killers as I can name; Ruth Osborne, who's always there to listen to me describe what I'm writing, no matter how gruesome (and Doug Osborne, for his patience); Dana DeVito, my coroner sister, who helps me to be even more gruesome; John Timpane, editor and friend, who has encouraged me every step of the way and provided some material that was difficult to find; Scott Paul, who invited me to consider the deeper personal consequences of ideas that emerged from political developments across the ages, and who let me talk even when he couldn't abide one more story about a serial killer; Gregg McCrary, who taught me so much about profiling and with whom I've had the most insightful and detailed conversations about this subject—

I'm also grateful to have had him as a sounding board for my ideas along the way; John Douglas, who gave me my first opportunity to learn from a profiler up close; Roy Hazelwood, who was able to answer so many of my questions because of his great expertise as a profiler and investigator; Robert Ressler, who was only too happy to discuss any of his cases and to offer much more than I even thought of; Robert Hare, whose work I deeply respect and who provided me with great resources for understanding psychopaths; Mark Hilts, current unit chief of the BAU, who made important corrections and explained how the profilers operate today; Richard Noll, who discussed psychiatric history with me; George Perovich, who pushed me into private practice and who shows such respect for my interest in psychopaths; Barbara Johnston, who sent me articles about serial killers whenever she saw them, and who never discouraged me from my "dark interests" as I grew up—or, at least, not that I remember; my student interns, Jamie DiPasquo and Trisha Dashner, both of whom worked on some of the stories with me and provided research support, and Rachel Kuter, who explored with me the cases of multiple personality disorder in the courtroom; Karen Pepper, who proofed the manuscript and whose enthusiasm matched my own; Karen Walton, who always reads my books, even when they scare her; the students at P.S. 300 who took my course on serial killers, and who indulged my constant forays into cases that grabbed my attention; the serial killer, who will remain unnamed, who first inspired me to become interested in this field of research; Ginjer Buchanan, my editor at Berkley, for her patience and encouragement.

A Brief Overview
of the Serial Killer

During the early 1400s, people ventured through a certain coastal area of southwestern Scotland with great trepidation. For over two decades, rumors featured tales of travelers who simply never came back. Occasionally a decomposing arm or foot might wash ashore, even an odd lump of flesh. While some area residents whispered about demons, the more practical villagers identified the problem as a roaming pack of wolves. When King John I of England (and IV of Scotland) heard the tales, he sent soldiers to investigate. The unfortunate result was that acquaintances of the missing were summarily hanged. But travelers continued to disappear.

One day, a band of thirty passed through the perilous area on their way home from a fair. From a distance they saw a man with a sword desperately defending himself against a pack of strange creatures. As they drew closer, they saw the attackers rip limbs from a bloodied corpse lying nearby and stuff raw pieces into their mouths. More astonishing still was that fact that these creatures were human.

The fair-goers drove off the pack. For the first time, someone—a man—had survived to describe the horrific experience. And what a tale it was—a depiction of savages more disturbing than anyone had imagined, with the dismembered corpse of the man's wife to prove it. Word reached the king, who sent troops with packs of dogs to track these feral marauders like the animals they were. As his soldiers searched the woods and coastline, they discovered the mouth of a cave at the bottom of a cliff, inaccessible during high tide. Growling and barking, the dogs picked up a scent. Something was *in* there. With trepidation, the king's party lit torches to follow the cave's twisting route, but after traversing a mile, they believed they'd made a mistake. It seemed to them that no one could live this deep underground—but then the smell of death from deeper inside suggested that they were on the right track.

The searchers soon encountered a pack of human mongrels in shredded clothing, both male and female, of all ages. Around them were skulls and bones, and overhead on hooks were drying dismembered limbs that turned out to be human. This spectacle sickened the soldiers, but they herded the group back to Edinburgh. The cannibals were Sawney Beane and his common-law wife, their fourteen children, and their thirty-two incest-spawned grandchildren. A quarter century earlier, Beane had moved into this cave and raised his family here. He'd fed them on his plunder from people he robbed and killed on the road, but when money became spare he'd turned to the meat he could get off his victims' bones. Unthinkably, these children and grandchildren had grown up on human flesh.

Because they were much like wild beasts, King John announced, there was no need for a trial. Between torturous dismemberment for the men and bonfires for the women, the entire clan was quickly wiped out. By the time the investigation was finished, it was concluded that this savage family was responsible for several hundred murders. Some reports put the number at over a thousand.

Or so the story goes. Many historians today dispute it as a myth, citing sparse documentation from those days and the manner in which bloodthirsty legends are generally exaggerated. It's a good story, to be sure, but could it possibly be true?

In a way, the answer doesn't matter, because we do have true accounts of people who killed hundreds, murdered for gain, or consumed the flesh of their victims. Readers will meet them in these pages. Pattern murderers have moved among us for as long as greed, lust, exploitation, and the need for aberrant arousal have been part of the human condition. Some eras even supported such deeds, but no matter when or where serial murderers may have started their cycles of killing, they all have this in common: Their actions derive from a complex interplay among three basic factors—specific cultural conditions, individual processing of those conditions, and opportunity. While these factors have always been present, increased global interaction and heightened conflict have inflated the first component remarkably, which has in turn influenced the second factor and its role in the exploitation of the third. Rather than spell out these factors more specifically here, I will show readers how our understanding of serial violence has been developed and refined over the centuries. There were times when we thought we had the answers about why they kill but did not, and we still may not even today, though we're probably fairly close.

This book is essentially a history of the world, highlighting conditions associated with serial killers. While it's impossible to cover all known incidents of serial murder (or all historical events) in a book this size, I selected key cases from different historical periods and cultures to demonstrate that we can gain fruitful insights from comparing diverse collective attitudes and conventions that may have influenced a killer's development. (I actually attempted to include more than four hundred cases, but the effect was encyclopedic rather than narrative, so I dropped many in preference for detail on key stories and better flow. Besides, after the 1980s, the activities of serial killers tended to get repetitive.) Placing serial killers from previous eras in a continuous narrative with their counterparts today offers a startling perspective, both on them and us.

Killers absorb a given culture's emotional nexus, and because they have low impulse inhibition, they are more apt to act out the nuances of covert dynamics, and the resulting arousal they feel keeps them going. The excitement of evil, greed, or need plays out physiologically, urging them to behave in those ways that most satisfy them.

This book studies how science and psychology weave through the history of episodic murder in a tri-stranded braid that offers direction for getting at the heart of this violent phenomenon.

Contrary to what many people believe, serial killing did not begin with Jack the Ripper in 1888. Even outright sexually compulsive serial killing did not start with Red Jack. In fact, in the context of serial murder, while Jack may be famous for his frenzied brutality and ability to evade detection, others from history outshone him in viciousness, grotesque appetite, victim count, cleverness, and sexual compulsion. Even women.

For example, there's a story, most likely a myth, that in the early seventeenth century, Queen Zingua of Angola in Africa declared a law of "vulgivaguability," which meant that on pain of death women were to make themselves available at all times for sex. She drew out her own sexual pleasure by offering the "honor" to each of her lovers of being executed as soon as she finished with them. At the very least, she represents remorseless killers who held positions at times and in places that allowed them to exercise their blood lust as an extension of royal privilege. Even as a fanciful tale, the form this one takes demonstrates the influence on some minds of a powerful position with no accountability. We'll see others like her in this book, both male and female. This queen is unlike Ted Bundy, Jeffrey Dahmer, or John Wayne Gacy. She doesn't even resemble female killer Aileen Wuornos. Yet she can be considered a serial killer in her desires, modus operandi, and attitude toward those she killed, and had she tried these same things in another country at another time, she would have been arrested and possibly executed—as was a twentieth-century woman in Mexico, Sara Maria Aldrete, who also required human sacrifice for her gratification.

Before we begin our study, let's clarify what we mean by "serial killer." The phrase was first used as a chapter title in Richard Hughes' book, *The Complete Detective*, published in 1950, and then during the 1960s in Britain to refer to "series crimes," or those crimes that were repeated by the same offender(s). A true crime writer used the term "serial murderer" in a 1966 book, a psychologist employed it in the mid-1970s, and around this time FBI Special Agent Robert Ressler reportedly overheard it and used it to describe the kinds of crimes he and his colleagues were evaluating as part of the Behavioral Science Unit (now the Behavioral Analysis Unit). "It wasn't from a specific case," he recalls. "It just became evident that I was dealing with a lot of cases that were repetitive. The media was calling all of this mass murder without any differentiation, and I and my colleagues became aware of the fact that this was too general."

According to the FBI's *Crime Classification Manual*, which many law enforcement agencies acknowledge as authoritative, there are three basic categories of multiple murder: mass, spree, and serial. The first involves a single extreme incident and the other two multiple incidents, but with different manifestations. Yet because classifications of human behavior are never clear-cut, some spree murderers are cast as mass murderers and some as serial murderers. Let's see how.

In strict terms, mass murder is the killing of a number of persons at one time and in one place, such as James Huberty's 1984 fatal shooting of twenty-one people at a McDonald's restaurant in San Ysidro, California. However, mass murder has also included cases where the killings were a few hours apart, or at different locales. In 1987 in Hungerford, England, Michael Ryan shot thirty people one afternoon along a two-mile walk (sixteen died). Yet if the same precipitating incident is linked to all the killings, offenders who take days or weeks to commit their murders are more aptly called spree killers. The serial killer, too, may commit multiple murders across several weeks, but is said to have a hiatus, or psychological "cooling off" period, between murders.

The distinction between a long spree and a series of murders attributed to a serial killer seems to rest heavily on method and motive. Serial killing is most often either a profitable crime, a crime for thrill and self-gratification, or a lust-driven crime where the killer may operate compulsively within an erotic ritual. Occasionally, it's about revenge, which might be included in the "thrill" category. In many cases, the killer is relieving pressure, either sexual or from some other type of need, and generally does not desire to be stopped or caught. Once the deed is done, the need subsides. In all likelihood, such killers cannot stop, although they may have a period of dormancy that can last years. Some have been psychotic, many were psychopathic, and others responded to a set of circumstances in such a way that killing became a habit or an easy way to achieve what they desired.

Yet even the term, "serial killer," suffers from conceptual confusion. Until 2005, when it was changed, the FBI's official manual indicated that to be thus classified, there must have been at least three different murder events at three different locations, with a cooling-off period between events, but the National Institute of Justice (NIJ) requires only two, and also acknowledges the idea of team serial killers. The FBI required different locations, but some killers murder their victims in the same place at different times. The NIJ's definition indicates that the motive is often psychological and that the behavior at the crime scene will show sexual overtones. While that's a common notion, it's too restrictive. Not all serial killing is sexually motivated. In addition, prominent criminologists have offered other definitions, and the many textbooks published on the subject demonstrate significant conflicts, from those experts who believe that serial killing is only a sexual compulsion and restricted to males to those who allow for more diverse motives in the context of repetitive crimes. I tend to accept the latter approach. To achieve clarity for my purpose, I define the terms thus:

1. Mass murder is a concentrated reaction to a single event or ideation, with at least four murders taking place in one basic locale, even if the killer travels to several loosely related spots in that area;

2. A spree is a string of murders or attempted murders related to a key precipitating incident but fueled by continuing and identifiable stress, that takes place in several locales, and that occurs across a relatively short period of time, no longer than a few months;

3. A serial killer murders at least two people in distinctly separate incidents, with a psychological rest period between, which could be considered a time of predatory preparation. He, she, or they also choose the murder activity, such as stabbing, strangulation, shooting, or bombing, and may either move around to different places or lure successive victims to a single locale. They view victims as objects needed for their ultimate goals, and manifest an addictive quality to their behavior, so that choosing murder is a satisfying act rather than merely a reaction or instrumental goal.

Not included are executions within a political regime, murder as terrorism, gangster hits, or acts of war, even if those acts are repetitive. Someone like Hitler or the Nazi henchmen are not part of this study, aside from their historical significance. Nor do I cover people sent on military, cult-inspired, or religious missions who killed repeatedly in the name of some ideal. When it's not clear whether a series of incidents would be considered "serial," and when that series has some historical impact, details are provided.

A history book that highlights serial killers must also note developments in law enforcement, investigation, and criminology in detecting and stopping offenders. History itself dictated these developments, with science becoming a valued occupation and certain techniques being discoverable only after the sixteenth century. Prior to that, politics and religion determined the nature of the beast, so to speak.

While the FBI responded in the 1970s and 1980s to the rising trends in serial crimes by establishing the National Center for the Analysis of Violent Crime, with its famed Behavioral Science Unit of criminal profilers, they know that even with their vast resources, predictive interpretations must nevertheless be flexible. At any given time, a serial killer could be or do something entirely unexpected, derailing carefully crafted analyses. Anomalies are consistent with human nature. Any investigative method must reflect this.

Distinct historical periods have framed the phenomenon of serial murder differently from one another, so laying out cases chronologically, with the inclusion of major historical incidents and dominant value structures, shows just how the behavior of these offenders reflects social and cultural dynamics. Many absorb a culture's pathology, creating an association that becomes a feedback loop between their individual modes of processing and the context in which they act that encourages more of the same behavior. Examining the various patterns gives us a way to understand serial killers in the context of their times and to suggest reasons why they may proliferate in one culture as opposed to another. The murdering heart is fed from several domains spanning physiology, psychology, and sociology, but it has taken specific scientific developments and investigative techniques to comprehend that fact. We'll begin with the most primitive ideas and responses and end with what we believe we know today. In between, we'll see the astonishing range of behaviors that links one serial killer to another.

Note: Sometimes a person suspected in a series of murders is prosecuted for and/or convicted of only one murder. Such people may then not be appropriately labeled as serial killers. Yet they may still be named in this text because of their historical association with the series (and, sometimes, their offers of confessions that were later recanted). In addition, in some cases a trial is still pending, but a suspect has been named in the press, so I include those reports.

CHAPTER ONE

The Darkest Ages:
The License of Privilege

Early Predators

The story of serial killing is a form of cultural narrative. It is as much about our collective self as tales of invention, war, and enterprise, because how we interpret given events reveals our social values. Even as some people accelerate cultural progress, others manifest a culture's pathogens, and both behaviors arise organically from the whole.

While it's likely that serial killers have always operated within human society, their notable manifestations in documented history have depended on the function they served in the social milieu. In other words, only certain stories made headlines. Some predators have exploited specific social conditions to seek out victims, and a number of cultural periods have even set up the conditions that encouraged serial violence. As history has unfolded, the modes of social tension specific to cultural and world events have influenced the increasing numbers of offenders who have killed episodically for their own gratification. Our first clear case occurred in Ancient Rome.

As humankind evolved beyond primitive conditions with at least the veneer of imposed order, homicide came to be included among those activities viewed with increasingly less tolerance. Warfare was one thing, but outright murder quite another. Still, with no computers to track them and no forensic techniques to prove anything, it wasn't difficult for clever people to get away with homicide—especially bloodthirsty members of society's aristocratic classes. In fact, in some cultures murder became something of an art form, and those who enjoyed doing it indulged often enough and with sufficiently predatory motives to be called serial killers by today's standards. While civilizations were forming around the world in ancient times, those that had the most influence on the evolving methods of documentation, capture, and disposition of serial killers were Greece and Rome.

The Greeks were mental achievers, pioneering medicine, mathematics, scientific thinking, legal structures, and philosophy. Free of enslavement or harsh rule, they encouraged the development of reason for tackling problems and enhancing resources. Socrates, Plato, and Aristotle showed the value of disciplined thinking in the realm of ideas, and specifically in understanding the nature of goodness, the divine state of one's soul, and the best course to achieve a life worth living. Gods were conceived of as ideal forms of men—a notion not lost on many contemporary serial killers.

As Greece fell to conquerors during the fourth century B.C. and Alexander the Great spread his empire across Asia to the east, Rome gained strength in Italy. Across several centuries, this empire grew to rule the world from Spain to Syria, from Egypt to Britain, passing along its law, alphabet, ideas, and language. There, amid rulers both noble and degenerate (but not including those Caesars who used murder as a form of entertainment), a type of serial killer was secretly indulged: predators who served the needs of the aristocrats.

The Republic and Empire of Rome endured from roughly 753 B.C., with the founding of Rome, until the final collapse of the Roman Empire in A.D. 1453, and during that time it was considered an organizationally cohesive world, although its true power waned around A.D. 503. Military garrisons were stationed across the empire to keep order and new roads linked far-flung provinces with Rome. The empire was ruled by common principles of law and conduct, with the knowledge that the authority of Rome would crush any who threatened it. Rome's powerful army was an intimidating force, and its soldiers moved out with a ruthless imperative to bring other lands under Rome's dominion.

In contrast to the intellectual creativity of the Greeks, the Romans valued functional ideals such as military organization and engineering. Rome's politicians prized a republic over a monarchy, so leadership was shared by a council of elders, the Senate, and citizens were granted certain rights.

During the middle stretch of this impressive reign

(which eventually devolved into decadence and cruelty), a few decades after the death of Christ, the notion of forensics was born. In 54 B.C., Julius Caesar effectively terminated the republic by becoming sole ruler of the Roman world. He tried to bring about reforms that would take from the wealthy to ease the burden on the poor, and for that, among other reasons, he was assassinated in 44 B.C. by a group of senators. The first known application of medical expertise to determine the cause and manner of death in a legal arena occurred when Roman physician Antistius announced which of the twenty-three stab wounds inflicted on Caesar had actually killed him. He declared this to the governing body, and in *Corpse*, Jessica Snyder Sachs points out that this is the origin of the word "forensic"—"before the forum."

Just over a century after Caesar's murder, we have the first documented serial killer, a woman, and it's likely that Julius Caesar and his power-hungry successor inspired her methods. Caesar had pronounced himself a god with absolute power. Upon his demise, his nephew, Octavian, took over as "chief citizen." After a war with Mark Antony in the east, Octavian acquired the title of Augustus and took over the offices of all the republican institutions. Yet while peace reigned from the Atlantic to the Persian Gulf, thanks to the social structure fatal intrigues among the powerful were in full force.

In Rome, the privilege of ruling was passed down through families, and the *patres* had legal, economic, and political privileges that the common *plebs* did not. Even when plebeian assemblies became part of the establishment, a class hierarchy remained. Not until A.D. 212 did all freeborn males acquire citizenship. Among the patricians, an aristocracy arose from the most ancient clans, with exclusive privileges that set them apart. Blood relations were honored above all else and patrons rewarded support in the assemblies with money or land. Roman law, tested and refined at this time, resulted in the science of jurisprudence, and orators such as Cicero clarified the rational principles that served as a legal base.

Following the reign of Augustus, who had established Rome as the hub of the civilized world, a string of successive dictators took charge, many of whom were unstable and corrupt. Historian Norman Davies noted the deleterious effects: "Societies, it has been said, rot from the head down, like dead fish. Certainly the list of early emperors contains more than its share of degenerates." From A.D. 14 until 41, Tiberius and Caligula fully indulged their perversities, and then Claudius took over. It was during his reign that Locusta and her crew of poisoners exploited the system of patronage.

Locusta, noted by many criminologists as the first documented serial killer, was born in Gaul, an outer province of Rome now known as France. Apparently, she was trained in the herbal arts, and did not have to work hard to find herself in demand in Rome as a "necro-entrepreneur." During that time of greed, rivalry, and hunger for status, many people sought the services of someone who could dispense poisons that made a death appear natural, so Locusta soon came to the attention of the wealthy. They paid her for her "remedies" and rewarded her with increased social status. While she erred at times and was arrested, her patrons always found ways to free her and keep her in circulation.

Eventually she landed an exalted assignment. The Empress Agrippina the Younger, fourth wife (and niece) of Emperor Claudius, had a son, Nero, from a prior marriage. She was determined that he, rather than Claudius's son, Britannicus, should become Rome's next emperor. At that time in 54 A.D., Claudius had been in power for thirteen years, following the assassination of the despotic Caligula. He wasn't going anywhere, but a woman like Agrippina was not content to wait. She wanted her son to assume command as soon as possible, but it wouldn't be easy.

The age-old weapon of choice in Rome was poison, dating to at least the fourth century B.C., and poisoning someone over a meal was not uncommon. Agrippina knew that Claudius loved mushrooms, so poison could be administered, but there was a problem. Claudius not only employed food and wine tasters to ensure the purity of his nutritional intake (he knew the dangers of being emperor), but he also had a habit of vomiting up what he ate; therefore, a poison would not have ample time to act. In desperation, Agrippina enlisted the famed Locusta to help.

As legend has it, Locusta was not only skilled, but cagey. At banquets, she noticed how Claudius liked to eat and purge so he could eat more, and saw that he accomplished this by tickling his throat with a feather. So she laced his dish with the deadly mushroom "death cap," *Amanita phalloides,* and for good measure added poison to the feather. One way or another, the toxin would enter his system. Agrippina managed to deflect the official food taster, and then she herself gave him the poisoned mushrooms.

When symptoms of poisoning appeared and Claudius wanted to purge, Agrippina gave him the fatal feather. When his distress continued, he called on Xenophon, his personal physician, for a purgative, but Xenophon was partial to Agrippina, so when he gave Claudius an enema, he injected some toxic colocynth. Poisoned from both ends, on October 13, Claudius succumbed to a tortured death.

Nero, then sixteen, was named emperor, and Locusta was arrested and put into prison. But Nero had his own plans for her, so he sprang her and put her to work. Having already acclimated himself to murder by stabbing men in the streets for fun, he wasted no time using the female assassin to dispose of his fourteen-year-old rival, Britannicus. This time, Locusta used a different method. The custom in Rome was to drink wine diluted with hot water, and when Britannicus complained that his drink was too hot, the tasters added cold water that Locusta had poisoned. The boy was soon dispatched.

Locusta now had a royal protector, himself a deviant torturer, who offered her a full pardon for her series of poisonings over the years and kept her as his consultant on poisons. She also acquired more business among the aristocracy, with no fear of being arrested, and opened a school in which she taught others how to poison. Nero even allowed her to experiment on condemned criminals. While she had five known victims, it's likely that she actually had many more. (Nero had his own legacy of murder: his mother, his aunt, and his first and second wives. He considered himself an artist.)

Eventually, in A.D. 68, the Roman Senate, under the new emperor, Galba, condemned Nero to death. Locusta reportedly slipped him some poison, but he killed himself instead with a dagger. Then his enemies closed in on the contract killer. It was an age in which entertainment consisted of gladiatorial combat and the use of animals for committing obscene sexual acts and for ripping people apart. In a supposedly public spectacle, Galba had Locusta raped by a wild animal (some sources say a giraffe) trained for just this sort of punishment. (The victim was usually smeared with the vaginal juices of the female of the species to provoke the male into bestiality.) Then Galba ordered that she be torn apart. Not long afterward, he himself was killed. It was a deadly era.

Transition

As Rome went through eighty short-lived emperors over a period of two centuries, its center weakened and barbarian armies invaded the empire's outer edges. The Goths took Athens in A.D. 268, and shortly thereafter a six-year plague wiped out a large percentage of the population. Famine followed, and then economic disaster. The power base of civilization was ripe for being conquered again, this time by a new religion.

During the time of Caesar Augustus, in Palestine, a

child named Jesus was born who was hailed by his followers as the Son of God. In approximately A.D. 29, a preacher named John the Baptist declared him the Jewish messiah who would free his people from foreign domination. Jewish priests, disturbed by these messages, found a pretext to eliminate Jesus. He was crucified, but his twelve appointed disciples carried his message far and wide to establish churches along major trade routes. Their records, along with the letters of Gentile convert Paul of Tarsus, formed the foundation for the New Testament of the Bible. Christ had defeated death, this religion claimed, and offered a way for anyone to be cleansed of their transgressions against God and man, and gain eternal life.

While Christian sects were persecuted throughout this period, especially because they refused to worship the emperor, the religion gained status with a significant event. During the Battle of Milvian Bridge in A.D. 312, Constantine the Great experienced a vision of a cross. He won the battle and subsequently converted to Christianity. This allowed the religion to thrive and to form an established church. From A.D. 324 to 330, Constantine established a new capital for the empire at the city of Byzantium, in the east, calling this city Constantinopolis, the New Rome, thus, according to some historians, ushering in what would come to be known as the medieval period. The collapse of the Western Roman Empire in 476 established this shift more firmly. While Islam gained ground as a religion in the Near and Middle East, Christianity continued to flourish as a government-sponsored faith. It gained strength when the Emperor Justinian insisted that all of his subjects become Christians. Religion then merged into politics as church leaders sought to influence ruling bodies and to fashion themselves into an elite class invested with God's authority. But after Justinian's death in A.D. 565, Eastern and Western Europe developed in quite different directions.

The five centuries between A.D. 500 and 1000 are called the Dark Ages. Many of civilization's gains receded as trade, intellectual life, and manufacturing declined. Warrior tribes attacked and lawlessness increased across the land. Christian scholars preserved the church's teachings, along with the Latin language, but they jealously guarded their skills and knowledge among an elite few, granting themselves ever-greater status and power. While they kept important traditions alive, they also viewed themselves as the sole arbiters of God's truth, and some political leaders affirmed that.

Thus, the basis for medieval civilization was religion, and what flowed from it into modern times in terms of ideas about good and evil would also influence how society viewed serial killers, as well as how quite a few serial killers would come to view themselves. Christianity spread into most of the great cities in the West and along the eastern Mediterranean, with the theological position that humanity was inherently sinful and could only be redeemed by Divine Grace, which took the form of Christ's sacrifice on the cross. His resurrection replaced reliance on external law with an inner life of the spirit, wherein people could be joined to God via the mystical body. The faithful participated in Church-sanctioned sacraments and baptism, and a hierarchy of priests developed who inherited the role of the twelve apostles and had authority over how to interpret the Word of God. This led to the formation of the Roman Catholic Church, established in the city of Rome, and the Nicene Creed became its unifying doctrine. The Bishop of Rome became the Pope, who ruled the territory around Rome and had ultimate authority over the Christian population. The Holy Roman Empire was established in A.D. 800 with the Pope's crowning of Charlemagne.

Yet despite its promise of salvation, the religious life was not so easy. Few people during this time could read or write, so their lives were strictly regulated by papal interpretation. The popes had the "Evil One" to consider: the fallen angel, Lucifer, who went about tempting the faithful to sin. In part, this entity derived from pagan religions that worshiped seductive gods or feared the Lord of the Underworld. In essence, the devil was the opponent of all that was good, the agent of sin and suffering. He acquired the name Satan and the appearance of a horned beast with a tail. To diminish his influence, which priests thought seeped into people's lives through errant beliefs, pagan practices and temples were gradually banned. As the Church moved to control both secular and sacred affairs, popes used the power of excommunication to force rulers to acquiesce.

So where, in all of this, were the serial killers? While poisoning, considered the "coward's weapon," continued to be favored by those engaged in clandestine repeat murder, the next person (aside from bloodthirsty dictators) who might be considered a predatory multiple killer popped up during the fifth century in Yemen—at least in legend. (It's likely that there were serial killers afoot between the first and fifth centuries, given society's perpetual chaos, but we have no extant record of them. Though we know that there was plenty of violence and death during clashes between different cultures, due both to political rivalries and to the persecution of the new religion of Christianity, a description of an actual predatory killer is hard to find.)

In keeping with the violent indulgences of those in power, according to some records a wealthy man in Yemen named Zu Shenatir lured hungry boys to his residence with food and money. There he sexually abused them and, once finished, tossed them out a window on the highest floor to their deaths, presumably, for his own enjoyment. But one potential victim apparently fought back and stabbed Zu Shenatir to death. Otherwise, given his status, he might never have been stopped. That was the course for such killers among the aristocratic classes. They made the laws and did whatever they pleased. Having a rigid hierarchy where the wealthy were clearly in power meant that when the killing impulse emerged in someone in a protected domain, he or she had no inhibitions to restrain them from repetitive murder. Coupled with the sexual urge, it would become an addiction.

At this time, nothing was known about the psychoneurology of repetitive acts, but many centuries later brain research came into its own, and nowadays it is easy to see how these aristocrats were similar in many ways to today's predatory killers. But we'll save that for later.

Light in the Dark

The first forensic science that would affect investigations was the art of interpreting the fingerprint. The Chinese recognized that fingerprints appeared to be unique to individuals and in the 700s began to use them to authenticate documents. During the eleventh century, as Europe awoke from the Dark Ages, Quintilian, a Roman attorney, proved that a set of bloody prints had been meant to frame a blind man for his mother's murder. In other words, he was able to use physical evidence in a forensic case to acquit someone. By around 1247, Sung Tz'u, a Chinese lawyer, was featured in *Hsi Duan Yu*—literally, "the washing away of wrongs"— the first work of forensic science. It included instructions on how to distinguish between suicide, homicide, and natural death, which made it the first record of this type of forensic medical knowledge.

As monks wrote books, learning spread and schools were formed, including universities. These developments would eventually inspire a new spirit of scientific and philosophical inquiry. But religion still held firm ground. With the expansion of trade and the growth of towns, missionaries continued to spread Christian doctrine. The Roman Catholic Church became a pervasive authority, but local kings, empowered by military might, founded separate nations.

In the feudal system, the king owned the land and granted estates to his loyal followers. These "vassals" received their own titles and privileges, in exchange for offering him warriors. But with peasants or serfs working their lands, the nobles often grew wealthier than the kings, so some kings financed their own armies and sought greater power by conquering other nations. England and France, in particular, often struggled over who would control the French.

The Crusades were also imperial in nature. While ostensibly the purpose of crusading knights was to spread the gospel, win converts, and recover the sacred places, they also invaded heathen communities and claimed land and resources. The first Crusade occurred in 1096, resulting in the defeat of Muslims and Turks for the greater glory of God. But then the Holy Land was lost. Two more Crusades, decades later, attempted without success to regain it, but the Fourth Crusade in 1204 sacked Constantinople. Christians also chased Islam from Spain, and the Sixth Crusade finally recaptured Jerusalem. By this time, Christianity had gained a lot of ground.

In 1387, the last remaining pagan state in Europe was converted. Yet thanks to the reestablishment of trade routes between China, western Asia, and Europe, during the fourteenth century the entire region had to deal with the devastating effects of massive outbreaks of the Black Plague, which killed some twenty-five million, worsened an economic crisis, and inspired peasant revolts. While religion tried to homogenize society, political power was on the rise in various places.

By the end of the Middle Ages, four powerful nations had emerged: France, England, Portugal, and Spain. Yet the strongest influence was still the Church's authority, despite factionalism that resulted in there being two popes, one in Rome and one at Avignon in France. Power and wealth were corrupting the Church, and discontent with it spread among laypeople, but still the clergy worked tirelessly to enforce orthodoxy across the land.

In 906, Abbot Regen condemned sorcery. Since there were rumors throughout Europe that some people with special powers could change shape and even fly, Regen stated that such notions were delusions inspired by Satan. That did not stop the rumors. The Catholic Church ruled Europe, but its authority was beginning to tarnish. Its acquired manner of representing Christ via the ostentatious display of wealth and imperial control seemed to the working classes a false understanding of the true faith. Starting in the eleventh century, movements such as the Albigensians and lollards arose that provided those who wanted it with a return to simpler, less worldly ways. The Church condemned these movements and struck them down. Not long after, during the thirteenth century, the first official inquisitors arrived on the scene to ferret out witches and other diabolical beings. Inquisitors were granted whatever power they needed to rid the world of evil, and every ruler was obliged to assist them. In 1257 the Church sanctioned torture as a means of forcing confessions. The Knights Templar, a wealthy secret society pledged to defend Christianity but unable to defend themselves against political envy, were tortured and burned at the stake, and the first witchcraft trials began.

Yet even with the high moral standards imposed by the ideals of Christ, aristocrats with a blood lust found ways to indulge it. From within the Middle Ages, several serial killers came to light, and their brutal atrocities far outpace the acts of more modern killers. Those with the highest victim counts possessed status as aristocrats that demanded obedience from savvy servants who protected them from discovery. Among these predators, ironically, was a close confidant to Joan of Arc.

Holy Monster

The ecclesiastical judges observed the black-bearded, defiant, thirty-six-year-old man standing before them and wondered how it had come to pass that one so devoted to the Church, having used his wealth to build cathedrals and preserve religious art, could be guilty of the depraved crimes laid before them. According to one deposition, he would sit on top of children and "take his pleasure" as he watched their heads being cut off. It seemed impossible that this highborn lord who had been granted the highest of military honors could be the beast that these accusations suggested he was. Only a decade earlier he had been a significant participant in France's history, anointing and crowning the king as he won France back from the English.

The task before them was not easy. They needed a confession, and to get that they had to understand what might have made this man do the shocking things that he and his accomplices had allegedly done. His brief life did not stretch back that far. But they knew it was inextricably linked with France itself.

During the fifteenth century, France had struggled to maintain dominion in Europe. The Hundred Years' War, a series of skirmishes and short-lived alliances, had begun in 1337 as the result of William the Conqueror's invasion of England in 1066. Already Duke of Normandy in France, William also became King of England. His English descendant, Henry II, married Eleanor of Aquitaine, the divorced wife of the French king Louis VII, and they took control of lands in northern France. Over successive centuries, the English lost this land and won it back.

Just as Henry V took the English throne in 1413, the French king Charles VI displayed mental instability in the form of paranoia, bizarre delusions, and episodic bouts of unexplained aggression, causing a power struggle. Henry decided to make a grab for the throne and the land, so in 1415 his troops crossed the English Channel and landed in Normandy, raiding their way to the battlefield of Agincourt.

King Charles VI was in a bad position. He had granted a great deal of power to the lords of different regions in France, such as Burgundy, Orléans, and Brittany. Each man had his own army, made his own laws, and coined his own money. Each had enormous wealth and no particular allegiance. They could throw their lot in with Charles, but they might as easily see an advantage with Henry. Charles did not know for sure whom to trust. At Agincourt, the French tried to overwhelm the English but failed.

Henry V thus established England's sovereignty in France. The psychotic Charles VI disinherited his son, the dauphin Charles VII, and named Henry heir to the French throne. However, because of Charles VI's madness, many nobles in France rejected this treaty and refused to honor Henry V as their ruler. Both Charles and Henry died in 1422, and Henry VI became King of France and England. But the dauphin Charles VII was determined to take back his lands and expel the arrogant English. Among his loyal supporters for this task were Jean d'Craon and d'Craon's eldest grandson, Gilles de Rais.

Gilles de Rais was born in 1404, just after the French government collapsed and the country was divided into fiefdoms. Charles VI was already delusional and the Pope in Avignon was at war with the Pope in Rome. De Rais's parents were distant cousins forced to marry to strengthen the family wealth, so he grew up with every possible privilege of the time, including private tutors and extensive military training. His parents had both died when he was ten, the same year that France lost the battle at Agincourt, so Jean d'Craon raised him and his brother. Gilles was thus heir to a great fortune.

He married for political purposes at the age of eighteen, and the addition of his wife's fortune made him the wealthiest man in France. With his glossy black beard, he cut quite a figure; he was described as "a youth of rare elegance and startling beauty." The records indicate that Gilles de Rais was an arrogant, egotistical bully who seldom showed maturity in responsible matters. He loved violence and warfare, yet he also generously supported the Catholic Church.

After France faltered, and with Charles VI out of the way, in 1425 the dauphin prepared to revive the Hundred Years' War. Gilles, who had taken over managing his inheritance, organized two hundred knights and set off for battle. He took the English stronghold at Lude and arrived in glory at the French court. His cousin, already installed as an adviser to the king, helped Gilles to gain prominence. Then, in 1428, the English laid siege to Orléans.

A year later, Joan, the Maid of Orléans, rode forth and declared to the dauphin that she would lead a victorious campaign against the besieged area. In addition, she would have Charles crowned in the cathedral at Reims, the ancient place of coronation for French kings. She was so persuasive in her visions that the dauphin gave her whatever she asked, dressing her in white armor and making Gilles her adviser. He rode with her and an army of ten thousand to Orléans.

Gilles was in awe of how Joan's prophecies came true in front of his eyes. They grew together as friends and allies while he guided her military decisions. He believed in her miraculous visions, watching as she recovered from a wound that would have felled many a man and then gave several more confident predictions that were uncannily accurate. Within four days they lifted the siege, forcing the English to abandon Orléans, and the dauphin made Gilles the esteemed Marshal of France, the nation's highest-ranking soldier—at only twenty-five, a first for someone his age. Gilles then personally crowned Charles VII at Reims as the new King of France. Henry VI was no more.

The king ended the campaigns, expecting Joan and Gilles to go home, but neither was ready for that. Joan continued to do battle and was wounded and captured by the Duke of Burgundy, an ally of England. She languished in prison, abandoned by all who could have ransomed her, including Gilles de Rais, although he made an aborted attempt to rescue her. In 1431, she was burned at the stake as a heretic, and some reports say that Gilles went into a near-psychotic rage at the news, especially as rumors spread that her heart had failed to burn.

That same year, Gilles slipped into depravity. Although he could have chosen to retire at any of five magnificent estates, he continued his military engagements and then for a thrill began to rob travelers. He made several political enemies, who watched for an opportunity to bring him down. Then, just over two years after he had crowned a king, he murdered a child. The following year, his grandfather died. Jean d'Craon, in his remorse for having raised a monster, snubbed Gilles by willing his lands to others.

Gilles had become accustomed to killing, and he liked it. Since he was not subject to the laws of others, he believed he could do as he pleased, which made him vulnerable to anyone who encouraged him to act on his depraved fantasies. Having been so close to a spiritual visionary, Gilles looked to the art of alchemy, outlawed by the Church, for his new magical resource. At Orléans, he had seen how Joan's prayer had shifted the wind to favor the French, and he believed he could make the elements work as well for him. He soon partnered with a defrocked Italian priest, Francisco Prelati, who told him that the blood of children could turn iron and lead into gold. Together they murdered a child, removed the eyes and heart, drained the blood to write a devil's pact, and performed a ritual. Although the devil did not appear that night, Gilles discovered that he achieved a sexual thrill from the torture and mutilation of children.

He turned his attention to towheaded young boys, and sometimes to girls. He admired the Roman emperor Caligula, whose blood lust was legendary, and he patterned his life after this immoral and sadistic ruler. Here and there across the land, he sent his servants to invite families to send their children to him, for their "betterment." But in fact, they were being sent to their deaths.

Several people who later offered detailed accounts were present at his dinner parties, where he'd often rape a child, hang him on a hook, and continue to violate him as the child died. This was one of his great pleasures. Or he might see the child on the hook, feign displeasure, cut him down, reassure him, and then cut his throat as foreplay for himself. He might also hold the child between his legs and watch with pleasure as a servant removed the head. He often stuck the heads on rods so he could admire them, and called in a woman to curl the children's hair and make up their faces. Afterward, he would compare heads and ask his servants which one was more beautiful, the winner being used for sexual purposes. He would save the children's blood and some of their remains for magical purposes, and toss the rest into a sewer or fireplace.

Finally, he was stopped, though not because of these practices. Gilles assaulted a priest to whom he had sold some property. It was a trivial matter, a conflict over the property, but he came under the jurisdiction of the Catholic Church, and his enemies took the opportunity to file a suit with the bishop of Nantes. Gilles's relatives, afraid that his dwindling estates would diminish their own wealth, supported this action. In 1440, he was taken into custody. Once the investigation began, more charges were filed, including sorcery, violating the immunity of the Church, and sexual perversion with children. The parents of ten of the missing children related that the lord's henchmen had coerced them to part with their sons, promising that the children would be educated. But those children were never seen again.

A search of Gilles's holdings, documents indicate, produced the remains of some fifty children in a tower on one of his estates and a similar cache of bones in another castle. Evidence indicated that many more had been cremated. In the end, the indictment claimed that Lord Gilles de Rais had brought 140 children to harm.

When asked to respond to the charges, Gilles lashed out, refusing to make a plea. So he was summarily excommunicated. He feared for his immortal soul, so two days later he appeared before his judges and tearfully admitted his crimes. He was reinstated in the Church. Still he refused to admit to sorcery, so the prosecutor produced witnesses who said that they had seen Gilles de Rais conjure up the devil. After five days of this, Lord de Rais finally agreed that the testimony should be published as a warning to others.

Yet this was still not good enough. The officials applied various methods of torture at the dungeon at La Teur Neuve to de Rais and his accomplices, extracting yet more confessions. Gilles admitted to murdering 140 children for his own pleasure, saying that he alone was responsible. When asked what had led him to such crimes, he said, "It was my imagination alone that led me to them. I conceived them from my thoughts, from my daily pleasures, and solely for my own amusement and delectation."

His words affirm what contemporary criminologists know, that the acts of serial killers begin in violent fantasies. In addition, those who heard his admission noted that he took erotic delight in reliving his crimes—also quite like killers today: ". . . these children I caressed as they died, delighting in the most beautiful." His audience was so disturbed by this description that someone reportedly pulled a veil over the image of Christ that hung in the room. Many wept. Yet even after they were satisfied as to his remorse, Gilles continued his account.

He begged forgiveness from the wronged families. He admitted that he had placed the hand, eye, and heart of a child into a vessel to summon a demon. He also said that he had "pleased himself in every illicit act." He begged for their prayers for his soul. He then participated for the last time in the sacraments of the Church so that he could be buried on sacred ground. His lands were seized, and after a monthlong trial he was sentenced to death, along with two of his accomplices. On October 26, 1440, he offered his last words in the form of a sermon to the crowd gathered to watch his end. In an eloquent speech, de Rais admitted his sins and blamed his lenient upbringing (like many a serial killer, seeking to blame an outside influence). He exhorted the parents who were there to be strict with their children and faithful to the Church.

The hangman placed a noose over his neck and he fell to his knees. Just as the torch was put to the wood beneath him and the stand pushed out from under him, he called out to St. Michael. When Gilles de Rais was ascertained to be dead, six women in white-hooded robes placed his remains in a metal coffin and eventually a procession carried him to a Carmelite cemetery. For three days, the people fasted. In years to come, they devised an anniversary reminder for children by whipping them on the date of Gilles's execution until they bled. Although historical accounts differ on the final tally of his victims, depending on which account one reads, de Rais is credited with anywhere from one hundred to eight hundred murders of children.

Yet oddly enough, although people had witnessed his atrocities, no one had alerted authorities . . . not until he risked the family estates with his extravagant lifestyle. Only because he had threatened the status of his relatives and proven himself inept at politics did his crimes come to an end. Indeed, some of his relatives showed no emotion as they watched the castles being cleared of the children's remains.

By some interpretations, the enemies of Gilles de Rais had turned him in merely to get their hands on his lands, and he had never been a killer at all, but these explanations fail to account for all the bones found in his home. Like serial killers before and after him, Gilles reveled in stripping people of their human components and emptying them into himself. He acted out his own mind's ability to form twisted fantasies, showing how a protected arena can offer the imagination a way to bring even the darkest of images to life.

Gilles de Rais was called a monster, although he did not view himself as such, for his violent impulses were cushioned by an aristocratic system that granted status to those with wealth and connections. He shared with other serial killers from the noble classes across time the opportunity to exploit the social structure as a means of absorbing others' lives. While they emerged from the aristocracy in societies with limited social mobility and concentrated power, they would eventually show up among the lower classes.

In 1484, Pope Innocent VIII issued a papal bull for inquisitors to squelch witchcraft in Germany. Inquisitor Jakob Sprenger published the *Malleus Maleficarum* in

1486 as a guidebook for witch-hunters across Europe. By the following century, while blood lust continued to inspire some aristocratic atrocities, escalating conflicts between Christianity and pagan practices would precipitate such strong inner torment over deviant fantasies that some men would come to believe they had transformed into genuine monsters. In several countries, vampires and werewolves arrived in force.

CHAPTER TWO

The Alliance of Ignorance

Creating Monsters

Experts on serial murder disagree as to whether such tyrants as Vlad the Impaler from Walachia should be part of the pantheon of serial killers. While his behavior was sadistic and he was certainly responsible for a high death toll, his acts can be attributed to a leader's strategy for diminishing the enemy's population and marking himself as a fearsome warlord. Some scholars insist that he was the model for Bram Stoker's later classic, *Dracula*, but others are adamant that he was not. Nevertheless, the myths surrounding his deeds have inspired other authors whose work may influence popular culture, and thus Vlad's deeds have become part of the mind-set of those serial killers who adopt the vampire as a role model.

But to be accurate, Vlad Tepes was not a pattern murderer within the limits of the definition adopted here. He was a member of an aristocratic family of a Romanian state next to Transylvania, and in the middle of the fifteenth century he acquired a reputation for indifference in the face of tortured and dying men, impaled grotesquely on stakes, skinned, or boiled alive. Though his reign was brief, the stories of his atrocities endured. By some counts, he had killed tens of thousands before the Turks stopped him. But if he is to be counted, then so should other warlords from every era and country.

As the European population recovered from the plagues and prosperity slowly rose, banking systems and increased trade exposed people to other cultures. A new sense of optimism bolstered exploration and discovery, and modern ideas eroded ancient authority. An artistic renaissance, started in Italy by such people as Leonardo da Vinci, eventually swept through Europe. When Johann Gutenberg perfected movable type in 1453, he helped others to educate the masses and change modes of communication on an international scale. A new respect for the scientific method, based in theoretical mathematics, inspired discoveries such as the behavior of gravity and inventions like telescopes, which assisted Galileo in confirming that the Earth and other planets revolved around the sun. These new methods for examining nature also revealed how the body—until this time considered too sacred to be dissected—functioned. In 1628, William Harvey explained blood circulation.

Philosophers challenged the Church with humanistic ideas, while Luther birthed the Protestant revolt. The

Catholic Church fought back by banning books and persecuting those whose ideas contradicted their doctrines, but it could not impede the momentum, especially when such rulers as Louis XIV and Charles II supported that momentum. Scientific progress soon became a fashion. Seafaring ventures brought diverse cultures and whole continents in contact with one another, and Europeans settled other lands with merchants and missionaries—often to the detriment of the native culture. Industrialism had its foot in the door of heretofore agrarian societies, easing daily life with new inventions. Overall, humankind was experiencing a more central role in the universe.

Forensic science also took several steps forward. Around 1590, two Dutchmen, Zacharius Janssen and his son Hans, made the first crude series of lenses in a tube for magnification, perfected in the next century by Antonie van Leeuwenhoek in Holland as the precision compound microscope. In France in 1609, Francois Demelle published the first study on handwriting analysis, while toward the middle of that century Germany's University of Leipzig offered physicians a course in forensic medicine. Around that same time, pattern ridges of fingerprints were described by Italian biologist Marcello Malpighi, which would inspire innovators yet to come.

Yet despite excitement over science in learned circles, the masses were still embroiled in superstition. In those countries that remained loyal to the Pope, the Protestant revolt had inspired a counterrevival of spiritual fervor. Thus, while the moral life of the common person remained grounded in Dark Age traditions, the Church sought more forceful ways to instill its vision. Among them were campaigns in Central Europe against satanic entities. Between 1521 and 1600 several men were prosecuted in court for "lycanthropy," or *therianthropy* (becoming a wild beast), and such cases were recorded into the eighteenth century. In fact, during one extended period some thirty thousand cases of werewolf possession were reported to authorities. In God's name, inquisitors sometimes hacked these people apart to search for the telltale wolf hair supposedly planted inside their bodies. No one was immune from arrest, and some witch-finder generals fully indulged their lust to torment others or exercise power over life and death. With no real accountability for these agents of the Church, latent sadism found leverage and burst forth on thousands of victims.

Witch-hunters were especially active in France, a country fighting for its former political glory. At that time, the criminal personality was thought to be the result of demonic influence or possession, with the devil inspiring his followers to take different shapes. Some viewed themselves as cursed with an animal compulsion. They not only killed but also consumed their victims' flesh and drank their blood. In fact, during this time, cannibalism and necrophilia were not uncommon—at least, according to (frequently torture-induced) confessions of the time.

In the French countryside, governing bodies issued proclamations to warn citizens about werewolves and to instruct them in how to arrest and punish the beasts.

Scholars argued in print over the correct definition, but in essence, "shapeshifters" were people engaged in sorcery or lycanthropy and leading degenerate lives that endangered others. Yet despite the Church's firm attempts to convert everyone to the "true faith," mystical practices calling on nature deities continued to flourish, especially in outlying areas. While these practitioners may have used herbal medicine and prognostication merely as a way to feel some control over nature, their practices were considered a threat to righteous doctrines. The more adherents these movements attracted, the more the Church insisted that the devil was rising up in greater strength against God.

In other words, these practices were taboo, and taboo subjects often acquire an erotic aura. Some men dressed themselves in wolf-skins at night, according to scholar Montague Summers, as a way to contact Satan for the beast's special powers. Those who could manage "the change," states the lore, were granted a period of complete abandon into blood and violence. Tales were told around Europe of hunters who hacked off the paw of a wolf, only to then find a woman's hand in their pouch and a woman in town with a mysteriously bandaged arm.

But since such lustful behavior was viewed as contrary to God's ennoblement, those who were attracted to it (or condemned to it by excommunication) were outcast. For those with a strong sexual drive and poor impulse control, however, a pact with the devil was a perfect excuse, a way to "accept" that whatever they did was beyond their control. In fact, the entire history of serial killers is framed by whatever excuses are in vogue at the time for mitigating accountability in vile acts. For this era and region, the beast within was the guiding theme.

In 1521, Pierre Burgot and Michel Verdun were tried in France, and quickly blamed their murderous behavior on demons. They had pledged obedience in exchange for money, they claimed, and had been anointed in a ceremony with unguents that changed them into savage animals. Together they had torn apart a seven-year-old boy, a grown woman, and a little girl, all of whose flesh they consumed. They so loved lapping up the warm blood that they could not help but continue to kill. They also had sexual relations with female wolves, "as Dogges follow a Bitche." In fact, Verdun had supposedly been discovered in the guise of a wolf. It seems that a traveler had wounded him before Verdun could kill him and had followed his trail to his home, where Verdun's wife was bathing his wound. He was executed, along with Burgot and a third man, for sorcery.

Years later, Gilles Garnier had a similar story to tell. He was a reclusive man living in Dole, outside Lyons, with a wife and several children. Trying to feed them, he entered the woods to hunt and encountered a "spectral man," who used an unguent to show Garnier how to become a wolf. Garnier then proceeded to kill. After the case came to trial, a pamphlet was printed at Sens in 1574 to warn people about such practices. It described Garnier's confession: Supposedly, shortly after the Feast of St. Michael, a ten-year-old girl had wandered into a vineyard. In the form of a wolf, Garnier seized and "killed her both with his hands, seemingly paws, as with his teeth." He dragged the body to the woods, stripped off the clothing, and indulged his lust for raw flesh. Then he tore off some to take home to his wife. He tried this again with another little girl, but the approach of some people interrupted him. About a week later, he attacked a young boy, ate flesh from the thighs and belly, and tore off a leg. Then he apparently made the mistake of attacking a child while he was still in human form, and witnesses saw him. Garnier was subsequently arrested.

The Parliament of Franche-Comtè, shocked at the incidences of werewolf attacks in the area, decided to set an example. In 1573, Garnier was burned alive as a creature of Satan. While he quickly blamed a force outside himself, it failed to affect the decision. He was not an animal, the court said, he was a human corrupted by dark forces. He had to be purged from their midst, lest Satan use him again, so his body was burned.

And it was not just men who did such deeds. Several women confessed to participating in rituals in which they killed children and other women. Francois Secretain admitted to all this and more: She had also had illicit relations with the demon, in the shape of a black man. She, too, was executed.

That same year, another notorious case came to the courts. The "Demon Tailor," or "Werewolf of Chalons," was arraigned in France on murder charges so shocking that after the trial in 1598 all court documents were destroyed. The unnamed man allegedly lured children into his shop in Paris to subject them to torture and sexual perversion before slitting their throats. He would then dismember them, dress the flesh, and consume the remains. When he could not get victims that way, he supposedly roamed the woods in the form of a wolf to find them, and he was alleged to have killed several dozen children. Officials raided his shop and found barrels full of bleached bones in the cellar, along with other foul items.

The stories from these times were generally the same. Some woman or child would be found torn and partially eaten, and wolves were seen bounding away—sometimes in packs, because they were members of the same family. Confessions always followed, but how freely they were given in those days of hideous torture is open to question. According to the written documents (which likely served the Church's purpose more than truth or justice), the captured person inevitably offered precise details of killing a child just where a mutilated child's body had been found. That was evidence enough. In one case, however, the Church decided that a man who could barely speak should be confined in a hospital rather than burned. In other words, it may well be the case that many of these alleged killers were mentally defective in some manner and unable to do anything but tell inquisitors what they wanted to hear.

In 1603, some six hundred alleged shapeshifters were burned. By this time, voices had been raised in opposition and learned men had published books to try to quell the madness. Yet the tortures continued. As late as 1764, the bloodsucking "Beast of Le Gevaudon" started a three-year panic in France. Reportedly, it was a large wolf that could walk erect and that favored women and children as its prey—apparently in the hundreds. A posse killed it with a silver bullet.

Former FBI profiler Gregg McCrary theorizes that the state in which some mutilated victims were found before people understood criminology may have spawned these werewolf myths. "There's a reluctance to admit that someone in our community would be capable of the kind of evil we see in brutal murders," he says. "Evil is so overpowering that we want to attribute it to some 'monster,' but the reality is that many good people can have some terrible flaws."

Germany had a similar problem. Around the middle of the sixteenth century, the town of Bedburg, near Cologne, was generally a quiet place. Yet over the course of twenty-five years, from time to time a savagely mutilated body would be discovered. These victims had in common having had a disagreement with an otherwise unassuming man by the name of Peter Stubb (or Stump or Stubbe). But young girls who did not know him had also met such a fate. During one period, dismembered limbs were found on a regular basis out in the fields, and the townspeople feared a marauding wolf.

Finally the authorities used hounds to track down the beast, only to discover, according to an illustrated pamphlet about the sensational case, Peter Stubb removing his wolf-hair girdle and transforming back into a man. He was caught and freely confessed a string of atrocities, from incest to murder to cannibalism. Apparently he implicated his wife and daughter in the crimes—they knew that he had feasted on the brains of his son—claiming that an "enchanted belt" had assisted his "change," and admitted that he would rape children and tear out their hearts to consume while still hot and beating. He was tried in 1589 with his wife and daughter as a "pack," and all three were convicted of murder. Stubb was tortured on a wheel with heated pinchers, his flesh was pulled off, and his limbs were broken with hatchet blows. Then he was decapitated and his head was displayed as a lesson to others pondering a deal with the devil.

It's difficult to know for certain whether these men and women were serial killers, lunatics offering false confessions, or people simply hoping in vain to escape or decrease the torture. Certainly a high body count with enough commonalities to tie victims to a single offender would implicate a serial killer. However, the superstition surrounding the events and the lack of physical evidence, along with the framework of religious hysteria, makes it difficult to know the truth. It's likely that there were killers similar to those we see today who are so caught up in lust that they drink blood, dismember corpses, rape, and bite with ferocity. The fact that the popular mind-set guided people to look for werewolves probably influenced the form a killing frenzy took.

But some monstrous killers were less like werewolves than vampires.

Lady in Waiting

During the Christmas season of 1609, King Mathias II of Hungary sent a party of men to the massive Castle Cse-jthe to investigate rumors of the kidnapping of several young women in the area. These men knew they had to be careful: The mistress of the manor was of royal blood and was especially well connected. Once married to a warrior count known as Hungary's "Black Hero" for his bravery in battles with the Turks, she was related to princes and kings, bishops and cardinals, and she was cousin to Prime Minister Thurzo—a member of the very party that approached her imposing domain with such stealth and trepidation that night.

It was cold out and difficult to see their way, even with a few torches, but they knew that their best chance lay in surprise. The rumor was that the woman they sought would be having one of her late-night clandestine gatherings, which would be a sight to behold if they managed to get that close. They might even catch her in a deviant act. People down the hill in the village often claimed to have heard female screams emanating from within the place, but no one had dared approach her until now. Finally, she had gone too far.

The men entering the castle had heard that the mistress was a practitioner of the Dark Arts and they feared that she might use a spell against them. All told, the party consisted of the prime minister, a priest who had lodged a detailed complaint, the local governor (also a relative of this woman), and several soldiers. Climbing the imposing hill on which the stone castle stood, they stopped to catch their breath. Most of the windows were dark, and there were no cries of alarm. So far, so good. They moved on toward the castle, preparing to break in.

To their surprise, the massive wooden door stood partly ajar, as if inviting them in, so they pushed it open and entered. To their right, a cat jumped out, spooking them. They had heard that the countess used these animals as her wicked emissaries, sending them to attack her enemies. The priest quickly crossed himself. He counted six cats in all, and would later have reason to remember them.

At that moment they saw, quite unexpectedly, what they had come for. There in the great hall on the cold stone floor lay a pale, partially clothed girl. The men went to help her, believing she might be ill or drunk, but discovered that she was dead. Not only that, she appeared to have been drained of blood—exactly as the rumors had indicated she would be.

And just a few paces away was another girl, sprawled faceup but still alive—barely. Her body had been pierced in many places with a sharp implement and she, too, was alarmingly pale. She would not last long.

The party moved on, and against a pillar deeper into the castle they found another female corpse chained to the post. On her were marks of beatings and burns, as well as bruises from a whip. She, too, had lost most of her blood.

What manner of sorceress was this? the priest wondered. What was she doing with the blood? It could only be for some dark ceremony, so common in these lands despite the Church's influence. Anxious now about their trespass into this domain, the men moved down the stone stairs to the lower floors to locate the dungeons. It wasn't long, as they made their way by touching the cold stone walls, before they heard plaintive cries. Rushing to the sounds, they located a cell full of women and children, most of whom had been subjected to bleedings.

The men freed the captives before venturing to higher floors to find the woman responsible for these carnal misdeeds. To their surprise, inside a large room they discovered a drunken orgy. There is no extant account of the details, reportedly because the scene was too monstrous to be written into a permanent record, but there was plenty to tell for those who would be called to the trial. The raiding party arrested these licentious revelers, freed the victims, and imprisoned the protesting sorceress in a room in her own castle.

Her name was Countess Erzsebet Báthory and she was a member of a powerful family from an estate at the foot of the Carpathian Mountains. The earliest accounts of this tale derive from an eighteenth-century history of Hungary by Father Laslo Turáczi, in a monograph published in 1744, and from a 1796 German publication. According to the account in 1575, at the age of fifteen, Erzsebet had married the great warrior Count Ferencz Nadasdy, joining two families with strains of cruel madness running through them. Báthory's kinsman, the Prince of Transylvania, was noted far and wide for his instability and savagery. Her aunt, a distinguished lady at the court, was reputed to be a witch. An uncle was an alchemist and devil-worshiper, and her brother was a reprobate. There were whisperings of incest and of Erzsebet's having an illegitimate child. To make matters worse, her nurse from childhood, Ilona Joo—one of those arrested—practiced black magic that required human sacrifice. Erzsebet had also grown up experiencing uncontrollable seizures, headaches, and rages.

By many accounts, she was a narcissist who spent hours admiring her legendary beauty in mirrors. No one denied her whatever she wanted and she demanded continuous praise for her pale skin, voluptuous figure, and black hair. Becoming Nadasdy's wife introduced Erzsebet to his special modes of discipline. One trick was to spread honey over a naked servant girl and leave her tied outside for the bugs to nibble and bees to sting. As a love token, Nadasdy sent magic spells for his wife to try at home from foreign lands where he was at war. He also showed Erzsebet how to beat the serving girls to the edge of their lives, a task in which she reportedly took great pleasure.

Nadasdy was frequently gone on military campaigns, so Erzsebet took male lovers, although she reportedly indulged in lesbian practices as well, and accumulated an entourage of people adept at alchemy and witchcraft. One nobleman with pale skin and long dark hair, who was reputed to drink blood, was brought to live at the castle to teach her about his predilection.

Nadasdy died in 1604, leaving Erzsebet a middle-aged

widow with four children. She moved at once to their castle in Vienna, but eventually returned to Hungary, where she had more privacy for torture sessions. In villages both near and far, pretty young women began to disappear. The victims' families felt helpless, because speaking against the nobility could bring more harm upon them; they had not forgotten how in 1524 the nobles had punished a peasant uprising. So they turned to the priests. They saw the Nadasdy carriage at night, they reported, drawn by black horses and carrying girls inside who never came back. Year after year, it was the same thing.

Finally, the crop of peasant girls ran out. Erzsebet, ever daring, turned her blood thirst to lesser aristocrats. Like many serial killers, she was eager to extend her reach, just for the thrill of seeing what she could get away with. She offered to teach "social graces" to young women from noble families. Some of them, too, disappeared. After the murder of one of these girls in 1609, which Erzsebet tried to stage as a suicide, the authorities decided to investigate. The king supported this action, since Erzsebet had been asking him to repay funds he had borrowed from her husband; if the rumors proved true, he would be free of his debt.

The rumors did indeed prove true, and Erzsebet's gory tyranny was terminated. As she awaited trial, officials searched her castle. They discovered bones and other human remains, along with the clothing and personal effects of missing girls. They also had the tales of survivors to go on, as well as detailed stories from a crew of accomplices. The men and women who had assisted Báthory in her bloody deeds jostled one another to be first to win clemency through cooperation. Erzsebet herself did not attend the trial. Instead she remained in her castle, maintaining her innocence.

Twenty-one judges were on hand on January 2, 1611, when the proceedings of the special tribunal began, with Judge Theodosius de Szulo of the Royal Supreme Court presiding. The principal testimony against Erzsebet came from four people who had served her in her bloody campaign. They were all asked the same eleven questions about how long they had been at the castle, whom they had murdered, and how many victims there had been. Ficzko, a dwarf, claimed he had been taken to the castle forcibly. He was not sure about how many women he had helped to kill, but he did know the count of the younger girls: thirty-seven. Five were buried in holes, two in a garden, two at night in a church, and so on. They had been lured from the country with the promise of employment, and women in some of the villages had actually provided girls in exchange for money or gifts. If the girls did not come willingly, they were beaten into unconsciousness and carried off. They were chosen, Ficzko said, for the softness of their skin—even of their tongues.

When asked about the type of torture used, he described it thusly: "They tied the hands and arms very tightly with Viennese cord, they were beaten to death until the whole body was black as charcoal and their skin was rent and torn. One girl suffered more than two hundred blows before dying. Dorko [another accomplice and procurer] cut their fingers one by one with shears and then slit the veins with scissors."

Erzsebet's childhood nurse, Ilona Joo, admitting that she had killed around fifty girls, said that she had applied red-hot pokers from the fire, shoving them into the mouth or up the nose of some hapless girl. The mistress herself, she testified, had placed her fingers into the mouth of one girl and pulled hard until the sides split open. Erzsebet had also stabbed them all over with needles, making them bleed, torn open their flesh with sharp pincers, and slit open the skin between their fingers.

Erzsebet, these accomplices stated, administered many cruel and arbitrary beatings and was soon torturing and butchering the girls. She might cut off someone's fingers, or beat her about the face until the bones broke. In the winter, women were dragged outside, doused with water, and left to freeze to death. Even when Erzsebet was ill, she would have girls brought to her bed so she could slap and bite them. She had made Ilona Joo place oiled paper between one girl's legs and set it on fire. There was often so much blood from cutting the girls in strategic spots that cinders were placed around the countess's bed to absorb it.

A third accused accomplice added that the countess liked to apply a red-hot iron to the soles of the girls' feet. It also came out that the kidnapped girls had been chained to walls in the dungeons and fattened up, because the countess believed this increased the amount of blood in their bodies—and blood was needed for her moonlit sorcery. They were also forced into deviant sexual activities with her. If they reacted with displeasure, they received torture and possibly death for it. Yet even those who did well eventually bored her, and they, too, would be dispatched. Sometimes, depending on the countess's whim, her favorite girls received the worst treatment. One had been forced to strip a piece of flesh off her own arm and eat it. Several were shoved into small cages full of spikes.

Even during an age when torture was commonplace, the judges who listened to these accounts were appalled, especially as those survivors able to testify offered firsthand accounts of being pierced, pinched, beaten, and burned. Many had been disfigured for life.

The trial lasted into February, reportedly growing more gruesome by the day. Based on the skeletons and cadaver parts found, Countess Báthory and her cronies were convicted on eighty counts of murder. In a second part of the trial, a newly discovered register was entered as evidence. It listed, in Erzsebet's handwriting, over 650 female names. The suggestion, which could not be proven, was that she had kept track of her victims and had actually killed that many. The number of formal charges remained at eighty.

While her accomplices were tortured and put to death in a variety of ghastly ways, from having fingers pulled off to being burned alive, the judges considered what to do with their mistress. King Mathias favored execution, which would mean a special statute to strip her of her royal immunity. Prime Minister Thurzo intervened on her behalf to insist that she was insane, and in the end Erzsebet Báthory was sentenced to be imprisoned for life in a set of

rooms in her own castle. There she stayed, with the en-
trances and windows walled up save for tiny slits for food
and air. After only three and a half years, during the summer of 1614, when she was fifty-four, she died there.

When they tore down the walls to retrieve her body,
they found a brief document to the effect that prior to her
imprisonment she had invoked a darker power to send
ninety-three cats to tear out the hearts of her accusers and
judges. The priest recalled the cats they had seen the
night they'd first entered the castle.

Erzsebet Báthory was the first person in court records
to have been murderously motivated by blood. What's
most notable about her is that whereas most killers
throughout history who have displayed vampiric appetites
have been male, Erzsebet was female. After her death, rumors spread about how she'd actually bathed in the blood
of her young victims. One enduring but unfounded legend indicates that Erzsebet slapped a servant girl one day,
got blood on her hand, and discovered that it made her
skin look younger. Alchemists apparently assured her that
this was a sign of her nobility, so to restore her waning
beauty, she made a practice of bathing in virginal blood.
These ideas were suggested in 1795 by Wagener, when he
wrote: "Elizabeth [Erzsebet] was wont to dress well in
order to please her husband, and she spent half the day
over her toilet. On one occasion, a lady's-maid saw something wrong in her head-dress, and as a recompense for
observing it, received such a severe box on the ears that
the blood gushed from her nose, and spurted on to her
mistress's face. When the blood drops were washed off

her face, her skin appeared much more beautiful—whiter
and more transparent on the spots where the blood had
been." Apparently due to this, "Elizabeth formed the
resolution to bathe her face and her whole body in human
blood so as to enhance her beauty." Her accomplices, he
said, would catch the blood in a tub so that Erzsebet
could "bathe at the hour of four in the morning. After the
bath she appeared more beautiful than before."

No official account mentions this bizarre fetish, and
it's more likely that she simply experienced a sexual thrill
from seeing blood and/or used the blood for her rituals
and ceremonies. Nevertheless, if the ledger with 650
names on it is what many believe it is, then no single person in the centuries to come surpassed her victim toll.
Her reputation remains as one of the most bloodthirsty
killers on record, in part because her noble status made
her untouchable in a society that protected its aristocrats.

Sacrifice

While Báthory's official death toll may seem like an as-
tounding number of victims, it was surpassed in France
during the reign of the "Sun King," Louis XIV, in the
seventeenth century by an alleged sorceress in league with
a renegade priest. Catherine Monvoison, also known as
La Voison, was married to a penny-poor jeweler in Paris.
To supplement the family income, she developed skills in
palmistry, face-reading, fortune-telling, and herbal lore.
She made the acquaintance of Etienne Guiborg, a chemist

who held several ecclesiastical offices, who joined her in clandestine rituals at which the devil supposedly appeared to empower those who did his will. The books they used were reportedly bound in human skin and the hosts for their perverse communion were desecrated with feces and urine. The drawback was that for the magic to occur, they had to mix the potion they drank with a child's blood—and it was expensive to purchase infants. La Voison apparently went along with this practice, even establishing a home for unwed mothers, who readily gave up their progeny. Because she offered potions for love or abortion (as well as for getting rid of troublesome spouses or mistresses), she was soon in demand, especially by aristocratic women with money to spend. She also grew wealthy and acquired a lover, Adam Coeuret, who became an accomplice.

Apparently she led black masses that numerous priests attended and acquired connections in prestigious circles. What she was doing was heretical and illegal, but so many came to her ceremonies from the king's own court—including his mistress—that it was difficult for officials to stop her. Yet they did arrest another woman.

While La Voison worked her ill-fated magic, another Parisian poisoner from that era, Marie Madeleine de Brinvilliers, was executed for the murders of an estimated fifty or more people in 1676. She had practiced first on her servants and hospital patients, then turned her skills against her father, lover, and brothers. She was lured away from a nunnery where she was staying, her quarters were searched, and a document was produced that itemized her various treacheries. It was a private confessional of self-accusations, sufficiently detailed to condemn her to death.

Three years later, the king, now wise to La Voison, appointed a commission to prosecute offenders like her. While many people were arrested, evidence against those whose prosecution would embarrass the king was suppressed, and some innocent people were imprisoned simply because they had inflammatory information. But La Voison was fair game. In February of 1680, she was tortured several times and executed, along with thirty-five others, in what came to be called the *affaire des poisons*. She apparently claimed to have slaughtered well over a thousand infants in her rituals (some sources say the figure was as high as twenty-five hundred).

Shortly thereafter, the king's military campaigns, aimed at increasing France's power and prosperity, only inspired alliances that forced him to give up the gains he had made. His failure and inability to inspire strong successors led in the next century to increasing national discontent.

The Age of Arsenic

The sixteenth through the eighteenth centuries were clearly good years for poison. Innkeepers poisoned travelers for their goods, and men and women alike dispatched unwanted spouses and relatives. In England, for example, Thomas Lancaster killed at least eight people, mostly his wife's relatives. La Tofania was active in Italy, and by 1723, she was implicated in the deaths of over six hundred victims. Reportedly a man-hater, she was alleged to have organized a sisterhood of poisoners who dispensed arsenic concoctions—"*aqua tofania*"—to those who could afford it for ridding themselves of tiresome relatives. (La Tofania confessed under torture, so it's anyone's guess how many victims she actually had.) Germany had poisoners, too: Gessina Gottfriend killed people unchecked for thirteen years.

The detection of poisons in a human body was to become the first significant discovery of clear physical evidence in the field of forensic science, primarily because poison became such a pervasive weapon. But that would not stop many from perfecting their techniques.

While an alleged biography of the Barber of Fleet Street, Sweeney Todd, claims that he was a real person during the late 1700s and was responsible for more than 150 murders, no one has proven his actual existence beyond Victorian fiction. But though eighteenth-century documentation on serial murders is sparse, a sensational murder case of the period did involve medical professionals offering expert opinions, primitive though they were, thus paving the way for an increased reliance on forensic science. The incident occurred in England in 1751. Mary Blandy had agreed to marry Captain William Cranstoun, a man of supposed wealth and position but in fact both poor and already married. Mary's father wanted to oust the bum, but she loved him, so she agreed to Cranstoun's plot to administer poison to her father to hasten her inheritance.

Arsenic has different effects depending on degrees of ingestion. It is absorbed from the bowels into the bloodstream and then into the organs. The liver, which takes up toxins, gets the brunt of its effect, but when delivered in one large dose, this poison quickly hits the brain as well. When delivered in smaller doses over a period of time, the poison affects the peripheral nerves, stripping their insulating sheaths. Victims will feel a prickly heat, like hot needles, and the skin may blister. They will also suffer severe headaches, nausea, numbness, and general weakness.

Mr. Blandy grew ill with gastric distress, so a servant examined his food. She suggested to the old man that Mary was using arsenic on him, but he allowed his daughter to continue to prepare his food, and soon he was dead. The plot was discovered and Cranstoun fled, but Mary was arrested and tried. Four doctors who had observed Blandy's internal organs at autopsy stated that their "preserved quality" indicated probable arsenic poisoning. The state of the art in medicine at the time supported their findings. One doctor applied a hot iron to the powder that the concerned servant had secured to analyze it by smell—a primitive test, but an attempt to be objective. The jury listened to the evidence, found Mary guilty of murdering her father, and sentenced her to be hanged.

Around this time, in 1764, criminology—the psychological analysis of criminal behavior—was also gaining ground in Italy with the publication of *Trattato dei délitti e elle pèna,* by Cesare Bonesana ("Beccaria"), republished in England as *Essays on Crimes and Punishment.* Beccaria had been inspired by the case of a Huguenot man accused of killing his son for converting to Roman Catholicism. Under torture the man had confessed, but Voltaire found the boy's death to be a suicide and had included his analysis in a published appeal for religious tolerance. He managed to obtain a posthumous reversal of the conviction, which provided grist for his plea to stop the torture of religious dissidents. Beccaria shared this ideal about justice and set out to free the legal system from religious domination. He hoped for a revival of the classical ideals of Ancient Greece, which grounded the state's power to punish wrongdoers in the collective welfare. Beccaria viewed crime as less the result of demonic influence than of the offender's rational decision. Thus, he believed that punishments should fit the crime, should decrease the risks of committing a crime, and should affirm the belief that crime does not pay. This philosophy of creating a healthier community through the legal structure was part of a new view of the relations of people to themselves and to society. It also turned the field of criminology into a separate inquiry.

Less than two decades later, another forensic science began to prove itself. In 1784, in Lancaster, England, John Toms was convicted of murder on the basis of a "matching test." In his pocket upon his arrest after a fatal shooting was a torn piece of newspaper that exactly matched the torn edge of a wad of newspaper removed from his pistol.

For murderers, those eras defined by ignorance and class divisions had provided all sorts of easy cover, as well as guises that offered killers a specific kind of identity, such as a werewolf. But science was displacing religion, and that would have its own unique influence on serial crimes. Instead of its diminishing incidents of the phenomenon, it led to a clear increase in them.

CHAPTER THREE

Murder and Science

The New World

As medieval darkness yielded to light, the known world started to change. So did the way criminals played their roles. In fact, the mechanization of Europe and its exploitation of other lands, while affirmed by philosophers as a greater good, provided a profitable social model for those with exploitive impulses. The more society emphasized an objective, controlled approach to human existence, the more its criminal undercurrent embraced this approach to justify its own momentum.

In 1453, the Ottoman Turks had recaptured Constantinople, which put them in a threatening position over the traditional trade routes with Asia and China. Better maps and navigation instruments encouraged exploration of lands across the ocean and those European countries best equipped set off to claim areas of Africa, India, and the

Americas. (The Vikings had already been there but did not stay.) Spain and Portugal monopolized South and Central America, so England, France, and others went farther north. France headed into Canada, while the Dutch settled the island of Manhattan. Then Spanish explorers established the first permanent European settlement of what would become the United States, in St. Augustine, Florida. But the British eventually claimed the advantage.

The King of England granted charters to British companies, which colonized parts of North America along the Atlantic coast. They made their initial inroads on Roanoke Island, North Carolina, in 1585, and two decades later in Jamestown. In 1624, Virginia became the first crown colony, with a governor. Tobacco and sugar plantations prospered, encouraging slave trade with Africa in the south, while Puritans sought freedom to practice their religion in the north. Eventually, Britain knocked out the Dutch, and the land along the Atlantic coast from New England to the Carolinas became theirs. Then France and Britain clashed from 1756 to 1763 securing the British most of North America east of the Mississippi.

Yet France dominated the arts, and French was the universal language for the educated, with writers such as Voltaire, Rousseau, and Diderot espousing ideas about justice and political reform. Thanks to the humanistic Enlightenment and the idea of rule by the people, the western hemisphere experienced an unprecedented number of revolts by those seeking better conditions. Human rights were emphasized and intellectual movements continued to challenge and erode religious authority. Emperor

Joseph II attempted to impose new policies on the Austrian populace, and Frederick II did the same in Prussia, while in America and France the emerging middle classes resisted aristocratic tyranny in any form.

In North America, Britain had thirteen colonies, and once they had defeated the French in 1763, the colonials collaborated twelve years later to throw off King George III. To achieve representation in legal and economic matters, they went to war and forced a British surrender in 1781. The new United States of America rejected the idea of rule by the elite and, as the first democracy of the modern world, voted leaders into power by the will of the people.

Within the chaos of these times, especially in the unsettled West, the first documented U.S. case of serial murder arose. A team of cousins, Micajah and Wiley Harp (changed from William and Joshua Harpe), who passed as brothers and who had fought in the Revolutionary War, perpetuated a string of brutal crimes. Growing up in an immigrant family from Scotland, Big Harp and Little Harp planned to run a plantation in North Carolina, but the American Revolution turned them into Tory outlaws. They fought for the British but deserted the army in 1781. After kidnapping two women for wives, they set out for the American wilderness. When their wives gave birth, they ruthlessly slaughtered the babies.

Crossing through the Kentucky and Tennessee territories, the two men killed relatives and strangers at whim, racking up anywhere between twenty and forty victims. According to historical accounts, they would put stones inside the abdomens of victims and dump them into rivers, or mutilate the bodies and leave them in the wilderness for the animals to scavenge. They also joined a team of river pirates with whom they felt encouraged to indulge their sadistic streaks, and in one incident they reportedly bound a man naked to a horse and sent it over a cliff. They made no distinction among children, women, or men as their victims, or between freemen and slaves. They simply raped, thieved, and killed as opportunities arose. The Harps eluded justice several times, frightening posses and escaping from prison before they were finally caught for good.

The older Harp was captured first, around 1800, and he confessed to twenty murders before his head was removed and displayed at a Kentucky crossroads. Little Harp survived four more years before making the error in Mississippi of seeking bounty on another man's head. He was recognized when he went to claim the reward, hanged, and decapitated.

The Harps had exploited these unsettled areas during the 1790s, as well as taken advantage of the difficulty primitive law enforcement had in locating killers in remote and mountainous areas. Such a task was dangerous for the newly formed U.S. marshals, appointed by President George Washington in 1789, and many were killed. Unlike the compulsive fantasy-driven killers of today, who tend to be repetitive, the Harps murdered people in a variety of ways, from shooting to stabbing to bludgeoning. But even had they behaved as the modern-day serial killer does, law enforcement had no concept then of solving crimes by observing offender behavior, so its inadequate investigation methods would likely have yielded few results.

Even as America was becoming a new country and the Harps were making their mark as its first known repeat killers, an important event in the history of forensic science occurred in Europe. In 1787, Johann Daniel Metzger devised a means for detecting arsenic in solutions. He discovered that when arsenious oxide is heated with charcoal, it forms a black mirrorlike deposit on a cold plate held over the coals. That substance is arsenic. His invention prepared the way in the next century for bringing science into the courtroom. But politics, too, was lending a hand in the more advanced countries by shifting the locus of power from aristocrats and clergy to the people.

In 1789, King Louis XVI made an unusual gesture that would change the destiny of Europe. He appealed to popular support by allowing a meeting of the long-defunct French Parliament. This resulted in the formation of a National Assembly representing the overtaxed middle class, and its members removed privileges from the nobles as they proclaimed that "men are born free and equal in rights." In short order, seeking relief from poverty, the masses rioted that summer, storming the Bastille prison in Paris. Eventually they beheaded numerous aristocrats, both as retaliation and as a warning to other countries rumored to be pondering invasion. In 1792, France became a republic, and after some years of chaotic rule, Napoleon Bonaparte arose to take power in 1799 as a military dictator.

During this time, several serial killers emerged in Bavaria. Anna Schonleben, neé Zwanziger, 49, was facing the prospect of growing old alone, and turned to house-keeping to attempt to win a man. First she murdered a woman intended as a wealthy man's wife, and then she moved on to the home of a younger man, who died when he failed to respond as she hoped. When she killed the wife of a lawyer, he dismissed her from his household, so she left arsenic behind in the salt boxes, poisoning the servants, the man, and his baby. They all survived, but Schonleben came under suspicion and her earlier victims were exhumed. The only known method for arsenic de-tection then was observation. The organs of these vic-tims showed an unusual state of preservation—sufficient proof that they had been poisoned. The authorities went in search of Schonleben, who was already on her way to other potential victims.

Yet even as this case was being investigated, the de-tection of arsenic advanced another step in 1806, when Valentine Rose discovered how to locate it in human or-gans. He used nitric acid, potassium carbonate, and lime, turning that mixture into powder form and treating it with coals to get the telltale mirror substance. The test might have been used on Schonleben's victims (accounts differ), and it would soon find its way into such cases, because the appeal of poison as a murder weapon showed no signs of diminishing.

With Schonleben still on the loose, in 1807 Bavaria saw another series of "lust murders." In Regendorf, Bar-bara Reisinger arrived at the home of Andreas Bichel to discuss an advertised position, and agreed to have her fortune revealed by looking into his "magic" mirror. Bichel told her that to accomplish this, her hands had to be tied and her eyes covered, but as she was eager to see what her future husband looked like, she complied. When she was ready, he proceeded to stab her repeatedly until she died. No one knew what to make of her disappearance, but they had no proof implicating Bichel. However, when another young woman associated with him also disappeared, local officials used a bloodhound to track a scent to the woodshed, where the dismembered remains of both women were uncovered. Bichel was arrested and brought to trial. His victims' remains were shown to him in court, whereupon he collapsed and confessed. He then said he had killed the women for their clothes.

In an 1865 book about lycanthropy by historian Sabine Baring-Gould, Bichel's blood lust is vividly described. Accordingly, the *"Mädchenschlächter"* (Bichel) reported that once he had begun to stab them, a strange passion seized him. "I opened her breast," he recounted in court, "and with an axe cut through the fleshy parts of the body. Then I arranged the body as a butcher does beef, and hacked it with a knife into pieces to fit the hole which I dug for it in the mountains. I may say that during the operation, I was so greedy that I trembled all over and could have ripped off a piece and eaten it." With that kind of testimony, his guilt was in no doubt, and he was convicted.

Then, in 1809, Anna Schonleben was arrested with a packet of arsenic on her person, which she called her "truest friend"—as much a confession as anything could be, short of her fully describing her crimes. She was held for trial and convicted.

In the same year that she was beheaded, London experienced not just a serial killer but a serial mass murderer. On a cold December 7 in 1811, the people in London's East End, around Ratcliffe Highway near the docks, had settled in for the night. Timothy Marr, his wife, and his apprentice were closing up their hosiery shop when an intruder entered. Along with the Marrs' baby, all were murdered as he bashed in their skulls and slashed their throats. They were discovered early the next morning, and the weapon used on them was determined to have been a seaman's maul, with the initials J. P. set in copper nails into the handle. However, nothing appeared to have been taken, aside from a bit of money, so the motive for this shocking massacre remained a mystery.

London panicked. While the Ratcliffe Highway area was far from genteel, the Marrs had been a hardworking family with no apparent ties to criminal elements. To make matters worse, there was no real police force. Criminal investigation methods had emerged in England with the "thief-takers," or bounty hunters, who were easily bribed. Then, in 1749, Sir Henry and John Fielding, successive magistrates at the court at Bow Street, had established the Bow Street Runners, the first official constables in London. Their job was to track down known criminals and deliver writs of arrest. Their success was such that the office had been expanded and proposals made for routine patrols around the city. Nevertheless, there were no organized bodies for investigation and no detective bureaus.

Things settled down on Ratcliffe Highway, although the crime went unsolved. Then, on December 19, in the same part of town just down the road, a family residing at the King's Arms Inn suffered the same treatment. The inn's owner, John Williamson, was bludgeoned to death on the cellar stairs, and in the parlor his wife and the maid were found laid out with smashed skulls and slit throats. With two such cases, it appeared that London had a mass murderer on its hands.

Soon circumstantial evidence pointed to an Irish sailor, John Williams. The constables searched his lodging house and found that a trunk there belonging to a sailor out at sea was missing a maul. That sailor's name was John Peterson—J. P. Two days before Christmas, Williams was arrested. The damning facts against him were that he'd had the opportunity to take the sledgehammer, he'd gotten mud on his shoes, and he'd returned to his room just after the killer had fled the second crime scene.

The courts in those days relied largely on logic and eyewitness testimony. If a narrative could be devised that fit the facts and made sense, then more than likely a person would be found guilty. Investigators did not yet think about or possess ways to process and match blood evidence, interpret blood spatter patterns, look for fingerprints, or make a soil analysis. The best they could do was surmise what must have happened, given what they knew, and then leave it for the courts.

However, Williams never got to trial. He hung himself in the Coldbath Fields Prison. But that was not sufficient for the populace. Just to ensure that his restless soul would never rise again, a procession of citizens hammered a stake through his heart before he was buried at a crossroads.

Science Inspires the Noble and Debased

Napoleon had crowned himself emperor of the French in 1804, shortly after America made the Louisiana Purchase from them, and he dissolved the Holy Roman Empire and extended France's frontiers across Europe. By 1811, the French empire ran from the Baltic Sea to the south of Rome, through Italy, Spain, Switzerland, and into most of Germany and Poland. These conquered lands were reshaped with new systems and laws. Under Napoleon's encouragement, manufacturing and industry prospered. So did forensic investigation.

During that time, as one story goes, the Empress Josephine, wife of Napoleon, discovered that his wedding gift to her, a priceless emerald necklace, was missing. It had been stolen from Malmaison, a small estate just outside the city where she was staying. Napoleon was furious. He ordered his director of police to spare no effort to find it. The director had more than three hundred men to work with, but none was trained for this type of task. The French police at that time were generally used as spies to report political uprisings. While they were also supposed to suppress crime, they had no experience with investigative techniques, so it wasn't long before they were stumped—an impasse that provided an opportunity for a unique man named Eugene Francois Vidocq.

It's difficult to pinpoint who Vidocq really was, since many authors from his time based characters and incidents on him, and since he remained mum on certain subjects while exaggerating others. Throughout his life his exploits were legendary, and his own autobiography was entirely penned by a sensationalist ghostwriter. He was aware of the notion that perception is truth and used it to his advantage. Supposedly, he once told author Honoré de Balzac the secret to passing as someone else: "Observe what you would become, then act accordingly and you will be transformed."

Born on July 23, 1775, Vidocq was the son of a baker but preferred the life of an adventurer. He joined the army, and on leave from the Bourbon Regiment, he interfered with an execution and was arrested. The daughter of a high-placed official intervened, and Vidocq found himself forced to marry her. Breaking it off, he posed in various places as a military officer and learned to become a successful card shark. Arrested for desertion, he escaped, and by the age of twenty he was a fugitive from justice.

It wasn't long before he was arrested again, over a scene he made in Paris upon finding his mistress with another man. For that, Vidocq was sentenced to three months in jail. There he met a farmer serving six years for stealing grain to feed his family. Taking pity, Vidocq forged a pardon for him—which got him a harsh sentence of eight years in the galleys. He escaped, was caught, and escaped again. Each time, his sentence grew longer, until he was ultimately sent to Brest's dreaded naval prison.

One day, he explained his plight to the head of the Lyons police, Jean-Pierre Dubois, who investigated it. Dubois realized that Vidocq was actually guilty of only one minor misdeed, so he released him and offered him a position in town as a police informer. Vidocq entered the Lyons underworld. He succeeded at his new occupation, and the Lyons arrest rate accelerated. Moving to Paris, he became a spy for the Criminal Division of the Paris Prefecture of Police. From within La Force prison, Vidocq would send reports twice a week about hidden contraband and planned crimes. He solved murders by listening to his "fellow" convicts discuss their deeds. After a year, he "escaped" and began to mingle with the criminal element outside the prison, succeeding as a spy in that world as well. Thus, by 1809, Vidocq's fortunes had changed. So had the future of law enforcement.

Now he was challenged with solving a crime that would get Napoleon's attention and demonstrate his skills. In disguise, he entered taverns where rogues gathered and got acquainted with them, keeping his ears open for the right information. Within three days (as the legend goes), Vidocq managed to do what the entire Parisian police force could not: locate the thief and the necklace. That got Napoleon's attention, and Vidocq explained his vision of forming a detective bureau. In 1813, Napoleon signed a decree that made Vidocq's *Brigade de la Sûreté* a national security force. He hired people whose identities were known only to him, including women. They all had criminal records, which annoyed the uniformed police, and they were paid for each arrest. Despite doubts from officials, they quickly proved themselves. In their first year, they made hundreds of arrests.

The *Brigade de la Sûreté* also made significant contributions to the art of investigation. Vidocq kept meticulous records about prisoners, including criminal backgrounds, modus operandi, and physical descriptions. He required regular written reports that documented the demonstrable facts of an investigation. His detectives maintained a card-style index for each case, used disguises, and paid their informants. Vidocq also instituted a form of plea bargaining, used psychological interrogation methods, and employed the "new sciences" of handwriting analysis, firearms evaluations, and plaster of Paris casts of shoeprints. On the side, he created indelible ink. He was assisted in this by an analysis of a questioned document in 1810 in Germany, where a chemical test to establish the authenticity of a particular ink dye was applied to a document known as the *Konigin Hanschritt.*

Others in France kept up with him. In 1813, Mathieu Joseph Bonaventure Orfila published a book, *Traite de Poison,* or *Treatise of General Toxicology.* In it, he summed up everything known about poisons at the time and offered classifications. He had tried to demonstrate the various tests for poison detection and had found them to be highly unreliable. He also refined Valentine Rose's method of arsenic detection to achieve greater testing accuracy and showed with animal tests that, after ingestion, arsenic gets distributed throughout the body. Orfila won a prominent position at Paris University and was invited to consult on several criminal cases. Forensic toxicology had still to develop, but this man was determined to use his scientific knowledge for social betterment.

The World Changes Again

There was a downside to French domination of Europe, in heavy taxation and trade restrictions that fed a growing desire for Napoleon's demise. Eventually Britain, his enemy since the 1812 war that had set the boundary between the United States and Canada, invaded France. Napoleon also took a devastating blow from Russia, and his retreat inspired other countries to join against him. By 1814, Paris had fallen and Napoleon was banished. He attempted to regain his throne, but the British and Prussian armies defeated him at Waterloo. France was treated well at the Congress of Vienna in 1814–15, however, and a royal ruler was restored.

During this time, poets, composers, and novelists had ushered in an age of feeling with the Romantic movement. Goethe, Wordsworth, Shelley, and Beethoven explored and celebrated intense emotional expression. Napoleon's exploits had been good subjects for stirring tales, and with his defeat the longing for national identity and pride further inspired artists. Dying for a cause became a noble goal and young men throughout Europe entered into revolutions in the name of glory and freedom. As an activist spirit burgeoned, the Industrial Revolution put more money and goods into the hands of people once forced to work for nobles, providing them with sufficient power to challenge traditional forms of authority.

Inventions were still encouraged, and in 1823 in the realm of forensic science the Czech physiologist Johan Evangelist Purkinje published a description of nine fingerprint types, and five years later William Nichol invented the polarizing microscope. Knowledge of human anatomy, too, was gaining ground, and that produced yet a new breed of murderer.

During the 1500s, the early anatomists who dissected corpses to study the body had gained support when the Emperor Charles V had decreed that medical expertise be used in all trials involving suspected murder or abortion. These professionals noticed how things like "rigor mortis" (state of muscle rigidity) or "algor mortis" (the body's cooling temperature) worked in the postmortem state, and to the list they added the progression of color changes known as "livor mortis," or lividity (blood settling in the body at the lowest point of gravity). Medical men continued to study this, and by the late 1700s French physician Pierre Nysten had observed the subtle changes in rigor mortis from flaccid to stiff to flaccid and penned "Nysten's law," which held that the process begins in the face and neck and moves downward throughout the body. In England, in the spirit of science and precision, Dr. John Davey used thermometers to measure corpses' diminishing body temperature.

Around that time, with the growing sophistication of scientific inventions, industrial technology, and medical discoveries, coupled with the breakdown of religion's dominance, a certain practice arose in the medical community that inspired a unique motive for repeat murder. Science was becoming the dominant force of the new humanism, and whatever was done to promote scientific knowledge seemed justified. That included treating the once-sacred human body as an object of study. However, sometimes scientists made their gains from nefarious deeds, turning a blind eye as they paid for cadavers that came from places about which they did not wish to know. A living could be made from the darker side of science, and this encouraged certain men already committing crimes "for science" to become killers.

Body snatching, or removing fresh corpses from graves, had long served the purposes of religious cults that needed human organs for sacred rituals, so in 1604 King Henry had made this practice a felony in England. In part, this was due to the religious doctrine that to get into heaven the body must be intact. Medical schools were allowed four corpses each year from the gallows, but this supply was terribly inadequate, so in some places students were required to supply their own corpses. That meant raiding the cemeteries. Since they could not afford to be arrested, the students often paid "resurrectionists," or "sack 'em up" men, to take the risk for them. Some of these resurrectionists grew quite adept at spiriting a body out of a grave without being discovered; indeed, one gang of ghouls stole nearly eight hundred bodies in the course of two years.

But there was always an easier way for those who didn't

mind it. Some body snatchers turned to outright murder and some killers skipped the cemetery altogether but pretended they'd gone the usual route. Realizing that a "marked" corpse lost value, one team devised a clever technique. William Burke ran a boardinghouse, Log's, in western Edinburgh, Scotland, with his partner, William Hare. Together they would get their victims drunk and grab them in an armlock around the throat or sit on their chests while holding their noses closed until they died. This method, which came to be known as "burking," left no bruises or punctures.

In nine months, Burke and Hare managed to kill sixteen people, selling them, one after another, for an average of ten pounds. Citizens began to notice that poor and homeless people were missing in significant numbers, and one boarder discovered a female body in a straw bed at Burke's home. He was caught red-handed, although he and Hare were able to quickly sell the corpse to Dr. Robert Knox. But to save himself Hare turned king's evidence and testified against Burke, who was convicted and then hanged on Christmas Day in 1828 in Grassmarket. Ironically, his corpse was turned over to the anatomists at Surgeons Square. Thirty thousand people witnessed his execution and anatomized body, which was put on public display to deter others from emulating his foul deeds. People pressing forward to get a view nearly caused a riot. For his protection, Hare was smuggled to England, while Dr. Knox was burned in effigy.

That same year saw the execution of another serial murderer in Germany. Having been arrested in the deaths of

the wife and five children of her employer, Gesina Gott-
fried admitted that she not only had no remorse as she
watched people die by her hand—through poisoning—
but that she took a great deal of pleasure in it. She had also
used arsenic to dispatch her three husbands, her two children, three other relatives, and a friend. Her mistake was
to let one person live, because he turned her in. She was
convicted of the six counts of murder associated with the
man's wife and children—although clearly she was guilty
of more—and beheaded.

More Revolution

Back in France, the Romantic painter Eugene Delacroix
expressed the spirit of freedom and equality that the people sought, and in 1830 French citizens revolted again
and replaced the king with Louis Philippe. They wanted
the freedom to trade, to represent themselves through
voting, and to think for themselves rather than have "authorities" dictate to them. To avoid violence, Britain offered the people a political voice through Reform Acts,
and several other countries followed suit.

In 1833, Eugene Vidocq, now fifty-eight, submitted
his resignation from the *Sûreté*, but he did not retire. The
following year, he established the world's first private detective agency, remaining active until he was eighty years
old. His success with innovative investigative methods
influenced the formation of detective squads across France
and in other countries; his techniques paved the way for

forensic scientists to introduce new inventions into the methods of law enforcement.

Also during the 1830s, James Marsh tested the coffee of a victim of poisoning, but was unable to convey to a jury how he had detected arsenic in it, so he decided to make his methods more demonstrable to uneducated minds. In a closed bottle, he treated poisoned material with sulfuric acid and zinc. From this bottle emerged a narrow U-shaped glass tube, with one end tapered, through which arsine gas emerged to hit zinc and escape. The escaping gas could be ignited to form the expected black mirror substance. This method became known as the Marsh Test. It was sufficiently precise to test small amounts of arsenic, and sufficiently visual for juries. Mathieu Orfila later used the Marsh Test to analyze cemetery soil for the presence of arsenic, so that exhumed bodies that had absorbed it from the surrounding dirt could be distinguished from those that had been poisoned aboveground.

Light and Shadow

In 1829, the British Crown assented to Sir Robert Peel's Metropolitan Police Bill, which was the beginning of an organized, full-time police force in London. Called Peelers or Bobbies (both derived from Peel's name), they were housed at Whitehall Place near Great Scotland Yard (and later moved to another building called New Scotland Yard). During the 1840s, a separate Detective Department was established, and over the course of the next few decades, most of Britain had replaced parish constables with local police forces.

In 1835, Bow Street Runner Henry Goddard made the first successful bullet comparisons to catch a killer. He noticed an odd mark on a bullet taken from a victim's body, so he pocketed it. With suspects in mind, he looked for a bullet mold at the residences of those individuals that would match the blemish. In one suspect's home, the bullet mold showed a flaw that was matched to the mark on the bullet, effectively tying the man to the shooting. Confronted, he confessed, and Goddard became the forerunner of a long line of experts in forensic ballistics, although it would be many decades before this field became a rigorous discipline.

Back in the United States, which had expanded again in 1819 with the acquisition of Florida from Spain, the British system of justice was put in place, and the 1820s had seen two confessed repeat murderers executed: On the Indiana frontier, John Duhmen was arrested for two murders, but admitted to having killed more people in Europe and America, while Samuel Green was hanged for "numerous murders" in New England. Then attention shifted to the South in what was to become a sensational case of "mad doctors" and excessive brutality.

In New Orleans, a Creole-style mansion in the midst of the French Quarter on the corner of Royal and Governor Nicholls Streets was the home of Dr. Louis Lalaurie and his wife, Delphine. She was a beautiful woman with long black hair, and they were renowned for their extravagant parties. They had many slaves and seemed a respectable pair, but little did townspeople know what Madame Lalaurie did to make her slaves submissive. She had been in court over charges of brutality, and on one occasion several slaves were removed from the home, but few people would speak out against such a wealthy couple, so they remained free of arrest. Then one night in 1834, a fire brought a volunteer brigade to the home, and the Lalauries' disturbing secrets were discovered.

As they put out the flames, firemen broke into a locked attic room, and were stunned by what they saw. According to several accounts, dead slaves were chained to the walls, but the piteous cries coming from cages revealed several who were still alive—if barely. Once the fire was contained, they were rescued, but some of them were in such a state, it might have been more merciful to let them die. Most had been severely maimed by medical experiments. One man had been surgically transformed into a woman, and one woman was so deformed she looked like a human crab. Her arm and leg bones had been broken and reset at odd angles. Another woman's arms had been amputated and her skin peeled off in a spiral pattern, while the lips of a third were sewn shut. A few had skin grafts and some had been dissected, with their organs still exposed. One man had a stick protruding from a hole in his skull. Scattered around the room were pails full of body parts, organs, and severed heads. Among those who had died were males whose faces had been grotesquely disfigured.

A lynch mob was formed that night, but the Lalauries had apparently realized that the fire spelled the end of their experiments. During the chaos, they escaped, and they were never heard from again; some believed they went back to France. Renovations years later uncovered even more skeletons, but no one knows how many unfortunates they actually victimized. This pair of sadistic killers became part of the city's legend, their former home the residence of ghosts.

While the Dark Ages may have yielded to the rise of science and the Enlightenment, it's evident that in many places shadows still ruled. Even so, those who hoped to contain evil were making progress. Killers came face-to-face with real adversaries in the form of clever detectives. Vidocq had inspired improvements in physical science, now known as criminalistics, and he also relied on psychological analysis, which would become a cornerstone in learning how to locate and trap a serial killer. The subject would also become a beacon for the media, as Vidocq had, and the disseminating of information on criminals in the form of compelling stories would have its own influence on criminal behavior. And soon, a serendipitous discovery by the manager of a near-failing American newspaper was about to shift how the popular mind perceived both murder and its investigation.

CHAPTER FOUR

Crime, Police, and Reporters

Farther Than the Eye Can See

As crime detection became more efficient, criminals also grew savvier. With the increased sense of confidence and power that accompanied the spirit of invention at one level of society, its underside generated a dark mirror. Without the supernatural doctrines that long had defined good and evil, certain human beings—criminals and victims—became a new kind of devil and angel. And that went hand-in-hand with social progress, which gave people more time to pay attention to stories.

England grabbed the lead during the Industrial Revolution, which accelerated with the steam engine's invention and the production of coal as cheap fuel. Factories were built to house larger machines and produce readily available goods. Markets once limited by rural needs increased in size and variety, and banks supported their growth. Roads and transportation improved, as did overland travel conditions and the use of canals for connecting industries with those markets. Tracks were laid for railways in what would become a massive network across Europe, and yet higher living standards arrived for some at the cost of slave-labor conditions for others. Everyone scrambled for position as wealthy merchants challenged the privileged classes for social status. Changes were inevitable, from the lowest levels of society to the top political positions, and better industry meant better military . . . and more aggression. The world slowly mobilized, with growth and invention providing a bridge for future conflicts on a grander scale.

In 1826, a Dutch steamship crossed the Atlantic without a sail. It signaled humankind's freedom from dependence on nature for power. The U.S. began laying track for a network of trains, while waves of emigration to new lands took European culture and technology with them, settling Australia, South America, South Africa, and the western territories of North America. More people began to read and respond to cultural trends. Toward the middle of the nineteenth century, newspapers in America, which reported primarily political, economic, and trade news, were about to make a dramatic shift into a particular form of public entertainment.

A Winning Formula

Mrs. Rosina Townsend, proprietress of a bordello in Manhattan, heard the last "visitor" come in for the night, so around 1 A.M. that Sunday, April 10, 1836, she went to bed. At the time of the incident, politicians, lawyers, journalists, and wealthy merchants were "courting" her nine girls. Two hours later, she awoke to the smell of smoke, which turned out to be a fire in Helen Jewett's upstairs room.

Although there would not be an organized fire department in the city for another decade, or even a full-time police department, a night watchman on Thomas Street heard the cry of alarm. He grabbed a club and ran to the scene. Once the fire was extinguished, they saw a dead woman in bed, her nightclothes mostly burned. It was Helen Jewett, and it appeared that someone had bludgeoned her with a sharp implement.

The key suspect was Richard P. Robinson, nineteen, a cultured young man and frequent client. He was arrested and taken to see the corpse, but he denied any involvement. Robinson stood trial nevertheless, and this incident serendipitously mated crime with journalism in a unique new way. To this point, crime reports had been succinct, factual, and distant. But that was about to change.

Several newspapers were a mainstay among the thriving businesses in the area. The *New York Herald,* edited by James Gordon Bennett, was one such paper. He was a sardonic Scotsman who entered the business in the 1820s when newspapers had no banner heads, bylines, interviews, charts, foreign reports, columnists, gossip, photographs, or cartoons. Bennett thought the press was dull and drab, so to increase both circulation and readability, he decided to find exciting news and deliver it moments after it occurred. His competitors among the penny sheets, the *New York Sun* and *New York Transcript,* devoted no more than half a column to police reports, but Bennett sensed that the populace would be interested in the tragedies of fellow humans. When the murder of Helen Jewett came to his attention, he turned it into the most sensational piece of journalism to be seen to date in the country. In fact, the very first direct interview for a newspaper appeared on April 16, in Bennett's newspaper.

The subjects of sex, crime, and scandal, heretofore believed to be unfit material for those of higher moral character, were about to become the primary targets of enterprising reporters. Bennett's success with "yellow" journalism, as it would later be dubbed, forced other papers to follow his lead. His accounts shocked his readers, but transfixed them as well. Even as they criticized, they demanded more salacious content.

Bennett himself boldly went to the crime scene, and as he approached the violated house, he spotted a crowd of young men outside. He entered and listened to Mrs. Townsend eagerly repeat her tale. Then he viewed the body, covered with a sheet. An officer revealed the dead woman for Bennett to see, and in his paper he offered an innovative first-person report. He detailed the sensual contours of the body, stiffened now with rigor mortis, and selectively mentioned aspects of the woman's beauty, comparing her to the "Venus de Medici." He noticed how the fire had "bronzed" her skin along the left side, making her look like "an antique statue." He also noted the bloody gashes that had brought about her "dissolution."

These erotic elements set the public imagination on fire. Bennett's spicy death scene observations increased his newspaper circulation so fast he could not keep up. To ride this tide, he researched the backgrounds of the principal parties and provided heartfelt editorials about morality and the likelihood of Robinson's guilt. He then interviewed Mrs. Townsend for a "scoop," and decided that she was a likely suspect as well, so he reprinted the interview verbatim in his newspaper—to her dismay. Now he was not so certain about young Robinson—another twist.

The *Sun* and the *Transcript* then sided together against the *Herald's* suggestion of Robinson's innocence and showed sympathy for Helen. As a result of all this interest, another market was created, among artists and lithographers. Several developed images of the principal parties and the murder scene itself. These sold for high fees and a few became famous around the world. In addition, a cultlike movement started in which young men who sympathized with Robinson donned cloaks and caps like those he had often worn, to show their identification with him. These men were at the forefront of the "sporting male" culture, which promoted aggression, entitlement, and indulgence. Robinson was their idol, a symbol of their sexual freedom. Helen, too, had her supporters—women who donned white beaver caps with a black band of crepe. They opposed the defenders of her accused murderer.

The *Herald* kept the case front-page news, and city papers in Philadelphia, Boston, New York, Baltimore, and Washington, D.C., were pressured by reader demand into reprinting Bennett's detailed accounts. Then another sinister development occurred.

A two-volume diary was discovered in Robinson's room that bore the warning: "Whoever shall pry unbidden into the secrets of this book will violate the whole of the Ten Commandments." It wasn't long before editors gleefully posted excerpts. Robinson acknowledged in the diary that while he looked innocent and naïve, he was a depraved profligate. He was subsequently identified in print as a "consummate scoundrel," while Helen was now a beautiful girl shamelessly seduced. Heroes, fallen heroines, and villains were meshed in larger-than-life scenarios for public consumption.

The trial itself began on June 2, 1836, less than two months after the murder, and for the first time in American history, representatives from out-of-town newspapers were present at a murder trial. The marshals allowed a thousand spectators at a time into the chamber and then rotated them out to bring in more. On June 8, the jury found Robinson not guilty, which caused controversy around the country. After this case, thanks to keen public interest, journalism would never be the same—especially as it approached the age of the modern serial killer.

Forensic Science

As society was beginning to realize maximum production from minimum effort, those principles were applied to social patterns as well. English lawyer Jeremy Bentham outlined a utilitarian program that included the prevention of crime, improved law enforcement, and hard labor in prisons. With organized police forces available, the sporadic establishment of detective bureaus, and a growing demand for public safety, scientists continued to make discoveries. In 1839, reliable procedures for the microscopic detection of sperm were published and photography was invented in France with the first daguerreotype. But toxicology failed in a notorious case in England.

During the 1830s, Thomas Griffiths Wainewright, aka "Wainewright the Forger," an artist and former contributor to *London Magazine,* was suspected in the killings of three relatives and a friend for profit. He hid out in France, but returned to London, where he was recognized and arrested for defrauding the Bank of England. About the murder of his sister-in-law, he reportedly said, "It was a dreadful thing to do, but she had very thick ankles." Yet because the poison he'd allegedly used had been strychnine, which was difficult for toxicologists to detect at the time, he was not proven to be a murderer. Instead of going to the gallows he was transported to "Van Dieman's Land"—Australia—for forgery. The public was outraged, believing that he'd gotten away with murder.

In 1840, experts also entered a murder trial to provide toxicological testimony, and due to their mistakes the case was nearly lost, but the ultimate result was that this science gained even greater ground. The case involved the prosecution in France of Marie LaFarge, twenty-four, for the murder by arsenic of her husband, Charles LaFarge.

Just prior to his death, she had purchased a relatively large amount of arsenic "for rats." Servants reported that Marie had stirred white powder into her husband's food, and a pharmacist found the food to be poisoned, so the circumstances were clearly against her.

The prosecution's experts used the Marsh Test but were unable to determine if the contents of LaFarge's stomach contained arsenic, so they exhumed the body to test the organs. The results still came up negative. The court then retained the famed Mathieu Orfila, and he performed the same tests. He got positive results, proving the presence of arsenic in LaFarge's body as well as the fact that it had not originated in the soil surrounding the coffin. The other experts had simply bungled the task—a significant lesson for the courts. Based on Orfila's results, Marie was convicted and sentenced to death (later commuted to life in prison).

Doctors and pathologists were then recognized as the first forensic scientists, and certain procedures were formalized in terms of what had to be proven about poisoning for a conviction. As yet, the actual amount of poison in the body could not be measured, so prosecutors had to rely as well on building a convincing circumstantial case, but the LaFarge incident inspired those who hoped to gain support for science to take care with its techniques.

In 1843, the Belgian *Sûreté Publique* took the first known mug shots of criminals, making them the ancestors of judicial photography. The daguerreotype process involved a mirror-polished silver-plated copper sheet that was treated with iodine fumes, which converted its surface into a thin coating of silver iodide. After the plate was exposed in the camera, it was developed with a vapor of metallic mercury. While it was not clear for what purpose these early photographs (featuring both the faces and hands) were taken, the Swiss used it during the next decade for identifying released prisoners suspected of returning to their criminal profession. During the 1850s, efforts got under way in police departments across Europe and in the U.S. to compile and catalogue archives of prisoner images. When needed, they could be used on "Wanted" posters.

Psychiatry, too, addressed criminal issues, since many offenders suffered from mental diseases. One such case in Britain was to have historic implications for the justice system there and in America, especially in cases of extreme violence.

Criminal Insanity

With the rise of modern science and the emphasis on natural law and material substance, the appraisal of human character from external appearances became a fashion. Phrenology involved feeling the bumps or depressions on a person's skull to determine how different areas of the brain were functioning. The brain was considered dividable into thirty-five different organs, each associated with such traits as "cautiousness" and "adhesiveness," and the larger the organ, the more pronounced the trait was believed to be. Hubert Lauvergne, the prison physician in

Toulon penitentiary, observed that many convicts had unusual faces, which he believed must reflect their criminal instincts. For a time, prisoners would be classified according to their phrenological profiles—a listing of traits specific to them, based on skull formation. Theorists believed that a child could overcome a disposition toward delinquency and later criminal conduct by strengthening those brain organs that controlled the desirable traits.

Thus, brain damage supposedly caused insanity, and the mentally deficient were distinguished from the mentally deranged. Autopsies were often performed on mental patients to locate lesions that might account for some trait or behavior, and some professionals studied treatment outcomes. The superintendents of mental institutions during the nineteenth century, called alienists (from their expertise with *aliéné*, or mental alienation), were generally educated but lacking in standard diagnostic theory. They began the rudimentary practice of psychiatry and founded journals, encouraged scientific findings in their fields, and promoted the view that the insane were not monsters but people imprisoned by their condition. To that point, the mentally deranged had generally been locked up—even chained up—and forgotten save by those who ministered to them. The conditions were terrible, but the new enlightened view was that these people deserved better hygiene and more compassionate treatment.

Despite the growing emphasis on free will in criminal assault, there were clear instances in which someone acted from a delusion or uncontrollable impulse, and some experts who studied them were pleading for better understanding. In 1837, Matthew Allen published an essay on the classification of insanity. He discussed the role of stressful relationships as a precipitator and described one of the first cases of parole into an asylum. In that same year, American psychiatrist Isaac Ray published a tract, *Medical Jurisprudence of Insanity*, which laid the basis for forensic psychiatry. Shortly thereafter, the issue of insanity came up in a British court, resulting in a historic decision that reflected this new tolerance in a way that would have wide-reaching repercussions into the next century.

Sir Robert Peel, founder of the English Bobbies, was the target of a deranged man in 1843 who mistook his secretary, William Drummond, for Peel. Daniel M'Naghten suffered from delusions that the "Tories" were conspiring against him. Believing they were closing in to murder him, he acted preemptively in self-defense, shooting Drummond. M'Naghten was arrested and tried, but common knowledge about his history of delusions supported his defense of madness. His counsel claimed that he had not known what he was doing and had been unable to control himself. The prosecution offered no rebuttal to the psychological plea, so the court declared that the accused must be found not guilty by reason of insanity. He was then sent to an asylum.

The public reacted negatively to this finding, so a royal commission was appointed to study the issue. In prior centuries, reference to a mental defect as a defense in a crime had depended on various tests, such as counting a certain amount of coins or demonstrating a moral kinship with wild beasts. But no more. The commission established the M'Naghten Rule, and thereafter the House of Lords made it a requirement that to establish a defense on the grounds of insanity, it must be proved that "at the time of the committing of the act, the party accused was laboring under such a defect of reason, from disease of the mind, as not to know the nature and quality of the act he was doing; or if he did know it, that he did not know he was doing what was wrong." That is, such a defense had to demonstrate more than just cognitive impairment; it had to prove that the behavior was not within the subject's moral awareness or control. This ruling became the basis as well for dealing with such cases in the U.S. legal system.

In 1845 the *American Journal of Insanity,* published in New York, started to include articles about the notion of self-control in cases of insanity, as well as on such topics as the importance of sleep in preventing insanity, the influence of the weather on mental states, and homicidal impulse. It also included a description of the murder trial of Abner Rogers, the first in a U.S. court to successfully introduce an insanity plea. He was found not guilty and was committed, but shortly thereafter killed himself.

During this time, alienists grappled with factors related to insanity, especially homicidal impulse, by testing what caused it; publishing papers ranging from "Fright, a Frequent Cause of Insanity" to studies of head injuries or "sensibility in nipples"; and examining the differences in manifestation of insanity between males and females. Quite a few issues of the *American Journal of Insanity* were concerned with trials in which mental illness was introduced as a homicidal factor, as well as the role of mental illness in confessions. Eventually this knowledge filtered down in primitive ways to criminals, who, seeking mitigating excuses, sought ways to pose as being mad.

Historic Shifts

In 1844, Samuel Morse sent a message from Baltimore to Washington by telegraph, and it wasn't long before an underwater transatlantic cable was laid for communication between Europe and America. But Europe was still unsettled. Even as the U.S. won a war against Mexico and acquired California—prompting a gold rush—there were revolutions in France, Germany, Austria, and Italy. France became a republic once more, but the revolutions in Hungary and Italy were crushed.

Around that time, in 1849, a case entered the American court system that set a standard for the use of science in deciding guilt and innocence. Boston landlord George Parkman, fifty-nine, went off one day to collect his rents, plus money he had loaned to Professor John Webster at Harvard Medical School. Known for his compassionate attitude toward the mentally ill, Parkman had studied with French psychiatrist Philippe Pinel, who in the 1830s made the bold move of removing the chains from some patients at the La Bicetre asylum. Parkman hoped to introduce such reform in America, but his aspirations were cut short.

He entered the building where Webster had a lab, but

no one saw him leave. A police search turned up nothing. Webster's uncharacteristic behavior, however, inspired a janitor to sniff around. He broke through a wall at the base of Webster's privy and found a decomposing pelvis, a dismembered thigh, and part of a leg. When the lab was searched again, a large chest was opened, revealing a dismembered human torso hollowed out to contain another thigh. In the furnace were charred bones, including a jawbone with artificial teeth.

At this stage in forensic science, it was difficult to prove who this person was, let alone a cause of death. For the trial, an anatomist drew a life-size picture that approximated Parkman's build and showed how the measurements of the decomposing parts would fit. Dr. Oliver Wendell Holmes, dean of the medical school, testified that someone with knowledge of anatomy and dissection had done the dismembering.

But the real prize for fledgling forensic science goes to a dentist, Dr. Nathan Keep, who insisted that the false teeth found in the furnace were Parkman's. He had made a wax mold of the man's peculiar protruding jaw and used it to show the jury how the jawbone fit it. Another dentist called this "class" evidence—other people's jaws might fit the mold—rather than evidence unique to an individual, but other dentists insisted that a dentist knows his own handiwork.

The judge apparently instructed the jury members (some say erroneously) that in the absence of an obvious corpse, they needed only reasonable certainty that the victim was Parkman and that he had been murdered. On the same day the jurors went to deliberate, they found Webster guilty. He eventually confessed and claimed that he had acted in self-defense, but he was hanged that same year. Thereafter, the testimony of medical experts became more important in criminal cases.

In 1850, in France, insect analysis made its first appearance in a Western court case. A mummified infant was discovered inside the wall of a building undergoing renovation, pointing the finger of accusation at a young couple who resided there. But they had not lived there long, so Dr. Marcel Bergeret constructed a time line based on what was then known about insect activity, comparing it against the activity found with the remains. He established via logic and a naturalist's knowledge that the infant had been placed in the wall two years earlier—before the couple had moved in.

Bergeret's approach to this case inspired widespread interest among pathologists, notably Edmond Perrier Mégnin in France, who regularly visited morgues and cemeteries and who eventually recorded eight distinct stages of necrophilous insect infestation. He would go on to publish a book on forensic entomology that identified those insects that were significant in estimates about the time that has passed since someone has died: egg-laying blowflies, beetles, mites, moths, and flies that liked fermented protein.

Another 1850 trial opened up a new area for toxicology. The male victim showed clear chemical burns in his mouth, tongue, and throat. Researcher Jean Servois Stas searched the body tissues for three months for the agent.

Using ether as a solvent, which he then evaporated to isolate the substance, he found the potent drug: nicotine. It was, in fact, the murder weapon. The man's killer had extracted this toxin from tobacco and force-fed it to the victim. With Stas's testimony, the killer was convicted, making Stas the first person to discover poisonous vegetable extracts in a body.

Other toxicologists then developed tests using the Stas procedure to determine the presence of various alkaloids in an obtained extract. But with more work, a problem became evident: false reactions. At times, alkaloids might develop in the body after death that mimicked the test reactions for the vegetable alkaloids. These substances became known as "cadaveric alkaloids," and they created a need for the development of new tests.

Then, in London, a murder trial in 1859 dealt a blow to science in the courtroom. Dr. Thomas Smethurst was accused of murdering his wife with arsenic, and the "greatest living toxicologist," Professor Alfred S. Taylor, misread his test results, which he was forced to admit in court. Furthermore, he and two other medical experts contradicted one another on matters in which there should have been no dispute. Dr. Smethurst was nevertheless convicted and sentenced to hang. Medical authorities debated the case so vociferously, with petitions to the crown, that another noted authority was asked to evaluate the results and Smethurst, who nearly went to the gallows, was pardoned. Detractors of forensic medicine dubbed it a "beastly science," which forced greater accountability upon physicians.

The National Spirit

Throughout Europe, liberal reforms failed to take shape and royal rulers regained their footing, but not without having to take the people's representatives into account. Members of various countries viewed themselves in terms of a collective identity, and Romanticism added the emotional glue of a shared foundation in noble civilizations and common values. Collections of small states became large nations, and it was soon Germany's turn to gain political domination in Europe. And just as the U.S. had won independence decades earlier, Mexico and the countries of Latin and South America prepared to shuck the domination of Spain and Portugal. Emigration accelerated as places like Australia and New Zealand offered the chance to get rich from gold mining.

But the U.S. crashed into its own troubles. Although the importation of slaves had been abolished and people in the industrialized North opposed a slave-based economy, Southern states still relied on this cheap labor, and political discussions about the secession of a coalition of states grew into a four-year civil war during the early 1860s before the country was once again uneasily rejoined.

Across Britain and the rest of Europe, beleaguered working classes formed trade unions to pressure for better wages and workplace conditions, inspiring the formation of producers' co-ops to shed the need for capitalist backing. Socialist creeds denounced private enterprise monopolies over the production of needed goods and food.

Yet science continued to prosper, including those discoveries that would assist criminal investigations. London put on the Great Exposition in the astonishing Crystal Palace to showcase the century's achievements in art and industry. All nations were invited to exhibit in this seventeen-acre building with the largest roof ever constructed. Over a hundred thousand exhibits were offered, launching the first in a series of world's fairs that would pit nations against one another in striving for the largest and most awe-inspiring designs. From steam engines to matches to the common yellow pencil, this kind of event was the place to see both accomplishment and new discovery.

Between 1853 and 1856, Ludwig Teichmann of Poland invented the first microscope crystal test for hemoglobin, and Richard L. Maddox developed dry plate photography, which reduced exposure time and the amount of bulky equipment required for processing methods. His technique proved highly useful in photographing inmates for prison records. During the same period, Sir William Herschel, a British officer, authenticated documents with thumbprints. This would eventually inspire the use of fingerprints in criminal investigations. In 1859, the U.S. became the first country in which photographs were used as evidence in a court of law, while in Germany, Gustav Kirchoff and Robert Bunsen demonstrated that the color of a flame can identify a burning substance. They founded the field of spectroscopy when they built the first spectroscope, a prism-based device that separated light into its chromatic components, or spectra, and made it possible to study the spectral signature of chemical elements in gaseous form. Over the next few years, presumptive tests were also developed for detecting blood on surfaces or clothing.

Charles Darwin also published *On the Origin of Species by Means of Natural Selection* in 1859, in which he proposed his theory of evolution based on survival of the fittest. It hit the right notes for the times, as thinkers turned away from religion and sought a better understanding of human origins. Tensions emanating from the Church forced many to choose sides, but the momentum was strong to recognize the laws of biology and how they applied in other human endeavors, politics not excluded. Realism in art, theater, and literature helped to reinforce the new scientific ideas.

During this era, though France and England instituted procedures to make cities safer, they still had their share of serial murderers. In the 1850s, Dr. William Palmer allegedly used antinomy to poison fourteen people, from his wife to creditors to a gambling companion. The rope used to hang him was cut into pieces and sold for a good profit. A decade later in France, Helen Jegado was arrested as a poisoner, suspected in as many as sixty deaths. Employed as a domestic servant, she apparently decided to get even for her sorry lot in life. She killed seven people in three months, including her sister, but pretended to be horrified by the "jinx" that seemed to follow her from one position to another. When she was caught stealing in one home, everyone grew ill the next day, and in 1851, a physician finally examined one of her victims.

By the end of that year, she had lost her life on the guillotine.

But rather than the quiet art of murder, some chose a bloodier sport. Marie Pichon, a maid, met Martin Dumollard in the spring of 1861 in Lyons, France. He promised her high wages for domestic service, so she accompanied him back to his home. Before they arrived, he attacked her, putting a rope around her throat, but she was sufficiently agile to escape him and run for help. Her frightened complaint sent the authorities to Dumollard's house. He was already a suspect in a crime that occurred six years earlier, when the body of a woman had been found near his home. After Pichon's report, they searched his home and found three female corpses, along with a vast wardrobe of female clothing of different sizes. Dumollard's wife, Marie, admitted to officials that over the past decade she and her husband had lured young girls into the house because Martin took a sick pleasure in killing them. Then Marie either used or sold the clothing. Dumollard pointed out a few secret graves but confessed that he had flung most of his victims into the river. He was executed, while his wife was sentenced to life in prison.

That same year, a nurse, Catherine Wilson, was convicted in the poisoning murders of at least seven patients, as well as her husband, and when she was hanged, twenty thousand people turned out. Spain and Italy saw their own form of serial killings during this time, and in New Orleans, a violent woman was responsible for several murders. Mary "Bricktop" Jackson, a longtime prostitute already at the age of twenty-five, was a terror in her brothel.

When a man called her a whore, she took a club and bludgeoned him to death. Another man argued philosophy with her, and she stabbed him to prove her point. Partnered with a female companion, she knifed a man who did not like her foul mouth, and for that she went to prison. There Bricktop met a one-armed jailer named John Miller, who had replaced his missing limb with an iron ball on a chain. When she got out, they joined forces. Her role was to lure people into dark alleys, where Miller bludgeoned them with the ball. But one day he made the mistake of turning on her. She grabbed his ball and chain, dragged him across the room, bit him, and used his own knife to kill him.

Like Bricktop, Joseph Phillipe, the "Terror of Paris," was no one to cross. He savagely knifed between eight and eighteen prostitutes before being executed in 1866. Three years later, Jean Baptiste Troppmann, twenty-two, was stopped after murdering a family of eight for profit, killing them, sometimes three at a time, over several days. One victim died from prussic acid, another was hacked to death, others were strangled or stabbed. Their bodies were soon unearthed, and the killer was arrested. During this time, the newspaper *Le Petit Parisien* sold half a million copies per day and engravers drew large profits from their artistic renditions of the crimes. After Troppmann was hanged, his hands were removed for anthropological study, because he had such large thumbs.

Also in Paris in 1869, an incident occurred that demonstrated the power of science and deductive reasoning. The French detective M. Gustave Macé, of the *Sûreté*, was faced with a real puzzler for his first case. The legs of a missing craftsman were found in a well, stitched into a bag. Macé learned that a tailor named Pierre Voirbo had visited the household that used the well, bringing work to a woman in an apartment upstairs. He then determined that Voirbo had known the murdered man, and found some of the victim's items among Voirbo's possessions. Macé realized that Voirbo's rooms had been cleaned, which meant that evidence was destroyed, but then he noticed that the floors were tiled, with alleys between the tiles. He poured water on the floor to see where it ran, and then lifted the tiles in that area. Beneath them was enough blood to indicate that something of a violent nature had occurred in that room. Voirbo, who had observed this innovative demonstration, confessed. But before he went to trial, he committed suicide.

In the U.S. from 1846 until 1871 the "Learned Murderer," Edward Rulloff, was at large. A self-taught genius, he was skilled as a doctor, lawyer, and carpenter, but his actual expertise was philology, the study of language formation; supposedly he spoke twenty-eight languages. But he was also a burglar and a murderer. He was suspected in the poisoning deaths of two female relatives, as well as the bludgeoning of his wife and daughter. Lack of evidence allowed him to get away with it until he shot and killed a store clerk in Ithaca, New York. In New York State's last public hanging, Rulloff was executed, and his unusually large brain was removed for study and preserved at Cornell University. Reportedly, before his death he said, "You cannot kill an unquiet spirit." On the gallows he urged the hangman to hurry, as he wanted "to be in hell in time for dinner."

Perhaps the most infamous of the poisoners during this time was someone that no one suspected—at least not for two decades. The Industrial Revolution was revealing dirty linens beneath its fine clothing, with the emergence of a lower middle class off of which others were growing wealthy. While more food was available and several significant medical advances had been made, the burgeoning population spilled into unhealthy slums in those towns that became centers of industry. Cheap housing thrown up around the factories produced overcrowding, and along with that more crime. Children were put to work in terrible conditions, although naïve economists preached that everyone would eventually benefit. Improvements did occur, but slowly and at a cost to many individuals. The rise of disease inspired more people to take out insurance, and that, too, led to crime, especially fraud and murder. Some people viewed life insurance as a way to enrich themselves, and one woman demonstrated what nineteenth-century psychiatrists were calling "moral insanity."

Seven-year-old Charlie Cotton had died after a troublesome gastrointestinal illness. As the autopsy progressed, the village surgeon noticed signs in the body of malnutrition, and also saw symptoms of poisoning. It was 1872, in a poor area of West Auckland, Britain, where children often died from poor health—especially gastric troubles, which was a catchall diagnosis for ailments not more specifically diagnosable. Indeed, Charlie's stepmother, Mary Ann Cotton, had lost all of her children from four different marriages to this disorder. In fact, she'd lost her husbands to it, too.

The surgeon notified the constables, who arrested her and looked into her background. It seemed that she was something of a jinx. Over the past two decades, some twenty-one people associated with her had died. Three of those bodies were exhumed and arsenic was found in all of them. That meant that Mary Ann Cotton had systematically murdered more than a dozen children, several men, her mother, and some friends. As pretty as she was, she'd had little trouble moving on and finding a new husband, and her pattern of murder indicated that she had used arsenic as a social stepping-stone: When a better opportunity presented itself, she killed off those who hindered her from grabbing it.

For a while, no one seemed to suspect that something was amiss. But when Mary Ann nagged one husband to get life insurance, he grew uneasy. When he discovered that she had attempted to insure him on her own, as well as bled his accounts, he sent her packing. But her next victim was less fortunate. Frederick Cotton's wife had recently died, leaving him with two young boys. Mary Ann seduced him and then got rid of his sister, who had introduced them and who lived in Cotton's house. She married him and, in short order, insured the lives of Cotton's children; then, when another man caught her eye, Cotton mysteriously died of gastric fever.

During those times, village physicians paid little attention to the poor, so it was an easy matter to murder someone with poison. Mary Ann's new lover moved in, but then she spotted another man with greater social standing, which meant she had to relieve herself of her "burdens." Cotton's oldest son and Mary Ann's baby both died within a few weeks, as did her live-in lover—all of them from terrible convulsions. Now she only had little Charlie left—and an unborn child. With the murder of little Charlie, she was finally caught.

In those days, not much was known about how narcissistic psychopaths grow bored and move on, regardless of the cost to others. To Mary Ann Cotton, other people were merely pawns. While under arrest, she gave birth to a girl, who was removed from her. Then she went to court. Although she was tried only for the death of Charlie, the other arsenic poisonings were introduced as evidence and because she could not explain her purchase of the arsenic, she had no defense. The twelve male jurists believed she was guilty of at least fourteen murders. Mary Ann proclaimed her innocence and collapsed.

On March 24, 1873, one of Britain's worst mass killers, as she was called, faced the hangman. When he opened the trapdoor, her neck failed to snap and she struggled and choked for over three full minutes. Then her corpse was cut down and her hair was shorn so phrenologists could take a cast of her skull for further study. As the case passed into public gossip, a song was penned to commemorate her grim deeds:

> *Mary Ann Cotton*
> *She's dead and she's rotten*

She lies in her bed
With her eyes wide open
Sing, sing, oh what can I sing?
Mary Ann Cotton is tied up with string
Where, where? Up in the air
Sellin' black puddens a penny a pair

It was the age of psychiatric study of the criminal, and medical men looked earnestly for ways to recognize killers before they began their deadly careers. The idea was noble, but its manifestations once more put a blemish on forensic science.

CHAPTER FIVE

Puzzling Over the Worst Criminal Minds

Troubles in a Young Country

With the United States again a unified country after the four-year struggle between the North and South, recovery was a priority, with effort going once more into expansion. Settling the American Wild West inspired hundreds of cold-blooded killings, because it was difficult to keep law and order—especially when some lawmen were outright killers themselves. Billy the Kid and the Jesse James gang took many lives without remorse, and while they were not considered classic serial killers with predatory motives, there was an air in these badlands of "anything goes." Those lacking moral boundaries would often kill again and again, just because they could.

To the north, Canada united her French- and English-speaking regions into a federation, partly to keep the U.S. at bay, and a transcontinental railroad soon linked the diverse areas. The U.S. had accomplished this feat by 1869, which opened up trade via the West Coast with China. But America soon had plenty of problems with pattern killers, many of whom sought merely to enrich themselves.

In Manhattan, Lydia Danbury married young and had seven children, but when, in 1867, her husband grew depressed over unemployment, she poisoned him and then used the same poison on her children. Remarried in Connecticut to a wealthy man, she killed that husband within a year. Although she was now well-off, she married Horatio Sherman and in 1871 poisoned both of his children before killing him. A suspicious doctor sent out Sherman's organs for analysis, and when the presence of arsenic was detected, Lydia was arrested and sentenced to life in prison.

Around the same time in Kansas, still a frontier area being settled by immigrants, travelers passing through the southeastern part of the state found a warm welcome and roadside entertainment in the Bender family's log cabin. The Benders had arrived from Germany around 1870 and built their home as a way station along the road. Adult daughter Katie was apparently a spiritualist who claimed to summon ghosts, and she had sufficient charm to learn a traveler's financial state and persuade him to sit in a certain area for dinner. Behind him hung a canvas curtain, and behind that stood Old Man Bender with a sledgehammer. He would deliver the fatal blow, while Ma Bender, Katie, and John Jr. removed the victim's money and dropped him down a trapdoor.

Someone was bound to notice, and when Dr. William York disappeared in 1873, his brother came looking for him. The Benders soon abandoned the place, but when a heavy rain showed the clear outline of several graves in the orchard, the place was dug up. Ten bodies were exhumed, including a child who had been tossed into the grave alive and then crushed beneath her father's corpse. This story swept the nation, adding the "Hell Benders" to the tales of Indians and outlaws who posed dire threats to families hoping to settle in Western lands. Souvenir hunters took the Bender cabin apart, coming away with scraps of wood, nails, and anything else that could be sold for high prices. The Benders were identified in various locations, north and south, but no sighting proved accurate. One peace officer in Utah thought he had grabbed Old Man Bender and arrested him for murder, but the suspect died and decomposed before an identification could be made. Still, his skull was removed and displayed in the local saloon as that of the notorious criminal.

The following year, 1874, a ten-year-old girl went missing in Boston. Her disappearance was to open up a case the likes of which had not been known anywhere in the world . . . yet. The mystery of her whereabouts was solved only after a young boy in the same town was found murdered and horribly mutilated. Horace Mullen was only four years old. He lay near a swamp on the outskirts of town, stabbed and slashed so savagely that he was nearly decapitated.

Suspicions turned at once to fourteen-year-old Jesse Pomeroy. He'd been sent to reform school for his vicious behavior against other children and had been released the year before, but no one had forgotten the stories of how he had lured other boys into the woods to torment and beat them into unconsciousness. Not only that, but in an age in which an odd appearance was viewed as evidence of a criminal temperament, Jesse had the look: a sloping misshapen head and a milky-white eye. When he was taken to the swamp and shown the violated body, he seemed undisturbed. Asked if he'd done it, Pomeroy responded with a nonchalant "I suppose I did."

It wasn't long before the missing girl was also found dead, buried in the cellar where Pomeroy's mother had a shop, and he confessed to that murder, too. He said he just liked the act of killing. In fact, Pomeroy is likely the first American pattern killer for whom thrill was a known motivator. Dubbed by the press "The Boston Boy Fiend," Pomeroy was convicted and sentenced to death. During his sensational trial, moralists blamed his violence on lurid dime novels. Some accounts say he confessed to over two dozen more murders, and that mutilated bodies were unearthed near his mother's house, but this was the nature of the sensationalistic legends that now developed around crimes. It was part of the entertainment. Specialists in mental disorder searched hard to find reasons why a child his age would behave so aggressively and show no remorse. They hoped he was an aberration and not a signal of things to come.

Since the 1850s, educators, clergy, and early feminists had started a movement to pressure society away from sending wayward youths to prisons. They wanted a homier atmosphere with a family influence, so that children would not grow hardened or recidivate. Young minds were malleable, it was believed, and capable of reform. Thus was born the reform school—a place where Pomeroy had already been. Massachusetts was the pioneer in setting up the earliest of such institutions, and children who went there were assigned to cottages with matrons and father figures to serve as governing influences. Unfortunately, reform schools often became places for abuse via corporal punishment, and failed at the goal of rehabilitation.

To try again, a separate juvenile court was proposed to distinguish children from adult criminals. The court's paternalistic purpose was to learn the "disposition" of the case and to understand why the child had come to such a pass. He or she would get no criminal record and whatever condition they had would be treated as doctors treated illness. Yet it would be 1899 before such a court was instituted in Illinois.

In the meantime, also in Boston, another young man was experiencing a periodic urge to kill. On May 23, 1875, five-year-old Mabel Hood Young disappeared from her parents' side at the Warren Avenue Baptist Church. A search was organized and several people went into the belfry, where the child was found. She appeared to have been bludgeoned twice over the head. Immediate suspicion linked this murder to Thomas Piper, twenty-six, who was the church sexton. He was arrested, but he denied any wrongdoing. Although he had fled the scene, he claimed that he had merely propped up the heavy belfry trapdoor, which must have fallen accidentally on the child's head.

Throughout two trials, the "Boston Belfry Murderer" held to this story, but he was nevertheless convicted of murder. Then his lawyer began to question him in prison about discrepancies in his story, and he suddenly confessed. But he did not stop with the murder of little Mabel. He went on to describe his part in the unsolved murders of three other women. He was given to drinking whiskey and smoking opium to ease head pain, he said, and that's when the urge to find a victim usually occurred.

He had killed two women on the same night because he had been interrupted during the first incident and had wanted to complete the experience. On December 5, 1873, he had clubbed Bridget Landregan with a plumber's hammer and had been set to rape her when someone happened along. So he found another girl, attacking and raping her instead. She, too, had died. Witnesses had seen him, but he'd worn a black cape to protect his identity. Six months later, he killed a young woman in her own bedroom, causing hysteria about this mysterious attacker throughout the city. To avoid being stopped and questioned, men had given up wearing their opera cloaks. Piper's lawyer wondered, as per the times, whether a lurid novel had influenced his client's behavior, but Piper denied having read any such publications. He was hanged in May 1876.

Around the same time, the "Nebraska Fiend" claimed an estimated nine lives before he was unmasked as Stephen Lee Richards and hanged in 1879, while in Austin, Texas, five years later, beginning on New Year's Eve, 1884, a bloody killing spree left the city breathless. It started with "negro servants." Mollie Smith was the first victim, killed behind the home where she worked. "Bloody Work!" was that day's headline for the *Austin Statesman*. Five months later, Eliza Shelley was found "with her night-dress displaced in such a manner as to suggest she may have been outraged after death." Both had been hacked to death, as was Irene Cross less than three weeks later. A fourth victim turned up in August, along with her daughter, and then in one night, four people were attacked by a man entering through a window and bashing everyone's skull with an ax. He pulled one of the four, Gracie Vance, out into some bushes, where she put up a struggle before she was "criminally assaulted" and finally silenced with a brick.

The newspaper reported, "This city is again agitated over four mysterious outrages which were committed west of the capital at 2 A.M. All were servants living together." Two died—the husband of the dead woman, Gracie Vance, was slain as he lay next to her in bed—and two survived, but they were badly wounded. A black man with blood on his clothing was arrested and tortured for a confession, then released when no real evidence against him could be found. Prosecutor E. T. Moore speculated that the murders had all been committed by a single perpetrator who hated women, but his ideas were mocked.

The last of the "Servant Girl Annihilator" killings took place on Christmas Eve 1885, but this time two white women were raped and slaughtered. "The Demons have transferred their thirst for blood to white people!" shouted the papers. Jimmy Phillips, the husband of Eula, one of the two white victims, was accused of killing his wife. He had been severely beaten himself during the attack, but he was nevertheless the best suspect, and he went to trial. It had been a copycat killing, the prosecutors said. His wife had been prostituting herself behind his back, so he had killed her in retaliation but had disguised it as part of the series of ax murders from earlier that year. However, his feet were smaller than the bloody prints found at the scene. The prosecution theorized that the larger prints were the result of the added weight of carrying his wife, so there in court to prove the point they forced the defendant to pick up his lawyer (which did not prove anything). The jury found Phillips guilty, but on appeal, he was acquitted. This set of murders was never solved, but they would become an issue in a famous series of crimes not long in the future.

The Science of Man

In 1876, an Italian anthropologist, Cesare Lombroso, a professor at Turin in Italy, published *L'uomo delinquente*. Experienced in the methods of phrenology (reading head formation), he had made numerous measurements and studied many photographs of criminal offenders. Believing that human behavior could be classified through objective tests, Lombroso was convinced that certain people were born criminals and could be identified by specific physical traits: for example, bulging or sloping brows, apelike noses, bushy eyebrows that met over the nose, small close-set eyes, large jaws, and disproportionately long arms. In other words, delinquency was a physiological abnormality that could be observed in someone's simian appearance. Also, only criminals bore tattoos, which Lombroso considered a reversion to ancient tribal rites, primitive races, and the craving to torture, mutilate, and kill. The police, it was suggested by those who supported these ideas, could make arrests more accurately if only they'd train themselves to spot the right traits. And the public could better protect itself from a stranger with an obvious criminal appearance.

Lombroso's ideas spread across Europe and America, supported by the new evolutionary thinking, and sometimes a defendant's presentation alone could be a factor in a conviction, or in his getting a harsher sentence. The theory of the born criminal inspired widespread prejudices that often victimized innocent people.

In addition to criminality, the issue of insanity continued to interest investigators, and some began to look at the notion of heredity. Sociologist Richard L. Dugdale did a study on an American family whom he called the "Jukes," whose members had supposedly resided close together since the earliest settlements. Looking across several generations for evidence of mental illness or criminal behavior, he found support for his theory. Out of some twelve hundred descendants of one woman, the Jukes showed a higher than average percentage of syphilitics, prostitutes, thieves, and murderers. This degenerate tribe was compared against another family of good Puritan stock, out of which had emerged mostly upstanding citizens, and even some presidents. It seemed a good argument for the "born criminal" theory, especially since Dugdale neglected to examine the influence of environmental variables.

In those days, not much was known about psychopaths, or those people who violated the social contract for their own gain, without remorse. Such people made others feel vaguely uneasy and precipitated ongoing discussions among alienists, or psychiatrists, about "dangerousness" and homicidal insanity. (One even suggested that the brain contained an "organ of murder.") People without remorse and yet with their reasoning skills apparently intact weren't exactly mentally defective, but something did seem to be lacking. Philippe Pinel introduced the label "mania without delirium" in 1809, and more than two decades later, British physician James Prichard called it "moral insanity," to indicate that one's faculty for moral behavior and reasoning had been affected. He thought it was caused by illness or trauma. In 1881, German psychiatrist J. L. Koch introduced "constitutional psychopathic inferiority," which covered a multitude of disorders but emphasized the loss or impairment of the power of "self-government," and four years later William Stead called such people "psychopaths"—those to whom nothing is sacred. It would be another half century before psychology crystallized the disorder for practical purposes. Yet some nineteenth-century physicians were making the attempt, and in the process, they were documenting serial killers.

Alienists believed that lawyers needed assistance from

psychiatry to fairly sentence criminals with mental illness, but the legal system had little respect for their expertise. Richard von Krafft-Ebing, a German neurologist, an alienist at the Feldhof Asylum, and a professor of psychiatry in Strasbourg, was aware that without a clear way to diagnose and categorize the various manifestations of mental illness, psychiatry would not achieve the status of medicine, so he produced works influential during his time. In 1879, he published *A Textbook of Insanity*, in which he outlined an elaborate system for categorizing mental diseases. His next significant text, published in 1886, was the one for which he is known today, *Psychopathia Sexualis with Especial Reference to the Antipathic Sexual Instinct: A Medico-Forensic Study*. This book, which documented 238 cases, was translated into English in 1892 and has gone into many printings.

In this book, von Krafft-Ebing addressed the disorders of the sexual instinct, providing cases and categories, as well as a "vocabulary of perversion" that would be passed along to subsequent centuries. He is credited with clarifying terms such as "necrophilia," "sadomasochism," and "fetishism," all of which were manifestations of certain sexually deranged killers.

He also provided details about several of Lombroso's patients, specifically in the category of "lust murder." One man had indulged in strangling prostitutes after sex, admitting that it was sport for him. Another tried to rape a female relative, and when her father and uncle held him back, he killed them all. Then he went to a prostitute, but this visit proved insufficient to calm him. From there, he slaughtered his father and several oxen. A third man slaughtered and dismembered a four-year-old, and carried her forearm around in his pocket.

Among the noted cases in the book are several serial killers, including Vincenz Verzeni, twenty-two, who had been imprisoned in 1872. He was accused of several attempted murders and was suspected in several actual ones. His case began with the mutilation of a fourteen-year-old girl along a village path. Her intestines had been torn out and tossed some distance, a piece had been torn from her leg, and her mouth was stuffed with dirt. Another woman in the area was likewise killed and violated, and a third nearly met the same fate but survived to finger Verzeni.

His head was examined for evidence of physical abnormality, and the cranium was found to be asymmetrical and larger than average. Both ears were defective, and the right one was smaller. In addition, his penis was "greatly developed." Lombroso concluded that there were signs of degeneracy in the arrested development of the right frontal bone in the skull, and in Verzeni's ancestry. Two uncles were "cretins" and another was missing a testicle. A cousin was a thief, and other members of the family showed numerous abnormalities.

When Verzeni finally confessed to his deeds, he admitted that the murders and mutilations offered a pleasant feeling and gave him an erection. Putting his hands around someone's neck was sufficient to arouse him, and if he climaxed before they died, they were allowed to live. He did the same thing with chickens. He admitted that he had sucked blood from the thighs of one corpse and that he had carried around pieces of another because he derived a powerful sensation from them. He showed no remorse.

Lombroso evaluated another such killer in Spain— "Gruyo," who had strangled six women for the same reason as Verzeni. The man had also reached into their vaginas to tear out their kidneys and intestines—sometimes while they were still alive. These men were the ultimate menaces to society and were used as examples of supreme degeneracy.

A thinker in another discipline had an entirely different outlook. While alienists studied the criminal mind, German philosopher Friedrich Nietzsche inadvertently offered a form of justification for violence. He proposed ideas toward the end of the nineteenth century that would have ramifications far into the future on how certain psychopathic criminals perceived and excused themselves. In 1886, Nietzsche published *Beyond Good and Evil,* in which he spelled out how morality is illusory and then postulated that crime might be regarded as an invigorating condition to make the human species stronger. Exploitation within society is normal, because "life itself is essentially appropriation, injury, overpowering of what is alien and weaker." In other words, life is a "will to power," his title for a more forceful book in which he described the human ideal as an intense Dionysian affirmation of the world as it is, including violence.

Morality, Nietzsche said, was a system of judgments that coincided with the conditions of the moralist's life. There was a master morality and a slave morality. People who could assimilate the will to power would survive, accept the aggressive instinct, become leaders, and determine themselves what is good and what is evil. The greatest enjoyment, Nietzsche said, was to "live dangerously," i.e., to live on one's own terms. In the century to come, those who learned these ideas and desired to "live dangerously" would adopt Nietzsche as a patron saint . . . or sinner.

Criminalistics

Crime detection, too, benefited from more rigorous study and experimentation. Alphonse Bertillon, a file clerk for the French police, had grown frustrated during the late 1870s over the enormous and chaotic collection of police photos. As well, he had to deal with more than five million imprecise files that dated back to the time of Vidocq. Bertillon was determined to devise a way to categorize them and to better serve the legal system. Despite resistance from his superiors, he set out to formulate a way to tell when law enforcement was dealing with repeat offenders. He knew that one could not trust information from the criminals themselves, but he realized that they couldn't very well lie about what they looked like.

As offenders were arrested, Bertillon used a tape measure and calipers to take eleven to fourteen separate measurements, from the length of the foot to the width of the jaw to the distance between the eyes, classifying each person as small, medium, or large and recording the measurements on cards placed into categories. His system was based on certain assumptions derived from mathematics and anthropology: The adult human bone structure does not change and the chance of two adults having the same value for all eleven measurements was more than four million to one. He was determined to show that science could be applied to police work, and in 1883, he was given three months to prove it. After measuring almost two thousand men, he found a repeat offender he was able to identify strictly by measurements: The man gave a false name, but Bertillon was able to reveal who he really was. His method continued to show success, so the police adopted it.

Bertillon also introduced the profile angle into mug shots (his *photographie métrique*), which offered the jaw, ear, and more of the face for identification. Along with these measurements he made notations on the prisoner's card about such things as appearance, posture, and details of his life and crimes. Bertillon introduced the scientific method into criminal investigations. His technique was part of anthropometry, but it soon became known more precisely as *bertillonage*. This method quickly became popular throughout Europe, especially as Bertillon and a growing host of others asserted that it could identify someone with complete certainty. He also introduced more precision into crime scene photos, insisting on getting images before the scene was disturbed and photographing them in a way that allowed one to reconstruct evidence. He had mats printed with metric frames to mount on the photos, and for some he included both front and side views of specific objects.

Yet certain problems arose with Bertillon's system, notably that not everyone taking the measurements was careful and the process was time-consuming. Bertillon took pains to teach others his approach, but a new method for criminal identification was emerging that began to erode the ground from under him.

In 1877 in the U.S., Thomas Taylor had proposed that markings on palms and fingertips be used for identification. Three years later, Scottish physician Henry Faulds, who had discovered how to make fingerprints visible with powders, suggested that fingerprints recovered at the scene of a crime could identify the offender. In one case, he successfully eliminated a suspect and helped to convict the true offender. Along with his groundbreaking work, other researchers discovered the significant fact that fingerprints did not change over time. Also, getting a set of prints from an arrested criminal proved much easier than taking measurements.

The first modern trial in which a fingerprint was used was in Argentina. Juan Vucetich, a police officer, devised his own fingerprint classification system and in Buenos Aires in 1892 opened the first fingerprint bureau. Within two months, he took his ideas into the courtroom. Francisca Rojas claimed that a man named Velasquez had murdered her two children in her home. A search turned up several bloody fingerprints, but they did not match those of the accused. However, they did match those of the accuser. Confronted, she confessed and was sentenced to life in prison.

That same year, Sir Francis Galton published the first book about fingerprints and their forensic utility. He proposed that prints bore three primary features and that from them he could devise sixty thousand classes. For the next few years, he worked with Sir Edward Henry, head of Scotland Yard, who came up with a classification system based on five pattern types that influences the system used today. Henry had started his own fingerprint classification system in India, which he would publish in 1900. Then he became assistant commissioner of police at New Scotland Yard, where he established the Fingerprint Office. Nevertheless, *bertillonage* hung on, so reliance on fingerprints as indubitable proof for identification had to await a defining case, which was years away.

Super-Sleuth and Super-Killer

In 1877, Dr. Joseph Bell was a professor at the medical school of Edinburgh University and personal surgeon to Queen Victoria in Scotland. A strong proponent of the new forensic science, he impressed upon his students the importance of close observation before diagnosing a situation. To demonstrate, he picked someone about whom he knew nothing and made several accurate judgments about that person's occupation and recent activities. At least one of his students grasped the significance of this approach: Arthur Conan Doyle, Bell's clerk at the Royal

Infirmary, who had also observed how Bell made such deductions about patients.

Some time later, when Conan Doyle took up a medical practice in Southsea, England, he began to write. In 1886, he completed a story about a "consulting detective" named Sherlock Holmes, who resembled Bell and who relied on observation and logical deduction to help solve crimes that people brought to his door. Holmes resided at the fictional 221B Baker Street in London, and his intellectual prowess in several engaging cases was recorded by his sidekick, Dr. John Watson. The first of what would become a series of tales was "A Study in Scarlet." The story, then titled "A Tangled Skein," was rejected numerous times before Ward, Lock & Co. included it in 1887 as part of a Christmas annual. It attracted little attention, but was published as a book in 1888, receiving more exposure. Readers saw how, with sheer deductive reasoning, Holmes cracked a code and solved a murder, exposing the motive and the culprit. They wanted more.

The series would run until 1927, and among the reasons why the Holmes character endured was the technical expertise that Conan Doyle added to the tales, as well as his clear explanation of the thinking process. Drawing on what he remembered about his former teacher, he made Holmes's quick and accurate observations seem miraculous, until they were explained. As forensic science merged with crime investigation, Holmes became the prototype of the brilliant detective who has an edge over the ordinary "copper."

However, in those early days another literary work overshadowed the Holmes tales and became just as enduring for its own insights into human nature. In 1886, Robert Louis Stevenson published a gothic tale called *The Strange Case of Dr. Jekyll and Mr. Hyde*. Based on a dream he'd had, it featured an upstanding citizen, Dr. Jekyll, who experiments with an elixir that, when drunk, brings out Mr. Hyde, the darker side of Jekyll's personality. It was a popular literary rendering of a psychological truth about humanity: No matter what the public persona, people can harbor frightening secrets, fantasies, and behaviors. The brief novel proved to be a classic tale that offered a way for criminologists in the future to make sense of perplexing behavior—the uncontrollable urge within a person who appears normal. The novel became a stage play, which was showing in London's West End on the very night in 1888 when the first of a series of sensational murders occurred across town in the seedy, immigrant-populated area known as Whitechapel.

On Friday, August 31, just after 1 A.M., Mary Ann "Polly" Nichols, an alcoholic mother of five, went out into the street to earn the four pence she needed for lodging. She was one of hundreds of prostitutes who routinely worked the area. But on that night she never earned her keep. Quite suddenly, a man grabbed her and slit her throat with two powerful strokes. When she was found, her skirt was pulled up to her waist, her legs were parted, and severe cuts had been inflicted in her abdomen and throat; in fact, her head was nearly severed from her body.

Whoever had killed her had come at her quite suddenly in a vicious attack. To investigators unfamiliar with sexually compulsive violence, there appeared to be no motive.

Several weeks before that, on August 6, Martha Tabram, also a prostitute, had been found stabbed thirty-nine times with at least two different implements. But her unsolved murder was not linked to that of Nichols. Nor was it covered by the press the way the Nichols case would be, or those that followed.

The next victim after Nichols was Annie Chapman, discovered on the morning of September 8. Her dress was pulled over her head, her stomach was ripped open, and her intestines were pulled out and draped over her left shoulder. Her legs were drawn up, knees bent as if posed, and spread outward. Her throat was cut, too, with what appeared to have been a sharp surgical type of knife with a narrow blade, and it looked as if the killer had tried to separate her neck bones. Since there was no sign of a struggle, it seemed that she'd been quickly subdued. Coins and an envelope had been arranged around her as if in some ritual, and a closer inspection showed that the bladder, half of the vagina, and the uterus had been removed and taken away.

A note that arrived at the Central News Agency nearly three weeks later on September 27 and was forwarded to the police raised hopes of a lead. Addressing the note to "Dear Boss" and signing it, "Yours Truly, Jack the Ripper," the author claimed that he "loved" his work and would continue to kill. In retrospect, many experts came to believe this message was the work of a tabloid journal-

ist trying to drum up further sensation, but the gruesome moniker stuck.

At the end of that month, on September 30, there were
two victims on the same night. The Ripper slashed the
throat of Elizabeth Stride, forty-five, only a few minutes
before she was found, and then disemboweled Catherine
Eddowes less than an hour afterward. Some crime analysts believed that the killer had been interrupted with
Stride and had then completed the act with Eddowes. He
was growing bolder and/or more mentally ill. With Eddowes, the intestines had been pulled out and placed over
her right shoulder, one kidney had been cut out and
taken, and her face was oddly mutilated. Two upside-
down Vs were cut into her cheeks, pointing toward the
eyes, her eyelids were nicked, and the tip of her nose was
cut off. And, of course, her throat was slashed.

Two weeks after the "double event" came a letter and
box "from Hell" to the head of the Whitechapel Vigilance
Committee, with a grisly trophy: preserved in wine was
half of a kidney that turned out to be afflicted with
Bright's disease—a disorder from which Eddowes was believed to have suffered. The note's author indicated that
he'd fried and eaten the other half, which was "very nise."
It was believed that this note was from the killer, who
even offered to send "the bloody knife" in due time. He
closed with the taunt "Catch me if you can," indicating
his utter arrogance.

The police faced another problem. Among the thousands of letters that arrived with advice on how to investigate the case (such as that detectives should wear collars

with paralyzing electrodes while disguised as prostitutes) were numerous correspondences ostensibly from the killer but clearly faked. In fact, it became a fashion to send a "Jack the Ripper" letter to the police, and it was difficult to sort out which notes might be authentic—if any—from those that had been written for someone's own amusement. In addition, the rivalry between Sir Henry Smith, London's assistant commissioner, and Sir Charles Warren, metropolitan police commissioner, sometimes stymied the investigation's effectiveness. Warren himself destroyed a message written on a wall where a piece of clothing from one victim was found.

The police realized they had an unbridled killer on their hands, driven by rage, who killed at random and seemed unstoppable. Expecting something to happen on October 8 and 31, since the killer had struck on September 8 and 30, they stepped up patrols, but there were no more murders of that same type that month—at least not in the East End. On October 3, as the New Scotland Yard was being constructed to house a growing metropolitan police squad, someone had deposited the headless, limbless corpse of a woman inside a vault in the unfinished foundation. The arms were found in the Thames. Newspapers speculated whether this was part of the series, but police spokesmen said that there were too many divergences. This woman had been killed elsewhere and carried to the spot, and had been dismembered rather than mutilated abdominally. She became the "Whitehall Mystery" of 1888, while Red Jack's crimes were "the popular mystery."

It was the last official victim, Mary Kelly, twenty-four, who took the brunt of this offender's disorganized frenzy. On the evening of November 8, the prostitute apparently invited a man into her room, and at some point he pulled the sheet over her head to stab her through it. Then he slashed her throat, ripped open her lower torso, pulled out her intestines, removed her breasts, and skinned her chest and legs, spattering blood all over the room. When police arrived the following morning, they found a severed breast on the bed table, reportedly decorated with other cut-off parts in a mocking rendition of a face. The contents of her abdomen were spread over the bed and thrown around the room. Her heart was missing and flesh had been cut from her legs and buttocks clear to the bone. Doctors estimated that this frenzy had gone on for at least two hours.

Alienists (and spiritualists) devised psychological analyses of the killer, but the most notable one came from Dr. Thomas Bond, a surgeon. He had assisted in the autopsy of Mary Kelly, so had a good idea of just how demented this killer was. Investigators had requested a specific description of the wounds and modus operandi, but in notes dated November 10, 1888, Bond offered much more.

The murders had escalated in brutality and were sexual in nature, he indicated, with an intense element of rage against either women or prostitutes. Except for the last one, they were clean, quick, and out in the open, and often the victim was disemboweled in some manner. All five murders had been committed by one person alone who was physically strong, cool, and daring. Bond thought the man would be quiet and inoffensive in appearance, middle-aged, and neatly attired, probably wearing a cloak to hide the bloody effects of his attacks. He would be a loner, without a real occupation, eccentric, and mentally unstable. He might even suffer from a condition called satyriasis, a sexual deviancy. Very likely, those who knew him would be aware that he was not right in his mind. Bond believed that the killer had surgical expertise and anatomical knowledge. In addition, he suggested that the offer of a reward would garner clues from people who knew the man. A few months later, he was certain the same man was responsible for the murder of a sixth woman, Alice McKenzie, whose autopsy he performed as well.

To many Londoners, this beast was the devil himself. He'd savaged six (and possibly more) women with an unmatched frenzy, attacked in darkness, eluded police, disappeared as if by magic, and even sent a note "from Hell." The London populace was concerned, despite the fact that the victims were prostitutes in a crime-ridden part of town, because the press drew them in. The Ripper's crimes were novel and episodic, but the middle class also feared a social uprising from the lower classes, and those newspapers that viewed themselves as a social voice worked to form the public conscience. Part of that agenda was to demand conditions that would hinder the work of such vicious criminals.

Many criminologists say that Jack ushered in the modern age of the serial killer. In part, this is because he had struck in a large city during an era when media coverage coincided with public entertainment and when communication systems had become internationally accessible. In fact, more than 250 newspapers around the world carried the story, and some journalists speculated over whether Jack the Ripper might have traveled from other areas such as Jamaica, Tunis, or Nicaragua where there were similar unsolved crimes. Austin, Texas, the site of the Servant Girl Annihilator murders, was another possible link and one suspect who had been in both London and Austin was a Malay cook who often worked on ships.

But by January 1889, the murders appeared to have ended, and Sir Melville Macnaughten of the Criminal Investigation Division speculated that the killer's extreme indulgence might have caused a "brainstorm," compelling him to commit suicide.

But Red Jack apparently inspired others. Three more similar murders occurred in Whitechapel over the next two years, while copycat killings disturbed Moscow and Vienna. In Chicago, a secret "Ripper Club" was formed that involved businessmen in a macabre fan club for murder mysteries. It became something of a game to employ amateur sleuthing to try to determine who might possibly have been the mad dog offender.

In 1892, some people came to believe they finally had their man. In Canada, a young chambermaid named Kate Gardner was found dead in a privy with a bottle of chloroform next to her. She was linked to Dr. Thomas Neill Cream, an abortionist. He avoided prosecution and moved to Chicago. When a girl died there, Cream was arrested, but again he did not have to answer for what he had done. Next he poisoned the husband of a beautiful patient with whom he was carrying on a sexual relationship. This time he went to prison, but he was eventually released. He ended up in England in 1891, far too late to have committed the Ripper murders. Yet he was himself a serial killer, in South London, using strychnine to murder several young women. Arrested for one of the murders in 1892, he was convicted and sentenced to be hanged. As the hangman drew the bolt, Cream allegedly announced, "I am Jack the—" just as the noose broke his neck.

During Red Jack's spree, the London Metropolitan Police Force took a beating from the public and press. They were supposed to protect people from such crimes, and to solve them. Yet no matter who they put on the case, no one could identify the perpetrator. They had several suspects under surveillance, from a Polish Jew to a suicidal barrister to a quack doctor, but no proof against any of them could be discovered. However, this very public failure had a bright side: It inspired reorganization in the force and more emphasis on the scientific investigation of crime. Scotland Yard hoped to set a standard for police forces around the world. It did not hurt that Sherlock Holmes was a British character. The Yard's determination came at an appropriate time, for the close of the century brought a swell of serial violence. Given the many international alliances and animosities arising around the world as countries vied for economic and political domination, it's no surprise.

CHAPTER SIX

The Century's Turn . . . and Twist

Progress and Regress

As one century closed and another opened, while industrialized nations raced to acquire other lands, a rash of murderers provided the public with shocking entertainment and analysts of all types with fodder for theories. From refined gentlemen sadists to secretive Bluebeards to women who could dismember grown men, multiple killers cropped up around the world. Saucy Jack had ushered in the modern age of the serial killer, and the psychology of such crimes became a focus.

Cesare Lombroso published another book, *L'Homme Criminel*, in 1895, to reaffirm his status as the world's premier criminologist. As he focused on the body as a dispositional index and social risk, he distinguished between the epileptic criminal, who had an abnormality of the brain, and the insane criminal, who was mentally deficient due to "atavism," a reversion to primitive evolutionary states. Lombroso stated that society exacerbated these conditions by ostracizing such people. He described other categories as well, such as the occasional criminal, who indulged in petty crimes, and the criminaloid, who was warped by social conditions. Lombroso called female criminals "monsters." When the influences of "maternity, piety, and weakness" fail in a woman who commits crimes, he stated, "we may conclude that her wickedness must have been enormous before it could triumph over so many obstacles." Biologically, he believed, such women were more like men. He would eventually have cause to evaluate one such monster in America.

When in 1895 Max Nordau published an English translation of Lombroso's book, titled *Degeneration,* the "degenerative personality" became a preoccupation throughout Europe, with many people worried about their latent heritage showing in their offspring. Social progress and refinement were measured by such things as sensitivity to pain or the degree of dilation of blood vessels in the skin. Two strands of criminal psychology arose from this work: one looking to physiological causes and the other to the mind. By the turn of the century, in academic circles at least, the idea of the born criminal was losing ground, and gaining ground was a tendency to attribute criminal behavior to social conditions. But another new theory emerged as well.

By the last years of the century, Sigmund Freud had offered concepts about human motivation and behavior that would ignite a revolution in the field of psychology. He had introduced the idea of the libido, the ego, and the superego as structures of the self, and childhood trauma as a precursor to neurotic disorders. The outraged press labeled Freud a pornographer, but he attracted a number of followers who helped to ensure that the "talking cure" and all that it entailed spread throughout Europe and into America.

In criminal circles, insanity became a popular excuse and a way to escape the gallows. Another suspect in the Ripper crimes surfaced in Australia. His arrest arrived on the heels of the discovery in cement inside a Melbourne home of the body of a woman whose throat had been cut. That led to Frederick Deeming, and then to England, where Deeming had lived in another place ripe with the putrid odor of death. Dismantling it, the police discovered Deeming's first wife and his four children cemented into the floor, all with their throats cut. In fact, Deeming had recently gotten engaged to another woman, who apparently was just barely saved. He confessed to an overwhelming impulse to kill women with whom he was involved—urged on, he said, by his dead mother. To thwart investigators, he plucked out every hair of his mustache and devised an act to convince the court that he could not appreciate what he was doing. But there was no authentic evidence of mental illness, so he was convicted. Before a cheering crowd of twelve thousand, Deeming was executed in 1892.

In a burst of imperialism, England colonized Africa,

France moved into Indochina, Germany grabbed several colonies in the Pacific, and Russia advanced across Asia. Western medicine, religion, and manners permeated native lands through "civilizing" missions. European culture dominated many parts of the world, supported by Darwinian ideas that superior nations ought to rule inferior ones. The European white male was the standard against which all others were arrogantly measured. Japan and China successfully rebuffed these advances, although China had reluctantly surrendered Hong Kong to Britain. Japan invited the modern world inside through trade agreements with the U.S. and in 1894 asserted power over China by taking Korea. Kaiser Wilhelm II in Germany united with Russia and France to resist this "yellow peril." When Japan attacked and defeated Russia, Europe realized it was no longer invincible. In fact, to the west, the United States was quickly becoming a world power.

By 1900 the U.S. was the world's largest producer of steel, making possible the swell of fortunes for entrepreneurs such as Andrew Carnegie, John D. Rockefeller, and Cornelius Vanderbilt, and this economic power inspired its own form of imperialism. The U.S. government had purchased the Alaskan territory from Russia in 1867, and three decades later it annexed the Hawaiian Islands and took over the Philippines and Puerto Rico. It was a heady age of building and growing for this young country.

Culturally, Europe entered an age of repressed sexuality, strict conformity, paranoia, and class conflict, which had an effect on the field of forensic science. While scientists proclaimed the neutrality of their methods, human bias nevertheless infected interpretations. Alphonse Bertillon participated in the 1894 anti-Semitic court-martial of Captain Alfred Dreyfus, falsely accused of spying for Germany against France. In order to be on the "right" side, Bertillon contradicted his own analysis of the suspect's handwritten document, initially stating it was unlike the handwriting of Dreyfus and then saying it matched. He covered his "mistake" by suggesting that Dreyfus had disguised his handwriting during dictation meant to expose him. Dreyfus was imprisoned, while a military cover-up protected the real perpetrator. Few were fooled, and the shameful affair divided France and inspired scorn for so-called expertise in handwriting analysis.

During that same period, the murder of Anna Sutherland brought negative attention to the field of toxicology. Sutherland had owned a saloon, and had married a man named Robert Buchanan, who was in debt. When she mysteriously died, he was arrested. At trial, toxicologists determined that Sutherland had died of morphine poisoning, although she failed to display the characteristic narrowed pupils. It was discovered that to foil the experts, Buchanan had put drops of atropine in her eyes to dilate them. With this knowledge and the toxicological test results, the evidence seemed overwhelming, but for the defense, Professor Victor Vaughn showed how a cadaveric alkaloid mimicked morphine in qualitative tests. In the end, based on self-incriminating testimony, Buchanan was still convicted in 1895, but the jury ignored the prosecution's toxicological evidence. This forensic fiasco inspired toxicologists to look for new methods of demonstrating the presence of alkaloids in the body, so that in the long run a setback became an asset.

There were forward strides as well. Austrian lawyer Hans Gross, who was versed in a variety of sciences from physics to psychology, opened the Criminalistic Institute at the University of Graz, offering police science as a collaboration of diverse specialists. In 1891, he published *Criminal Investigation,* the first comprehensive description of the use of physical evidence in solving crime, which influenced the methods of England's early "Murder Squad." By the end of the century, these detectives were categorizing criminals by modus operandi. They would soon see the value of preserving crime scenes and properly handling evidence, and would demonstrate, thanks to Alexandre Lacassagne at the University of Lyon and Paul Jeserich in Germany, that the grooves on a spent bullet could be matched to the spiraling in the barrel of the gun that fired it.

Yet even as science became more sophisticated, so did the repeat killer. One of the most fiendish devised a plan that exploited America's drive to become a recognized cultural giant. While the 1893 World's Fair (the Columbian Exposition) sought to "out-Eiffel" Eiffel's tower, erected for the Paris World Exhibition in 1889, a man near the fairgrounds in Chicago was creating his own technical marvel for more nefarious purposes.

Doctors and Madmen

It was the discovery of a murder in Philadelphia in 1895 that opened the door to a case that few could quite believe. A onetime cellmate of a man who went by the name H. H. Holmes (born Herman Webster Mudgett) informed an insurance company of a recent scam. It had involved insuring Benjamin Pitezel for $10,000 and then faking his death in a laboratory explosion by substituting a cadaver. All participants were then to split the insurance money, but Holmes had reneged. When company managers checked, they found that Holmes had indeed identified a body and collected the money, so they sent the Pinkerton Detective Agency after the scoundrel. As these agents tracked the man, who had abducted three of Pitezel's children, they gathered information about his various frauds, thefts, and schemes, including insurance scams in Chicago that had provided him with funds to build a three-story hotel. They finally caught up to him in Boston.

Since the scheme had occurred in Philadelphia, detectives from there helped to arrest Holmes. On the way back to the City of Brotherly Love, Holmes bragged about his criminal career, admitting that he'd done enough in his life to be hanged twelve times over. He claimed to have the ability to hypnotize people to do whatever he wanted, and when reporters heard this, they attributed supernatural powers to the wretched scam artist.

The police soon realized that Holmes had actually killed Pitezel. Suspicious about the children, who were no longer with him, Detective Frank Geyer went on a highly publicized expedition to find them, and discovered that each had been murdered. Not only that, Holmes apparently had quite a list of other murders to his credit.

In the industrialized city of Chicago, investigators found even greater crimes. Not far from the site of the "White City," the name by which the World's Fair was known, Holmes had used his three-story hotel to let rooms to young women arriving in town to attend the fair. Some twenty-seven million people went through the exposition during its six-month venue, overtaxing the city's resources and inspiring plenty of crime, most of which the police could not investigate. Holmes was among those who took advantage.

His "castle" included soundproof sleeping chambers with peepholes, asbestos-padded walls, gas pipes, sliding walls, and vents that Holmes controlled from another room. The building had secret passages, false floors, rooms with torture equipment, and a specially equipped area for surgery. There were also greased chutes that emptied into a two-level cellar, and a very large furnace. Holmes would apparently place his chosen victims in the special chambers, into which he then pumped lethal gas as he watched them react. Sometimes he'd ignite the gas to incinerate them, or place them on the "elasticity determinator" to see how far the human body would stretch. It appeared that, when finished, he slid the corpses down the chutes into his cellar, where vats of acid and other chemicals awaited them. He would deflesh them and sell the bleached skeletons to medical schools.

Investigators discovered several complete skeletons and numerous incinerated bone fragments in the Chicago castle, but Holmes insisted that he had nothing to do with them. Those people had either taken their own lives, he claimed, or were killed by someone else. Nevertheless, newspaper headlines decried the "chamber of horrors." The *Chicago Tribune* announced "The Castle Is a Tomb!" and the *Philadelphia Inquirer* described skeletons removed from the "charnel house." It wasn't long before true crime pulp paperbacks were published to slake the public's thirst and turn a profit. Authors searched far and wide for even more murders that Holmes might have committed, going as far back as 1879. In Philadelphia, the "Holmes Museum" opened to the curious.

To exonerate himself, Holmes decided to pen a book, *Holmes' Own Story,* but it was so transparently self-serving that readers preferred the more lurid tales provided in newspapers. Inspired by a payment from the Hearst newspaper syndicate, Holmes then wrote out a lengthy confession for the *Philadelphia Inquirer.* Aiming now to become the most notorious killer in the world, he claimed to have murdered over one hundred people. Having second thoughts, he reduced that number to twenty-seven, including Pitezel. He insisted that he could not help what he'd done.

"I was born with the Evil One as my sponsor beside the bed where I was ushered into the world," he lamented. Indeed, he believed that his face was taking on an elongated shape of the devil himself. Though he felt no remorse, he then recanted the confession, and in fact it was learned that several of his "victims" were not dead at all. Yet so many people who'd rented rooms from him had actually gone missing that sensational estimates of his victims reached around two hundred.

At trial, Holmes tried to defend himself during the first day, but proved unable to establish points in his favor, and after many dramatic moments the jury convicted him of Pitezel's murder. From a distance, a phrenologist, John L. Capen, made an analysis, which was published during the trial in the *New York World*. He described the "repulsive" face and pointed out that great murderers "have blue eyes." Holmes's expression, Capen said, was cruel and inhuman, and his ears, twisted out of shape, stamped him as a criminal. This was all evidence of deviltry and vice. In other words, Capen convicted a man not yet found guilty based on appearance alone—and not even from his own physical examination.

On May 7, 1896, H. H. Holmes went to the hangman's noose. Even there he changed his story. He claimed to have killed only two women, and tried to say more, but the trapdoor opened and he was hanged. In short order, another American phenomenon occurred that arose from society's fascination with sensational crime. Thousands of people lined up to see the Chicago murder site, so a former police officer remodeled the infamous building as "Holmes's Horror Castle," an attraction that offered guided tours to the suffocation chambers and torture rooms. But before it opened, it mysteriously burned to the ground.

Across the country in San Francisco, another sensational case had caught the nation's morbid attention. In 1895, William Henry Theodore Durrant was tried for murder. He'd been a doctor in training at the Cooper Medical College in San Francisco and a superintendent of Sunday school at Emmanuel Baptist Church. Handsome and polite, Durrant appeared to be anything but a cold-blooded killer.

But the bodies of two women had been discovered in the church. Minnie Williams had been raped, stabbed, and stuffed into a cupboard, and the blood decorating the walls recalled the crimes of London's Ripper. Another woman, Blanche Lamont, was found in the belfry, nude, strangled, and laid out with care. Durrant was the common denominator.

The six competing city newspapers vied for dominance, and some even fabricated details that then became part of the legend, such as one tale that described Durrant's propensity to visit prostitutes and have them slice open chickens. William Randolph Hearst's *Examiner* was among the top three papers, along with the *Chronicle* and the *San Francisco Call*. Yellow journalism was rampant, although some papers pronounced themselves guardians of journalistic integrity. Potential jurors could not help but be affected, especially when on the same pages in which Hearst promoted U.S. involvement in a war with Spain, the *Examiner* turned the unfolding Durrant incident into a guessing game for readers.

Female reporters also covered the trial, getting exclusive interviews. One woman, Carrie Cunningham, nearly persuaded Durrant to confess, so she became a trial witness. This image of the "new woman" who acted like a male disturbed those invested in the status quo, but the salacious event was too good to pass up. Between four and five thousand people viewed the twin white coffins of the victims, and many women got into line more than once. Their open curiosity invited the same moralistic judgments as those made against females who were riding bicycles and becoming shockingly independent. Many felt that the turn of the century signaled a decline in morality that would be the demise of good society.

Indeed, there was talk that Durrant had utilized hypnosis on the young women, similar to the evil Svengali in *Trilby,* the novel by George du Maurier that had been serialized the previous year in *Harper's Monthly.* In that tale, a young woman had come under Svengali's control to become a famous singer, but when he died, she had no memory of what she had done. Hypnosis was considered to be that commanding.

It was Franz Anton Mesmer, late in the eighteenth century, who first brought hypnosis into popular consciousness, making unwarranted claims for its power. Jean-Martin Charcot, head of the Salpetriere Hospital in Paris and a leading neurologist during the 1870s, had used hypnosis to heal psychopathology that he believed was rooted in degenerative brain alterations. He had influenced Sigmund Freud, who went on to emphasize the eroticized dependent relationship between analyst and subject. During such a sexually repressed era as the late nineteenth century, that made hypnosis appear to be a tool of seduction.

The key issue discussed as Durrant awaited trial was the possibility that a man so charming, who never showed an ounce of violence, could commit rape and murder twice in the same month. Many theories were offered from criminological experts, and some insisted that the signs had been evident all along and the murders had been predictable. A "chiromancer" looked at a photograph of Durrant's hands to make pronouncements about his brutal disposition. Others believed that the shape of his head, which was a bit small and awkward, categorized him as a degenerate criminal type, although a comparison between his ears and those of killers such as H. H. Holmes failed to reveal much. A photograph of Durrant having fun with friends was published as evidence of his obvious degeneracy.

Durrant was quickly dubbed "The Monster of the Belfry." His three-week trial commanded front-page headlines. At the same time, in England, the trials of Oscar Wilde for gross indecency had ended with his conviction, and his behavior affirmed for many in San Francisco that the world was indeed growing more depraved. It didn't help matters that women of all ages flocked to the courthouse to glimpse this good-looking killer. They crowded into the courtroom's front rows, gawked at the prisoner, and giggled during the proceedings. An elderly woman even brought a pair of binoculars. Mrs. Rosalind Bowers attended each morning, carrying a bouquet of sweet pea flowers to send to Durrant, and it wasn't long before she became the "Sweet Pea Girl" in the press.

It wasn't just women who were entranced. Men and

women alike from the wealthy class decided that it was high fashion to show up for a day at the courthouse and to bring back stories for entertainment at "Durrant parties." Some were privileged enough to have a seat next to the judge, and no one considered that to be problematic.

Despite all this attention, Durrant's repeated claims of innocence, and his defense attorney's efforts to throw suspicion on the church pastor (who would also become the focus of a book a century later, proposing him as Jack the Ripper in hiding), it took the jury only five minutes to convict the young med student of both murders. He was hanged on April 3, 1897.

Soon thereafter a tramp named Joseph Vacher, twenty-nine, was tried in France for his crimes against fourteen people, including eleven murders. He had been arrested after a seventeen-year-old shepherd was found strangled, stabbed, and with his belly ripped open. Vacher wrote a confession for the judge, claiming that he suffered from an irresistible impulse and committed murder during frenzies. He thought that, having been bitten by a rabid dog when he was a child, his blood had been poisoned. As his victims died, he said, he drank blood from their necks. Despite the century's "enlightenment," people were still committing mythical crimes.

A team of doctors examined the defendant. Because his memory was clear about the crimes and because he had run off, they decided that Vacher had demonstrated sufficient awareness to be judged sane and therefore responsible for what he had done. Yet he had a history of "confused talk," spells of delirium, persecution mania, and extreme irritability. Indeed, he had once been treated in an asylum, when in 1894 he had killed a woman and had sex with her corpse. He also had once removed the genitalia from both a boy and a girl. If anyone had a claim to insanity, he did, but in 1898, at the Ain Assizes, he was convicted, and within two months he was executed.

Ironically, during Vacher's stint as a bloodsucker, *Dracula* was published in 1897 in England, introducing into mass consciousness the image of the predatory life-sucker. This archetype would become central to much horrific entertainment in a way that would influence murderers and criminological assessments alike.

But women, too, could be murderous fiends. Baby farming became a trend during the 1890s, arising from the social climate and economic conditions that inspired young women (or their families) to get rid of illegitimate infants in order to avoid social disgrace. Baby farmers charged high fees to take these children and place them with other families, or so they said. Once the baby was beyond anyone's concern, some of the more unscrupulous entrepreneurs simply pocketed the money and did away with the child.

In 1895, when a train conductor in New Zealand saw a woman board with a baby but leave without it, he alerted authorities. Their investigation led them to Williamina "Minnie" Dean, who was already known to police for taking in two babies that later died of "natural causes." A search of the gardens around her home unearthed the corpses of three infants. Dean was convicted and became the only woman to be legally hanged in New Zealand.

The following year, a bargeman found a bag on the Thames that contained a dead baby with a piece of tape knotted around her neck. The police set up a sting operation in which they caught Mrs. Amelia Dyer agreeing to take money to "adopt" a child. Dragging the river produced five more tiny strangled bodies. An alienist testified that Dyer suffered from delusions, but another doctor countered that they were feigned. She was convicted and hanged.

Even into the next century, women were caught in this nefarious business. In London, Annie Walters aroused the suspicion of her landlord, a police officer, who followed her to Whitechapel, where he saw her dispose of a small corpse. He arrested her and found that she had a milk bottle full of poison. It turned out that she was frequently seen carrying babies to dispose of, so she and her midwife partner, Amelia Sachs, were hanged for their deeds.

New Century, Old Methods

Thanks to the New York City police commissioner, Theodore Roosevelt, law enforcement in that city had cleaned up its act and the profession was becoming a noble calling. In fact, in 1895, New York became the first place where women were included on the force. Roosevelt also kept his finger on the pulse of reform, insisting on the use of photographs and Bertillon measurements for all prisoners. Yet even as he was introducing these methods, new discoveries were being announced. Pathologist Karl Landsteiner first detected distinct human blood groups in 1900, and the next year, in Germany, Paul Uhlenhuth devised the precipitin test to distinguish primate blood from that of other animals. He would soon make another discovery efficacious for crime investigation.

On the island of Rugen, off the coast of Germany, two young boys failed to come home one day, so their parents organized a search. Soon several body parts were found scattered in the woods, and eventually the searchers located the boys' disemboweled remains. The parents were devastated, and the villagers were terrified over the marauding beast that had done this.

Earlier that day, Ludwig Tessnow, a carpenter from Baabe, was spotted talking to the boys, and although he denied any involvement, a search of his home was made, which turned up recently laundered clothing with suspicious stains. He claimed that they were from wood dye, which he used daily in his profession. Unable to prove otherwise or to find other incriminating evidence, the police left him alone. But then an investigator recalled a similar crime.

Three years earlier in Osnabruck, Germany, two young girls had been butchered in the woods. The man loitering nearby was Tessnow. At that time, too, he had claimed that the stains on his clothing were from wood dye. Now his story sounded even more suspicious. The local prosecutor then heard a farmer report that one day a man who looked like Tessnow had fled from his field, leaving behind seven slaughtered sheep. That was sufficient circumstantial "coincidence" to bring Tessnow in, and the farmer identified him.

Still, the police needed better evidence to link him to the double homicide. They heard about a test recently developed by Paul Uhlenhuth that could distinguish blood from other substances, as well as mark the difference between human and animal blood. Tessnow's clothing was given to Uhlenhuth for thorough examination, and while he did find dye, he also detected traces of both sheep and human blood. With this evidence, Tessnow was charged, tried, convicted, and executed.

That same year, there was a startling case in Massachusetts that involved toxicology. Minnie Gibbs died on August 13, 1901, and her cause of death was listed as exhaustion, due to grief over losing other family members. But her father-in-law, Captain Gibbs, was suspicious. A nurse and family friend, Jane Toppan, had administered to Minnie's entire family during the weeks before her death, and every one of them had died. Gibbs enlisted the help of Dr. Edward S. Wood, a renowned toxicologist and professor at Harvard Medical School. Minnie was exhumed, and tests showed high levels of arsenic in her organs. However, there was arsenic in the embalming fluid, so they had to test for other poisons. They then found dangerous levels of morphine and atropine. By that time, two more suspicious deaths had been associated with Toppan, so she was arrested for the murder of Minnie Gibbs. After several more exhumations, she was charged with killing Genevieve Gordon and Alden Davis as well. She pleaded not guilty.

Three respected alienists examined Toppan, and she confessed to the murders but showed no remorse. She said that she killed because of an "irresistible sexual impulse"—dying people excited her. The experts determined that mental weakness ran in Jane's family and that her lack of moral sense had been evident since childhood. This had possibly derived from her abandonment by an alcoholic father and her adoption into a family that treated her as a servant. She could not appreciate the seriousness of her crime, they stated, she showed no fear, and she had no loyalties. In short, Toppan was diagnosed as suffering from a mental disease of a moral type.

As the doctors probed her background, they learned that during her training as a nurse in Boston she had experimented on patients with drugs, many of whom had died. "Jolly Jane" also had a reputation for lying and theft. She enjoyed administering morphine, which caused a patient's breathing to slow and the pupils to contract. Then she gave them atropine, which produced the opposite effects. Much later, one patient told a tale about her experience with Jolly Jane. Amelia Phinney said that Toppan had given her medication that had sent her into a semiconscious stupor. The nurse had then crawled into bed with her and held her as she slipped in and out of consciousness, but something had interrupted Toppan and she had left.

In 1892, Toppan had become a private nurse. Despite

her reputation as an excellent caretaker, she continued to dispatch patients whenever the mood struck her. She also poisoned her foster sister, Elizabeth, because she wanted Elizabeth's husband. Toppan admitted to cuddling with her as she was dying. Eventually Toppan met the Davis family, who owned a large estate and rented summer cottages. They began to die, one by one.

Toppan's trial was brief. The judge instructed the jury that "in view of the testimony of the three psychiatric experts, only one finding was possible: Miss Toppan was not guilty by reason of insanity." She was sentenced to life in Taunton Insane Hospital, where she became paranoid about her food. Afterward, Toppan's senior counsel revealed a shocking secret: She had given him the name of thirty-one victims. They were the only names she could remember; indeed, it has been alleged that Toppan actually poisoned more than a hundred people. As a female murderer, she was unique in that she killed people not for gain but for erotic enjoyment.

Other multiple poisoners from that period were male, one of them notable as an active Bluebeard, the other for a different type of notoriety.

Caroline Huff had become ill in Wheeling, West Virginia, and although her husband, Jacob, tended to her, she'd died. Reverend Haas thought he saw the man give her some white powder, but it seemed of no significance until Huff left his clothing and a suicide note on the bank of the Ohio River and disappeared. His wife's money was gone as well. It wasn't long before the reverend spotted Huff's photograph in the Chicago papers as a stockyard swindler who went by the name Johann Hoch. He alerted authorities.

The police launched an investigation and found that the man had gone through a string of wives in various places. Some had been abandoned, others had died of mysterious illnesses. When Caroline Huff's body was exhumed to test for arsenic, investigators discovered that her internal organs had been removed. But without evidence, they could not prosecute, so Hoch was freed. He returned to his former ways, giving police another opportunity. He married Marie Walcker, killed her within a month, and then proposed to her sister, who inexplicably accepted and handed over all her money. Hoch then disappeared, so Marie was exhumed and her body found to contain arsenic. Hoch was caught, convicted of one murder, and hanged, with his victim count hovering around 50 percent: At least twelve of his estimated twenty-four wives had died as a result of their association with him, and there may well have been more wives than is known. One source indicates that he had bigamously married fifty-five women.

In 1902, Maud Marsh became ill with gastric complaints and died. Her husband, George Chapman, had two previous wives who had succumbed in a similar manner, so he was arrested and tried. He had moved to England from Poland in 1888, and at the time, he had been a strong suspect in the Ripper murders. Upon his arrest in the death of his wife, Chief Inspector Frederick Abberline, a principal in the Whitechapel investigation, said, "You've got Jack the Ripper at last." However, in view of the vast differences between his MO and Jack's, few have seriously accepted his candidacy as a suspect. Convicted, Chapman was hanged in 1903.

More gruesome was the discovery in California of the bones of approximately twelve men buried near Joseph Briggen's Sierra Morena Ranch. There were also bones and a skull in the pen of his prizewinning pigs. The victims had all been ranch hands who had come and supposedly gone over the years. For their murders, Briggen was sentenced to life in prison.

In Australia, Martha Rendall moved in with carpenter Thomas Morris, and his five children soon showed signs of deterioration. Two died in 1907 and another the following year. A local doctor diagnosed various illnesses, but when police heard the stories neighbors had to tell, they ordered the bodies exhumed. It seems that someone had used hydrochloric acid to "treat" their illnesses, the symptoms of which imitated diphtheria. Martha was charged, found guilty, and hanged in 1909.

Fingerprints

As American industrialism enriched people and entrepreneurial adventurers encouraged expansion into Western territories, the United States was about to experience nearly as many serial killings as the European countries, and Russia, too, would be troubled. The twentieth century in general would see an increase in these crimes, in part because better record-keeping made linking crimes easier and in part because high-stress conditions inspired pathology and created opportunities. But law enforcement made strides, too.

Fingerprint evidence got a boost in 1903 when a convict named Will West came into Fort Leavenworth prison in Kansas for processing. An agent located his card, but West protested that he had never been there before. Yet his measurements matched those of the "Will West" on the card and his face was similar. Looking further into the matter, they found a William West in the prison, and were baffled by the coincidence. This was a blow to the system of anthropometry, but there was one thing that did distinguish these two men: fingerprints.

The incident supported fingerprinting as the leading tool for identification. That year, the New York State prison system began the first systematic use of fingerprints in the country for criminal identification, and by 1910, based on a print left in wet paint in a murder case, an appeals court would declare that fingerprint technology had a scientific basis. Five years earlier, however, British investigators had already succeeded with fingerprint evidence in a precarious case that drew the world's attention.

It was 8:30 A.M. in Deptford, England, when a young man entered Chapman's Oil and Colour Shop on High Street and found owner Thomas Farrow in a bloody heap under an overturned chair. His head had been bludgeoned and the place showed signs of a terrific struggle. The police arrived and found Farrow's wife upstairs, assaulted and in need of immediate medical attention.

An empty cash box revealed robbery as the motive.

Chief Inspector Frederick Fox and Assistant Commissioner Melville Macnaghten from Scotland Yard's Criminal Investigation Department (CID) deduced from the lack of evidence of a forced entry that Farrow had been deceived into opening the door. The robbers had then gone up to the bedroom, bludgeoned Mrs. Farrow, found the cash box, and fled. They had left behind stockings cut to serve as masks.

Macnaghten hoped for a good fingerprint analysis. He carefully took an impression from the underside of the cash-box tray and brought it to the lab. Scotland Yard took seriously Henry Faulds's ideas about fingerprints, as well as those of Francis Galton via Edward Henry, who had transferred his work with fingerprints from India to London to establish CID's fingerprint section. The print on the cash-box tray appeared to have been left by a thumb. Detectives compared it with the prints they had on record from housebreakers, but did not get a match. Witnesses identified brothers Alfred and Albert Stratton, so the inspectors took their prints. After hours of waiting, a match was made between the print on the tray and the elder brother's thumbprint. They took this evidence to court, along with witness identifications, and agencies around the world awaited the results.

The defense put up a good fight, but when Inspector Charles Collins from CID showed the jury with enlarged photographs how the prints from the scene matched those of the elder Stratton on eleven points of comparison, it proved a dramatic moment. Collins also told the jury that he'd been working for four years with files that numbered over ninety thousand prints. It took the jury members two hours, but ultimately they accepted the fingerprint interpretation, convicting both men. That case opened the door for other police departments to trust finger-printing techniques.

But forensic science still had a rough road in other areas, notably wound pattern analysis. One case that involved the ability to read impressions on skin threw the emerging science of forensic medicine into a crisis, with experts challenging experts and the public left to wonder who was right. On the afternoon of April 5, 1905, a woman entered a Paris hospital with a baby who appeared to have been choked. The child had been left in the care of Jeanne Weber, a relative. The doctor found a reddish mark on its neck, and he learned that four babies had died from apparent suffocation among relatives in this family. Jeanne Weber, thirty, was always involved, and her own three children were also dead. Three years earlier, two other children had died in her care, with diagnoses from diphtheria to convulsions to cramps. But this time she was charged with murder.

In January 1906, Jeanne Weber appeared before the Seine Assizes, where Dr. Leon Thoinot, the government's pathologist and the person who had examined four of the exhumed corpses, gave an assessment. He described studies from the past eighty years concerning marks left by manual strangulation. In 1888, a Dr. Langreuter had opened the skulls of fresh corpses, scooped out the brains, and watched what happened inside as his assistant choked the corpses or used cords to strangle them. He had recorded his observations for other forensic physicians, notably that a victim of manual strangulation would show specific bruises on the neck and dotlike facial and muscle hemorrhages, called petechiae.

Thoinot reported that his tests on the corpses were negative. While circumstantial evidence and witness reports pointed to murder, forensic science could not support it. Weber was acquitted, and reporters hailed science as a tool for the innocent. But the story was not over.

Under another name, Weber became governess to a man with three small children, and a year later one of them died from "convulsions." Once again, the telltale red ring of strangulation showed up around the child's neck. Weber's past was revealed and she was arrested and subjected to Thoinot's analysis. But he rejected the cause of death as strangulation and she was again acquitted.

But she was caught red-handed in 1908, attacking the son of an innkeeper and killing him. The examining doctor was careful to make an exhaustive photographic documentation, knowing that Thoinot would be asked to evaluate it. But Weber did not get another trial. Rather than admit to mistakes in earlier diagnoses, Thoinot now decided that the latest incident was the result of stress caused by her earlier accusations. Her motive: sexual ecstasy. She was committed to an asylum, where she eventually died while trying to strangle herself.

For forensic medicine, it was a sign that improvements had to be made. Results could not depend on anyone's reputation or fear of being wrong, but only on the method itself.

Femme Fatale

America, too, had its female fiends, as three Southern women known as the "Sisters in Black" set about killing their relatives. Virginia, Caroline, and Mary Wardlow, daughters of a judge, either married or found a profession but remained in close proximity to one another. Their respective children did not fare well. One was found burned to death, which paid off in insurance money. Then one husband died from acute stomach pain, and a daughter drowned. Money was handed over in each case, and finally the sisters were arrested. But their methods paled in comparison to the next American sensation.

A fire on April 28, 1908, gutted the farmhouse of Belle Sorensen Gunness, a Norwegian-American living in Indiana. She was inside with her daughter and two sons, and once the fire was extinguished, it became clear that all four had died. No one doubted at first that the adult corpse was Belle, although the figure was smaller than she . . . and was missing its head. The prime suspect in this apparent arson was a former hired hand named Ray Lamphere, whom Belle had unsuccessfully tried to have declared insane and committed. Spotted near her farm that morning, he admitted he'd seen the fire starting but said he had not felt compelled to warn anyone. Lamphere was arrested and detained.

Early in May, investigators searched the property for the possible remains of Andrew Helgelein, missing for three months. Belle had written letters imploring him to sell everything and come to her, and after he visited, he disappeared. The authorities dug in a soft spot and turned up a gunnysack containing his dismembered body. His legs had been expertly sawed off above the knees, his arms disarticulated, his head removed, and all of his parts shoved into the hole with his torso. Grasped in his hand was some curly brown hair. Another soft spot nearby yielded the skeletal remains of a young girl, and then the decayed remains of a man and two children. This discovery prompted more exploration, and before it was over an estimated twelve to thirteen sets of remains, mostly male, had been removed from the ground.

Belle's history was reexamined and reporters wrote about the sudden inexplicable death in 1900 of her first husband, Mads Sorensen, who had been insured for $8,500. Two of her adopted children had died a few years earlier from conditions similar to those involved in poisoning, and several of her insured establishments had burned down. Belle had traded her home in Austin, Illinois, for the farm in LaPorte, Indiana, and soon married Peter Gunness, who died eight months later when, as Belle reported, a meat grinder and jar of scalding water fell on his head (although no burns were present on the body and the blow to his head did not match up with the meat grinder). Belle then placed matrimonial ads in various papers to lure men with money—many of whom disappeared. That is, until they were found buried on her farm. Lamphere denied any involvement in these deaths.

Public interest ran high, as newspapers increased both their circulation and the amount of space they devoted to the grizzly tale. Thousands of tourists arrived to view the farm and catch sight of the bodies or parts, still held on the property. A reporter for the *Chicago Tribune* said that the "organized feast of the morbid and curious" on the Sunday following the murder was "without parallel." Indeed, the estimates ran to some fifteen thousand visitors in the course of a single day. Merchants hawked postcards of the grizzly finds, alongside refreshments for lunch. The authorities even allowed some people to file through the outbuilding that had been set up as a temporary morgue. Tourists grabbed pieces of brick or other debris from the incinerated ruins, while the spectacle provided fodder for moralists' sermons—especially on "females" who displayed an unseemly curiosity.

Strangely, the debates over Belle's fate aligned with political affiliations, with Republicans believing that Belle was dead and Democrats insisting that she had faked her death and gotten away—which was consistent with Lamphere's account. In one of his many renderings, he admitted taking her to the train station. The corpse in the burned building, they said, was likely a woman she had hired as a housekeeper—whom people had seen her with the evening before. In the ruins were found partially burned books on anatomy and hypnosis. When poison was found in the bodies, the Democrats considered this proof for their side.

Even experts from across the Atlantic weighed in. Cesare Lombroso indicated that among criminal types, females were worse than males. The mothering instinct present in normal females is suppressed or absent in these women, who generally use poison, he said, adding that, in fact, they take pleasure in torturing their children and their enemies. Nevertheless, Lombroso believed Belle had a male accomplice who assisted her with the killing and disposal, and that she probably rewarded him with sex. She suffered from either epilepsy or hysteria, like all great female criminals, and she exhibited "a superior intelligence for doing evil."

A key discovery, three weeks after the fire, was the upper and lower dental bridge, identified as Belle's, allegedly found in the ashes. Although the coroner now declared Belle to be dead, even then there was debate, since the bridge showed none of the effects from the fire that other metals did. Some people—those affiliated as Democrats—believed the bridge had been planted there to close the case.

On May 23, 1908, Lamphere was indicted on four counts of murder and one count of arson. He went to trial on November 9, after the elections. The law partnership of H. W. Worden and Lemuel Darrow took on his defense.

Prosecutor Ralph Smith decided to use the legal forum to get closure on Belle's fate. If the jury convicted Lamphere of her murder, then she would be definitively declared dead. In support, he had the coroner's declaration of Belle's demise and a report on the history of trouble between Belle and Lamphere. They also had Lamphere's statement as a witness to the fire, Belle's bridgework, and a set of rings identified as hers. For motive, they said that Lamphere and Belle had a falling-out over money that she was supposed to pay him for assisting her with the murder and disposal of Helgelein. In addition, he was jealous of Belle's attention to Helgelein.

The defense stood by the idea that Belle was alive. They even prepared a subpoena for her. They had witnesses who could counter any of the prosecution's "proof," as well as experts with their own theories. Worden effectively opened up holes in the prosecution's case. The man who had discovered the dental bridge in the ashes, for example, could not be found and several witnesses said they had seen him remove it from his pocket. Also, the whereabouts of the dead woman's missing head was never adequately addressed, and if the fire destroyed it, then it was too hot for the false teeth on the bridge to survive in good condition—and several people had done scientific experiments to prove this.

Worden believed that Belle had been under pressure because she had heard from Helgelein's brother that he was arriving to make inquiries about Andrew and she knew she had to act quickly. On the afternoon before the murder, she had in fact purchased a large quantity of kerosene, and the same method she used to kill Helgelein (strychnine and arsenic) was evident in at least three of the bodies burned in the fire (although the prosecutor contended that this could have been introduced via autopsy procedures that rely on arsenic).

On November 26, Thanksgiving evening, the jury brought back a verdict against Lamphere, finding him guilty of arson. While they offered a statement that they believed the body in the cellar was that of Belle Gunness, they apparently bought the notion that the woman had committed suicide; they did not think the prosecution had clearly proven murder. Lamphere was fined $5,000 and given a term of two to twenty-one years in prison.

Gunness was allegedly sighted numerous times around the country by people who knew her, but always managed to slip away. Then, in 1931 in Los Angeles, an elderly woman named Esther Carlson was charged with killing a man for money. Before her trial commenced, she died. Some accounts indicate that the police found a trunk in a room where the woman was staying that contained photos of children who resembled Belle's.

This may have been the last sensational case to which Lombroso managed to apply his theories, as he died in 1909, and four years later, Charles Goring published an article that discredited the idea of physical criminal features. In "The English Convict," he presented the results of his own measurements of criminal and noncriminal types, indicating that in the population at large there were no such differences.

Perhaps that's why no one noticed Eugene Butler's association with a number of young men who were disappearing when they went to work for him. He was already dead when authorities learned that he had been a murderer. He died in a mental institution in the early 1900s, probably suffering from paranoid schizophrenia, after which his house outside Niagara, North Dakota, was razed. At that time, the remains of six bodies were found buried in the crawl space beneath his house. Anthropologists determined that all had been males between the ages of fifteen and eighteen, and each had been bludgeoned to death with blows to the skull.

While it seemed that with each passing decade, murder was becoming more sensational, the conditions produced by two world wars would trigger even more, and they would include atrocities not seen since the Middle Ages.

CHAPTER SEVEN

Opportunities in Transition

Collective Anxiety

It was the era of sensation. Lindbergh's baby was kidnapped and killed, and two educated rich kids translated Nietzsche's will to power into murder. Einstein proposed the theory of relativity, while Henry Ford offered the Model T and thirty-four agents were appointed to the Justice Department's Bureau of Identification. The *Titanic* sank, the Wright Brothers flew, and Sigmund Freud gained ground. During a world war and the Great Depression that followed, men and woman alike exploited the chaos to indulge in dark deeds, even as gangsters and outlaws made killing a public spectacle. G-man Eliot Ness chased a dismembering fiend, U.S. crime labs were funded, forensic investigation made great strides, and multiple killers multiplied. In times of deprivation and need, most were motivated by profit.

For nearly a century, as European nations had generally developed in relative peace, an extreme sense of nationalism, inspired in many countries by increased voting privileges, stepped up weapons production for standing armies. The world was building up steam that could only seep through the inadequate vents offered in the Balkans crises. Without release, the tensions made citizens feel less secure and more aware of the possibility of large-scale catastrophe.

As those struggles played out, U.S. physiologist Thomas Hunt Morgan demonstrated that chromosomes carry inherited information, which would one day have implications for crime investigation. In 1910, Albert S. Osborne, another American, published *Questioned Documents* to show the forensic value of document examination, although courts still questioned if even expert interpretation wasn't actually subjective in nature. In France, Edmond Locard set up the first forensic police lab, using scientific analysis on trace evidence to solve crimes. His unique endeavor would motivate many others.

Inspired by Sherlock Holmes, Locard bought microscopes and studied forensic techniques. He believed that criminals had to leave traces of their presence at crime scenes. Few people listened to him until he took on a case in 1911. Swindlers in Paris were using counterfeit coins and the police had arrested three suspects. Locard went in with a pair of tweezers to examine their clothing. He removed specks of dust from their pockets, and under magnification he found minute traces of metal that matched the coins, implicating all three suspects. This case gave Locard publicity for his scientific approach.

At the time, most police officers did not rely on microscopes, but in 1912 that changed. The microscope became the first scientific tool to be used in a murder case in the U.S. when a Massachusetts-based homicide was solved with the microscopic analysis of threads from a coat that had lost a button at a crime scene.

But the solution to many crimes still relied on criminals simply making mistakes. Dr. Linda Burfield Hazzard opened a hundred-bed facility in Olalla, Washington, in 1911, where she claimed to offer enemas and extreme fasting to wealthy clients as "health treatments." Instead, she starved patients to death and took their money. Around the same time in Washington's port of Aberdeen, disembarking sailors disappeared in high numbers. When one sailor's body washed up from the ocean and was linked to the Office of the Sailors' Union, office worker Billy Gohl became a suspect. It turned out that he would ask incoming sailors if they were meeting family, and if they weren't, the "Ghoul of Gray's Harbor" killed them for their pay and dropped them down a chute into the ocean. He was convicted of two murders in 1913, but was suspected in forty-one.

From 1911 to 1920, serial killers appeared to be operating in over a dozen areas in the U.S. Ax killer Henry Lee Moore went cross-country killing families, while Georgia, Texas, Colorado, New York, Idaho, and Louisiana all suffered a series of murders from children to the elderly, from black women to couples killed in their beds. Most of these cases went unsolved, although some, like Lydia Trueblood's killing of her relatives, did not.

In Spain, a child named Angelita approached police in Barcelona with a wild tale. She had been held captive by a witch, she said, and forced to eat human flesh. The police followed her to where she had been kept and arrested Marti Enriqueta. The tale, it turned out, was true— Enriqueta would kidnap children to kill and dismember for use in her potions, and also consume parts of them. Her victim count was unknown, but by 1912 at least six children had been subjected to this treatment.

Just before James P. Watson, the "Monster of the Western Coast," was convicted in California of killing nine of his estimated twenty wives, another man in England made headlines for his method of wife disposal. Margaret Lloyd died in her bath in Highgate, England, in 1914. A relative of a victim of a similar drowning noticed her obituary and brought the matter to the police, who noted the criminal record of her husband, George Joseph Smith. Indeed, he had not only married Margaret Lloyd under an assumed name, but had married three times, and each wife had drowned in her bath. Until the third one, the incidents were considered accidents, but in fact Smith had killed them all by grabbing them by the feet and pulling them helplessly into the water. Then he enriched himself on their money or insurance. The "Brides in the Bath Killer" went to the executioner in 1915 shouting, "I am in terror!"

Back in the U.S., a small elder-care facility in Windsor, Connecticut, logged a suspicious number of deaths per year, even for that population. Amy Archer-Gilligan, who also had lost two husbands to a mysterious illness, ran the place. An undercover official collected evidence of fraud and foul play, which led to the exhumation of the bodies of Archer-Gilligan's second husband and several former patients. Finding high doses of arsenic in the bodies, officials charged her with six counts of murder. Then, consulting with physicians, they discovered that an average yearly death toll in such a small place would be eight to ten, not forty-eight. It turned out "Sister" Amy had persuaded some patients to pay an insurance premium of $1,000, for which she promised "lifetime care." Once she had the money, their "lifetimes" ended quickly. Archer-Gilligan was given a life sentence, which she served in an institution for the insane.

Stress Release

Germany quickly gained military strength, which forced France into an uneasy alliance with Russia. They were joined by Britain when outright war broke out after the 1914 assassination in Sarajevo of Archduke Franz Ferdinand, heir to Austro-Hungary's throne. Austro-Hungary attacked Serbia, and Germany offered support, declaring war on France and Russia, Serbia's ally. The opposing sides lined up in the Great War in parallel trenches to the east and west of Germany, with most of the fighting taking place through Belgium and northeastern France along a 450-mile front.

One Hungarian man conscripted into the war effort

was Bela Kiss. In 1916, officials learned about stores of petrol on his property near Czinkota, so they confiscated seven drums. But when they opened them, they were shocked to find that each one contained not the expected fuel but the preserved body of a naked woman, drained of blood. Autopsies indicated that all had been strangled, and each dead woman had wounds on her neck. Seventeen more barrels offered the same grisly contents, including Kiss's faithless wife and her boyfriend. During an investigation, officials learned that a "Professor Hoffman" in Czinkota had lured some of these victims with matrimonial ads. But authorities believed Kiss was dead, so they closed the cases. A battlefront nurse reported that she had attended to the fatally wounded Bela Kiss, seeming to confirm suspicions, but her description failed to match the man people knew, so it seemed that he had switched dog tags with a dying soldier and was still alive. Reports of him surfaced in Budapest, but like an elusive vampire, he was never caught.

The social stress created by war conditions seemed to infect certain individuals who needed only a slight trigger to act out. Red-bearded Henri Landru, for example, also exploited lonely middle-aged women in Paris—and there were many both during and after the war—through those handy matrimonial ads. Once he had snared and killed a woman, he took over her property. A suspicious relative of one victim informed the police, who caught Landru with items belonging to missing women. In his stove, they discovered human bone fragments. Even more helpful to the case, Landru had kept a notebook evaluating each prospect's assets. The press grabbed this story and exaggerated the number of victims of the "French Bluebeard" into the hundreds, perhaps because his stove yielded over two hundred bone and teeth fragments, but he was convicted of only eleven murders.

Three years into the war, Russia's soldiers mutinied and its people revolted against Czar Nicholas II. They set up a new government, which after a few months fell to Vladimir Lenin and the Bolsheviks, effectively removing Russia from combat. But the U.S. reacted to attacks on its supply ships by supporting the Allies. This increased military might turned the tide. Six months and the deaths of nearly ten million troops later, in 1918, Germany sued for peace. Delegates from thirty-two nations met at the Paris Peace Conference to decide the fate of the losing side. The Big Four—France, Italy, the U.S., and the U.K.— dictated harsh terms to Germany in the Treaty of Versailles, stripping it of arms and territory and exacting hefty reparations, which served to feed a smoldering Teutonic resentment. The land divisions also stepped up pressure in other places. It would only require leaders with vision to rally those humiliated nations in a new direction. Conditions certainly would not stabilize as they were left.

Several governments were dismantled. Along with the overthrow of Czar Nicholas II, Kaiser Wilhelm of Germany and Emperor Charles of Austro-Hungary lost their positions. Four years later, the Ottoman sultan, Muhammad VI, fell. Austria, Hungary, and Czechoslovakia formed new independent republics, while the Baltic States gained independence from Russia, and that part of the Ottoman Empire that did not become Turkey was parceled to the United Kingdom and France. The Communists held their ground in Russia.

Millions of Europeans were uprooted, and industries lost an enormous amount of manpower with the deaths of so many men. People became political refugees with no place to go. But women had grown empowered with new skills acquired during the war and did not relish leaving the workplace. Under pressure, many countries granted them the vote. The middle class exercised its voice, but with less confidence now in a Eurocentric vision.

A League of Nations was formed, but it had no power. In Russia, famine and a civil war threatened whole populations, so Lenin offered a New Economic Policy that encouraged a free market, as he founded the Union of Soviet Socialist Republics. When he died in 1924, Stalin took charge, ordered large-scale purges, and communalized farms, which would precipitate another devastating famine. The U.S.S.R. also concentrated on armaments, intent on becoming a world power as a communist state. For different reasons in different countries, a general feeling of dissatisfaction developed throughout Europe.

Two killers stand out from those times, in part for their barbarity. In Berlin, Georg Grossmann, a former butcher, was caught with the dismembered remains of four women. Throughout the war, he had brought home prostitutes for sex and then killed them. Often he sold the flesh to the hungry when meat was hard to get, and sometimes he ate it himself. The authorities estimated that he had killed around fifty women, although they charged him with only fourteen murders.

Moscow, too, had a "wolf," in the form of Vasili Komaroff. With his wife, he frequented the horse market, and people often disappeared after being seen in his company. When police caught him with a victim, he fled, but they found and arrested him, persuading him to confess to thirty-three for-profit murders. Twenty-two bodies were found, and he pointed out the graves of five more, but the rest had disappeared into the river. Komaroff and his wife were both executed.

These were hard times in Europe and Russia, but the war brought prosperity to America. With Henry Ford's development of mass production, the people saw nothing but material progress ahead. They invested with abandon in the stock market, so industries stepped up the production of goods. No one paid attention to the need for balance. It was the Roaring Twenties, after all, the Jazz Age.

And speaking of jazz, New Orleans had a scare over a few-month period in 1918 and 1919. The "Axeman" claimed most of his victims from among Italian grocers and their families. One legend says that this spree echoed incidents from 1911, in which three Italian grocers and their wives had been killed, but no records support it. The killer would enter the homes of victims during the night by chiseling out a door panel, then use an ax on the sleeping occupants. Suspicion fell on a man who had mysterious connections with Germany, and some blamed a violent Mafia band, known as the Black Hand. At one point, the local paper, the *Times-Picayune*, printed a letter, ostensibly from the killer, that warned everyone in the city to play jazz on St. Joseph's Night. He would then pass by and leave them unharmed. No one died that night, but during the spree, six people were bludgeoned to death, including a baby, and six more people were badly wounded. Eventually the attacks ceased, and a suspect was killed, but this marauder was never officially identified.

Crime Science

In the U.S. directly after the war, Luke May demonstrated the value of studying tool striations for comparisons between specific tools and the marks they made, while Charles E. Waite catalogued all U.S. guns ever manufactured in terms of construction, date of manufacture, caliber, number, and the twist and proportion of the lands and grooves, as well as the type of ammunition used. After three years, he had data on nearly all types of U.S.-made guns manufactured since the 1850s. He observed that no type was identical to any other and was able to scientifically distinguish which type had fired a specific spent bullet. He did the same for guns of European manufacture.

To look at the imprints left during the manufacturing process, Waite needed a good microscope. Optician Max Poser developed a device with fitted bullet holders and measuring scales. John H. Fisher then invented the helix-ometer to inspect inside a gun barrel and a device for making precise determinations about the lands and grooves. The final instrument came from Philip O. Gravelle, whose extensive work in microphotography inspired the comparison microscope, combining two microscopes in a single unit for side-by-side comparison of two bullets.

During the next decade in Germany, the electron microscope would be developed, using beams from fast-moving electrons to form an image on an electron-sensitive plate. This would enable scientists to see much smaller objects than was possible with a light transmission microscope.

In Russia, despite the upheavals there, paleontologist Mikhail Gerasimov calculated the past thickness of flesh on the face of a skeletonized victim. He started with fossil skulls, but then applied his ideas in forensic cases. Although not the first to do facial reconstruction, he originated the scientific approach to forensic art, and his methods assisted others in learning facial reconstruction from a skull.

Forensic evidence in the form of questioned document examination was highlighted in a famous case from this period. Nathan Leopold and Richard Loeb—both nineteen, brilliant beyond imagining, educated, and wealthy—were close friends. Loeb worshiped power and Leopold was willing to do anything for Loeb. Leopold was enamored of the idea espoused by the German philosopher Friedrich Nietzsche that superior men have no moral boundaries. He had proposed the idea of the *übermensch* who made and lived by his own rules. The two young men decided that they were among those exceptional beings, and set out to prove it by committing the perfect crime: They would kidnap and murder a child.

On May 21, 1924, they selected fourteen-year-old Bobby Franks. They hit him with a chisel and then smothered him with a rag. Afterward they poured acid on his face and genitals to prevent identification. Finally they tossed the naked mutilated body into a culvert and wrote a ransom note for $10,000.

Soon they were caught and tried. On the basis of a dropped pair of glasses and a close analysis of the ransom note, the police had leverage to get confessions and the two were indicted. The press reported this murder-for-thrill as unique in the annals of American crime. At trial, alienists were brought in to "explain" the degenerate behavior, and newspaper magnate William Hearst offered Sigmund Freud $25,000 to provide an analysis (he declined). After defense attorney Clarence Darrow masterfully argued against the death penalty, the judge gave both of them life in prison.

International Criminals

World War I had cost $186 billion and taken nine million lives, unsettling the social conditions in many countries. There was civil war in Russia, hyperinflation in Germany, and the rise of fascism in Italy. Survival was tough, so in France Antoinette Scieri poisoned and robbed a dozen elderly people, while between 1924 and 1929 the German press reported three shocking killers. They had not yet forgotten Georg Grossmann from three years earlier.

"Vater" Karl Denke, the "Mass Murderer of Münsterberg," struck at homeless people and guests at his inn, killing them and pickling their remains. He kept detailed records of their weight and poured buckets of their blood out in his open courtyard, but no one seemed to notice. After his arrest in 1924, he claimed he had eaten parts from as many as thirty-one people and that for over three years human flesh had been his sole source of meat. He committed suicide in jail, and soon after, the police discovered fingers, pickled flesh, suspenders made from skin, and other equally gruesome items in his quarters.

During the same time, Fritz Haarmann, the "Hanover Vampire," was arrested and convicted, and his crimes seemed particularly deviant. He was a trained butcher with a low IQ and a record of time spent in a mental institution. He would find wayward young men, invite them home for a meal, force sex on them, and then murder them. He teamed up with a male prostitute, Hans Graf, who could better lure the boys. Together over a period of five years, they trapped and killed an estimated fifty young men. They were finally stopped after someone found skeletal remains in a canal. Since Haarmann lived near there and had a previous arrest, investigators searched his home. They found clothing from several missing boys and saw bloodstains on the walls. Again, they arrested Haarmann, and this time he confessed.

While he excused himself by saying that he would warn the boys not to let him lose control, and that he had no premeditated intent to kill anyone, he admitted that once things reached a certain point during games of "terminal sex," he was unable to stop. He referred to his victims as "game" and described how he'd grab them as they dozed after a large meal or after intense sexual activity, and while sodomizing them would chew into their necks until the head was nearly severed. As he tasted their blood, he achieved orgasm. He would then remove the internal organs and cut the flesh from their bodies, eat some or store it under his bed, and sell the rest as butchered meat. The bones he dumped, usually into the canal. He claimed that he hated doing these things, but the obsession was too great for him to overcome.

Armed with grisly evidence for twenty-seven of the murders, investigators ensured Haarmann's conviction and he was sentenced to die in 1925. His attorney had requested a psychological analysis, but the judge had insisted that there was no place for psychology in the courtroom. Moments before the blade fell, Haarmann announced that this was his "wedding day." After the publicity on this case, people developed *menschenfleisch-psychose*, or the irrational fear of eating meat that might be human.

Haarmann's murders may have been his unique, albeit brutal, way of managing the cultural stress thick in the air, an anxiety that foreshadowed the state-sanctioned murders of millions of people soon to come. It seemed to be catalytic for certain types of aberrant behavior involving different kinds of drives and appetites. Scholar Maria Tatar linked these killers to the phenomenon in Weimar Germany of the appearance in art of the victims of serial murder. Having noted the sheer number of canvases from the 1920s entitled *Lustmord*—"sexual murder"—she found it unsurprising that someone like Haarmann developed as he did, and she viewed his behavior as symptomatic of something larger.

The artists, apparently, became quite involved in these paintings, as if they could capture the killer's perception and feelings. They turned the mutilated female body into an object of fascination, riveting and repulsive. Was there such hatred in the air for women at this time? Or was this artistic movement a disguised defense against losing so many men during the war? It seemed to be a violent strategy for managing collective social and sexual tension, and Tatar believes it was an intellectual attack on a woman's biology, both in hatred and in love. In fact, commentaries from those times excused murder as justifiable hatred against either Jews or women—those who threatened the social order, inspired self-doubt in males, or deviated from strict roles (such as women taking over male occupations or flaunting their sexuality). They had to be punished via disfigurement and death. Yet these violent artistic expressions may have been more a matter of internal panic for men than outright anger, a fear that letting females too close could deplete or overwhelm an already wounded gender. Better to kill and mutilate them instead.

Murder, then, became an "eroticized release for hatred" and supposedly an opportunity for transcendence. It was thought to be a "retaliatory pleasure" for those who perceived themselves as victims, taken at the expense of those who deserved it. In other words, Germany was smarting from humiliation, and getting ready to strike out to reclaim its status and punish those who had mortified such a proud country. For some men, the membrane between cultural forces and their own dormant aggression was thin. Their brutality, captured in popular ditties sung by children about "choppers" coming to make them into mincemeat, may have signaled just where the culture was heading. These killers were like leaks in a dam containing a collective psychosis that was moving toward payback.

Just a few years later, German citizens were treated to yet another gory series of murders, committed by a man the people of the Rhine River Valley called "The Monster of Düsseldorf." First, an eight-year-old girl was found nude and stuffed under a hedge. She had been stabbed thirteen times and an attempt had been made to burn her corpse. A week later, the body of a forty-five-year-old mechanic turned up, stabbed twenty times. Six months went by before two girls were murdered at the fairgrounds: The five-year-old was manually strangled and her throat was cut; the fourteen-year-old was also strangled, and then was beheaded. There were other attacks in which the victims survived, but then one night an adolescent girl was raped and battered to death with a hammer. Six weeks later, a five-year-old child disappeared and a letter arrived at a local newspaper with a map to the body. She had been stabbed thirty-six times. The letter also described the location of the corpse of another young woman who had been missing for several months.

The town was in a state of panic, and as with the Jack the Ripper case, the incidents inspired more than 150 copycat letters to the press. That in turn triggered condemnation against the press for its coverage. People felt that crime reporting had a negative effect on youth, while the police believed that the publicizing of the series of murders had triggered other types of insanity in society at large.

Then one day a young woman reported that a man had attempted to attack her with scissors and rape her, but had inexplicably let her go. She led police to the home where he lived with his wife. His name was Peter Kürten, and he was a carpenter. Once in custody, he confessed to everything. He explained that he'd committed numerous assaults and thirteen murders—including one when he was only six—and admitted to the excitement he got from drinking his victims' blood. He added an incident from 1913, where a child had been murdered at an inn. He described how as he choked the girl and cut her throat, blood had spurted into an arch over his head, which had excited him to orgasm. In fact, just before he was arrested, he had tied the stockings of one victim around his waist.

At his trial, defense psychiatrists declared him insane, but the jury ignored them. Kürten was sentenced on nine counts of murder to be executed in 1931. Just before dying, he expressed a desire to hear his own blood bubble forth after the blade came down. He called it "the pleasure to end all pleasures." Psychiatrist Karl Berg made a famous study of the man's sadistic temperament, among the first psychiatric analyses of serial murder. Another facet of Kürten's crime was his attention to the press reports. He said he liked notoriety and thus had behaved in a way to agitate the public. The journalists had inspired him toward greater acts of depravity, he insisted, and had made him what he was. His aspiration was to become the "most berated criminal of all time." Downplaying other motives, he said that what he had done was payback for his life disappointments. His trial accommodated physicians, psychiatrists, and more than a hundred journalists, for whom were provided specially installed telephone booths to facilitate the relaying of information.

Yet as bizarre as the four German butchers were, a group of Hungarian females outdid them. In Nagyrev, the death toll among males after they'd returned from the war was high, and bodies were sometimes found floating down the river. The area became known as the "murder district." Several people complained to the police about having been poisoned, so officials set up surveillance on the suspects, a midwife named Julia Fazekas and her assistant, Susannah Olah (who boasted of training snakes to attack people). Finally officials caught the pair in the act of distributing poison, and their shocking story unfolded.

When the men had gone off to war in 1914, the women

left behind had consorted with Allied POWs from a
nearby camp. But the men had returned, most of them
after the war, forcing the women to return to their tedious
roles. Restless, they turned to the midwives. Fazekas
boiled the arsenic off flypaper and sold it to those who
sought to be free of their marriages—or of their children
or other relatives, in some cases. Over a span of fifteen
years, with the first murder occurring in 1914, the death
toll reached over one hundred. Apparently, Fazekas and
Olah had inspired as many as fifty women to become murderers, or even serial killers, and had called themselves
"The Angel Makers of Nagyrev." Eighteen women were
convicted, with eight of them hanged. Perplexed police
officers declared it "promiscuity-inspired madness."

Guns, Glamour, and Gangsters

It was the golden age for American crime. In 1917, the
U.S. Congress had passed the Eighteenth Amendment,
which prohibited the manufacture, sale, and consumption
of alcohol. The amendment was ratified in 1919, and
along with the Volstead Act created not a nation of clear-
thinking people (its intent) but a nation of lawbreakers.
Many people made illegal liquor in private, but organized
crime began to bootleg it for large profits. Ethnic gangs,
banding together for power, turned city streets into bat-
tlegrounds. The era of Prohibition inspired "gangster
chic," with the newly invented tommy guns, fancy cars,
and speakeasies. And thanks to the amount of money that

could be made dealing in booze, police officers, too, were vulnerable to corruption.

The government fought back. During World War I, John Edgar Hoover, a Department of Justice lawyer, had been appointed assistant director for the Bureau of Investigation, established during the first decade of the century. After a shake-up of that institution in 1924 based on a violation-of-privacy scandal, he became acting director. At that time, there were over four hundred special agents manning nine field offices around the country. Pressured by Hoover's desire to train an elite force of professionals, the department became more disciplined, added more agents, and was eventually renamed the Federal Bureau of Investigation: the F.B.I.

Even as organized crime captured the public imagination, so did several independent murderers. The "Borgia of America," Martha Wise, fatally poisoned three members of her family when they opposed her relationship with a younger man. During questioning, she confessed and was sentenced to life. In Pennsylvania, Stella Williamson apparently killed and preserved the remains of five infants in a trunk in her house, which the authorities only learned about after she died years later. In the next state over, the police were dealing with more mysterious crimes.

On the night of November 10, 1925, Mrs. Frank Hall was hit from behind outside her Toledo home and bludgeoned repeatedly about the head and face. She survived, but five other women similarly attacked did not. Over the course of two weeks, a dozen women suffered the blows of this unknown assailant. The police issued a description of a monstrous-looking man with fiery eyes, and the press dubbed him the "Toledo Clubber." But his crime spree stopped as suddenly as it had begun, and he was never identified.

Not so with the next man also described as a monster. In San Francisco on February 20, 1926, sixty-year-old Clara Newman was found raped and strangled in the attic of the house where she let rooms. Her killer could not be found, but over the next year, twenty-two more such murders occurred in places as diverse as Philadelphia, Detroit, and Winnipeg, Canada. Most of the victims were landladies, all were raped and strangled, and all were hidden in small spaces or pushed under beds. Then in Canada, a fourteen-year-old and a married woman were murdered in the same area, and both were found under beds. At the same time, a barber in town noticed blood on the hair of a stranger who asked for a haircut. The barber's description enabled the police to catch Earle Leonard Nelson. He pleaded insanity, which was supported by stints in mental hospitals, but he was convicted and hanged in Winnipeg. Given his MO and descriptions of his distinct appearance, the American murders were connected to him, along with a triple murder in New Jersey in which three landladies had been strangled and placed beneath beds. Stocky, with protruding lips, long arms, and a sloping forehead, the "Gorilla Murderer" would have been an apt subject for Lombroso's theories.

Just as brutal but more wide-ranging was Carl Panzram, whose international one-man, eighteen-year crime spree spanned thirty-one countries and two continents. Arrested for drunkenness when he was only eight, Panzram lived a hard life. In his autobiography he referred to himself as "the spirit of meanness personified" and attributed his foul temper to endless abuse from family, religion, and prison guards. He murdered, raped, and sodomized people indiscriminately, sometimes several at a time, after luring them into situations of vulnerability. In West Africa, he hired six black men for a hunt, killed them, and gave their corpses to the crocodiles. He thought that killing people was fun, admitting to twenty-one murders and adding that he had sodomized over one thousand men. He wanted no hindrance to his death sentence, as he told a jury that if he were allowed to live, he would kill again, because he hated the whole human race. In 1930, he was granted his wish to be executed.

Panzram's case coincided with one of the most dramatic events in U.S. history. In October 1929, the optimistic American economy came crashing down. Many stock shares lost worth and more than five thousand banks were forced to close. Within two years, a third of the workforce was unemployed. This Great Depression spread overseas to Europe as well, and in some countries unemployment went over 20 percent, which inspired criticism of the capitalist system and greater emphasis on political nationalism. Whole families slept in their cars, if they had one, or went to the transient accommodations of tourist camps. They welcomed cheap entertainment, which arrived in the form of flamboyant "motorized bandits" who robbed banks. Outlaws in the mold of Jesse James, these men and women defied authority and punished the institutions that had caused such dire circumstances for so many. Appearing to be underdogs who were fighting back, they became heroes.

Yet another movement had also begun, grounded in the gangster era. The St. Valentine's Day Massacre in 1929, in which seven unarmed men were machine-gunned down in a turf war between gangs, provoked officials in the nation's "crime capital," Chicago, to do something. The first crime watchdog group, the Chicago Crime Commission, christened gangsters "Public Enemies" in April 1930. On the first list of twenty-eight, they placed Alphonse "Scarface" Capone at the number one spot. Newspapers and cinemas happily played out this polarity between good guys and bad guys, but it did not escape the public's notice that crime created celebrity—and sometimes paid.

A case in point was Herman Drenth. A noxious odor from an area in Clarksburg, West Virginia, in 1931 led to the exhumation of five decomposing corpses—two women and three children. The police had already arrested Drenth, a furniture dealer, for questioning about a missing person, and in the process uncovered a psychopath with a ghastly side business: marriage for self-enrichment. On his business trips around the country under the name "Harry Powers," he'd located wealthy widows via personal ads, married them, and brought them to his home, Quiet Dell.

But they ended up in his homemade gas chamber, which had a glass window. As he looked through it he would become aroused by his victims' struggles. He would then sell their property. He clearly had at least five victims, but he alluded to fifty.

On the forensic front, Calvin Goddard used scientific analysis to identify the weapons used in the St. Valentine's Day Massacre, and this feat inspired the nation's first multi-investigation crime lab, privately funded by businessmen. Goddard advised the FBI in 1932 on its crime lab, and its first pieces of equipment were a microscope and a helixometer. The agency had set up a national fingerprint file two years earlier, and was now moving into the modern age of crime investigation.

In 1933, John Dillinger arrived on the scene as a bank robber and was soon an internationally celebrated fugitive—and therefore, easily identified. To foil fingerprint experts, he had the tips of his fingers surgically removed—a uniqueness that only helped to affirm his identification after "The Lady in Red" betrayed him to authorities, who gunned him down in 1934 outside Chicago's Biograph Theater. Women who recognized him dipped handkerchiefs in his blood.

Baby Face Nelson, Ma Barker, Machine Gun Kelly, Pretty Boy Floyd: These were among the names that hit the news, cheered on by angry people who wanted someone to show them a way out of their mean condition. Bonnie Parker, a Texas waitress and avid reader of crime novels, fell for Clyde Barrow, and together they went on a killing spree. While they show up on some lists as serial killers, it's more likely that their killing was part and parcel of their bank robberies, although Bonnie was allegedly a hybristophiliac—one who finds violent adventures erotic.

In the attempt to fight crime with theory, Dillinger's brain, along with those of other criminals, was examined. None showed the expected defects described in then-current physiological theories, which had helped to spur a new movement in criminal anthropology. Harvard professor E. A. Hooten emulated Bertillon's measurement system to "prove" that the primary cause of crime was biological inferiority. He grouped the criminals he studied by nationality and types of psychoses. The public was thus primed for yet another sensational event that would harbor these racial overtones.

On a stormy Tuesday night on March 1, 1932, someone climbed into the second-floor bedroom of the home of Charles Lindbergh and kidnapped his twenty-month-old son. Although kidnappings were in vogue in those days as a source of quick cash, Lindbergh was a national hero for his historic flight from New York to Paris, so the kidnapping of his "princeling" outraged the country. Ransom notes arrived and money was paid in marked bills, but no baby was forthcoming. Investigators sought to use a new device, the polygraph, patented by Leonarde Keeler in 1931, to interview Lindbergh's servants, but he refused to allow it. Two months later the child's remains were found in the woods two miles from the Lindbergh home, and it took police two years to track down the man they believed was responsible: Bruno Richard Hauptmann.

He was in possession of the ransom money—paid in gold certificates that had been recalled by the government—and despite his protests that he had received the money from a business partner, he was arrested. He begged to take a polygraph, but since a federal appeals court had already banned the results of "systolic blood pressure deception tests" from the courtroom in 1923, it seemed of little use. His attorney had no interest in proving his client's innocence. Public sentiment went against this suspicious German immigrant with a criminal record, and after a one-sided trial, Hauptmann was convicted and duly executed.

The Eighteenth Amendment was repealed in 1933, ending the need for the Prohibition Bureau. Eliot Ness, who had led the nine-man squad of "Untouchables," retired and moved to Cleveland. But organized crime simply moved its business to other venues. The following year, Bonnie and Clyde were ambushed in Louisiana and shot more than fifty times each. Still in their vehicle, they were towed to town, and people arrived from miles around to touch the "death car." Schoolchildren ripped pieces from Bonnie's dress and grabbed her hair. This couple's demise signaled the end of an era.

As President Franklin Roosevelt's New Deal and ambitious road-building programs were helping to stabilize the economy to allow for growth, Albert Fish was being arrested in New York for the kidnapping and murder of twelve-year-old Grace Budd. Fish was fifty-eight at the time. He had ingratiated himself into the Budd family in 1928 as "Mr. Howard" before taking Grace to a "birthday party." Her family never saw her again. Six years went by and Fish sent an anonymous note to Grace's mother. He wrote about how he had taken Grace away, and strangled and dismembered her. Then he claimed that he had cooked pieces of her and consumed them.

A dogged investigator traced the stationery to Fish, and when the self-professed cannibal was arrested, he confessed in lurid detail: As he'd savored the stew he had made of Grace Budd's flesh for nine days, he had masturbated. His first murder, he said, took place in 1910 when he killed a man in Delaware. Believing himself to be Christ, and obsessed with sin and atonement, he had made a practice of beating himself with spiked paddles. He also stuck needles into his groin, threaded rose stems into his urethra, and lighted alcohol-soaked cotton balls inside his anus. In visions, he'd supposedly received commandments that made him believe he was Abraham from the Bible, and just as Abraham was called to sacrifice his only son to the Lord, Fish realized he would have to kill children—or at least to castrate young boys.

Fish admitted to the murders of three other children, but he sometimes claimed to have done away with around four hundred. Some experts place his death toll around fifteen. Despite his obvious insanity, the jury sentenced the "Moon Maniac" to death.

That same year, 1936, "Onkel Tick Tack" Adolf Seefeld was executed in Germany. He had confessed to killing a dozen children over nearly three decades. Indeed, although the U.S. was paying little attention, Europe was continuing to deal with multiple killers as well.

Buildup to War

On September 12, 1931, as the Budapest-Vienna express train crossed a viaduct near Torbagy Station, it exploded, killing twenty-two people. Sylvestre Matushka sued for damages, but when it was learned that he had purchased dynamite and that no one had seen him on the train, he was arrested. He confessed that he had caused the explosion, because it was the only way he could achieve sexual release. He had eroticized the image of bodies being ripped up by machines, but was caught before he could bring to fruition his agenda of causing one wreck per month: Indeed, this was his third attempt on a train. He was found guilty in 1932, but freed from prison during the Korean War to become an explosives expert.

As Matushka went to prison, a South African jury convicted European Daisy Louisa de Melker of poisoning two husbands and five children, while Georges Maître Sarret and his gang were tried in France for an insurance fraud that had cost four people their lives—two of them through being dissolved in acid. Sarret was executed, while the female gang members were allowed the excuse that they had been "mesmerized," and were freed.

From 1933 to 1936, Belgium, Australia, England, and

South Africa caught several multiple murderers, one of whom was a woman. Two insisted they couldn't help it and two appeared to just need money. Fifty-three-year-old Marie Alexandrine Becker killed her husband with digitalis and hired a string of male prostitutes to satisfy her needs. When money ran low, she poisoned her acquaintances. She had twelve victims before she was stopped and imprisoned. Melbourne-based family man Arnold Sodeman claimed an uncontrollable impulse when he was convicted of strangling four young girls, while Frederick Herbert Field initially avoided a murder conviction in England by confessing and then recanting, thus removing the only way in which police could associate him with the crime. When he tried to kill again, he got caught and this time was convicted. In South Africa, Ntimane Sandwene operated by day as a humble servant and by night as "the Killer of the White Mountain" who murdered eight shopkeepers. He was sentenced to death.

After the Great War, Germany had set up a democratic constitution, but when the mark lost value, the economy collapsed. Then, after a brief hiatus with better economic conditions, the Great Depression took its toll. The country craved a leader, paving the way for Adolf Hitler, who resented the peace settlement dictated in the 1918 Treaty of Versailles and hated Germany's enemies. Millions voted Hitler and his Nazi Party into power. In 1933, he declared the Third Reich, setting out to restore Germany's power, and three years later Spain fell into a civil war. Italy and Japan, too, had installed dictators, Benito Mussolini and Hirohito, respectively. All had resented the Allies since the Great War, and they soon began an imperial drive, making another large-scale conflict inevitable.

Between 1922 and 1939, serial killers popped up in other places: Poland had eleven victims, while in the U.S., a San Diego–based killer claimed as many as twenty-two, five women were beheaded in Pennsylvania, and Alaska's "Mad Trapper" killed a reported fifteen hunters.

Eve of Destruction

The years 1937 and 1938 saw developments that improved forensic investigation methods. Walter Specht did experiments with the molecule luminol, first synthesized in 1853, and saw that it offered a luminescent reaction in the presence of blood. If someone tried to wipe up evidence, an investigator could use luminol to locate the position and size of the former stain. Then scientists at the Institute of Experimental Pharmacy of the State University of Kharkov, Nikolai A. Izmailov and Maria Shraiber, developed a simple thin-layer chromatography, which aided toxicological analysis. With this process, a sample was placed in a vertical gel film and subjected to a liquid solvent that separated it into its constituent parts. This made it possible for scientists to replace the tedious process of extraction with direct testing.

Serial killers, too, made strides during this period. It took five years for the Philadelphia police to catch up with them, but in 1937 they arrested a ring of insurance scam killers. Dr. Morris Bolber started the practice with his cousin Paul Petrillo when they murdered a patient's husband and split the insurance money. They then recruited two more accomplices, including Carino Favato, the "Witch of Philadelphia" and serial poisoner. Before they were caught, they had murdered an estimated fifty men.

Not far away, in Cincinnati, nurse Anna Marie Hahn defrauded elderly male patients, fatally poisoning three of them. She had the honor of being Ohio's first female executed in the electric chair, while in Texas that year, Joe Ball brought his own crimes to an end with a bullet to the head. A former bootlegger, Ball had run a roadhouse with a poolful of alligators. The disappearance of a waitress triggered an investigation, but before any questions were asked Ball removed himself from the picture. Then evidence turned up for the murders of at least five waitresses, with the possibility that several were fed to the gators.

The "Cleveland Torso Killer," at work for four years, was much less fastidious. In September 1934, part of a woman's torso, with the legs severed at the knees, washed up on the shore of Lake Erie in Cleveland. A year later, in the garbage-strewn area known as Kingsbury Run, two headless, mutilated male corpses were found with their genitals removed. The younger one was identified as a small-time criminal, and the police dismissed his murder as just deserts. But then early in 1936, the remains of a prostitute were found in a basket behind a butcher shop, and then another decapitated male corpse turned up, inspiring the *Cleveland Plain Dealer* to dub the killer the "Mad Butcher of Kingsbury Run." Two more mutilated bodies turned up, making seven.

The city's director of safety was none other than Eliot Ness, former G-man and founder of the Untouchables. He assigned a dozen detectives to the case and burned down the slum from where many victims had come, but corpses continued to show up until August 1938. By then the number had reached a dozen, but still the killer eluded identification. Ness narrowed in on one suspect, who then committed himself to a mental hospital.

That same year, Martha Marek was convicted of fatally poisoning four people in Austria, and since Germany had recently annexed the country and restored its death penalty, she was decapitated. The following year, after a series of murders-for-profit, Eugen Weidman became the last person to be publicly executed in France. Also executed that year was failed actor Ramiro Artieda, who had lured and murdered seven eighteen-year-old girls in Bolivia. When caught he confessed that it had been his intention to kill as many girls as he could who resembled the woman who had jilted him. Artieda was suspected as well of having murdered his own brother.

And perhaps the greatest mass murderer of all time was quickly rearming Germany. As dictator, Hitler had used his Gestapo to stomp out all "enemies of the state." Many were sent to concentration camps, even as Party rallies and the buildup of armaments strengthened the people's spirit. But Hitler also envisioned the possibility of a purified master race of Aryans—symbolic of traits he felt he lacked in himself—so he instituted the wide-scale persecution of "inferior" races, notably the Jews.

In 1939, with the support of Germany and fascist Italy, General Francisco Franco won the Spanish Civil War. It was a serious defeat for democracy, inspiring Hitler, despite his promise in 1938 of "no war." He grabbed control of Czechoslovakia. France and Britain issued warnings, but Hitler ignored them and invaded Poland in September, igniting World War II.

CHAPTER EIGHT

The Unthinkable

The New World

War spread across the globe, signaling that nations had become a global community with mutual concerns. Any change in the balance of power triggered a hasty response, and rising tensions reverberated through every part of society. Some people with mental or sexual disorders and unchecked impulses acted out even before official forces mobilized for domination and control, as if they had absorbed the social undercurrents that fed political conflicts. (After this devastating war, the return to peace would yield a widespread wariness that would make the world a more dangerous place. It is no surprise that violence-prone people would seek relief in repeated acts of killing, especially sexual murder: They were playing out the internal rhythms of strife and imbalance.)

Thanks to improvements in transportation, arms, and

communication systems, this war clipped along, with amplified levels of lethality that brought more suffering to civilian populations. Hitler took Poland and warred with Norway and Denmark. Soon, his forces occupied Belgium and France. Winston Churchill rallied Britain to resist, and it managed to for a year, but then Mussolini joined Hitler, followed by several Eastern European countries. Hitler then invaded Russia, and the swiftness and success of his assaults took many by surprise. By 1942, as he occupied sixteen countries, he seemed demonically invincible. Secretly, he exterminated millions of Jews and other social or racial "misfits."

The U.S. maintained a policy of isolated neutrality until in December 1941 Germany's new ally, Japan, bombed the U.S. Pacific Fleet at Hawaii's Pearl Harbor. In less than a year, the sleeping giant was ready to enter the war. With this added manpower, several fronts gained ground and steadily drove back the Axis powers. Russia was especially successful.

Up until and during this time, in countries already beset by major stresses, pattern predators were secretly at work. Raymond "Rattlesnake" Lisemba, supposedly nicknamed for his murder methods, killed two wives and a male friend in California for insurance money, but among the most prolific killers over a fairly long period was Vera Renczi in Hungary. Born in 1903, she had married a wealthy man, who then disappeared. Taking another husband, who turned out to be a philanderer, she told people that he had left her as well. But the real story was revealed years later when a woman's husband was seen in Renczi's company and failed to come home. The frantic woman informed the police, who searched Renczi's lavish estate, including the cellar. There they discovered thirty-five zinc-lined coffins, each containing a dead man: two husbands, thirty-two lovers, and her grown son. Her lame explanation was that after getting involved with a man, she would suddenly grow jealous and afraid of rejection, so she would kill him and preserve the remains. More likely, this was her means of keeping control. Her son, she explained, had threatened to expose her, so she added him to her gruesome collection. When asked why she kept a chair near the coffins, the so-called Vampire of Berkerekul said that she enjoyed sitting among her men and gloating.

In America, *Arsenic and Old Lace* had its Broadway premiere, featuring the antics of two loony sisters who poisoned and buried twelve homeless men. At the time, people needed lighthearted distractions, and the comedy's multiple murders seemed too outlandish to be true. But they weren't. Even as Salie Linevelt's "alter ego" ordered him to bludgeon four women to death during five weeks in Cape Town, South Africa, a black man, Jarvis Catoe, was arrested in 1941 for the strangulation murders of ten women from New York to Washington, D.C. He was a roaming rapist-killer, and anyone qualified as his prey. Until he targeted *white* women, investigators ignored him, but when he pawned the watch of one such victim, he was caught.

Killers like Renczi, Linevelt, and Catoe are examples of the classic psychopath, with traits crystallized in psychiatric terms by psychologist Hervey Cleckley in 1941. He listed sixteen criteria for identifying them in *The Mask of Sanity*, such as their being manipulative, exploitive, self-centered, unable to bond, and lacking in empathy or anxiety. Also, compared with other offenders, they were more violent, more likely to recidivate, and less likely to respond to treatment.

Yet the concept of psychopathy was to evolve from the emphasis on personality traits to an analysis of behavior, and in 1952 the label "psychopath" would be replaced with "sociopathic personality," but for the moment psychiatry had at least gotten a handle on this class of criminals for study. That was important, for in the decades to come serial killers would increase in number and creativity. It became clear to the growing body of criminologists that people who committed repetitive homicides had motives that ranged from greed to anger to sexual compulsion, and that they could be of either gender and work alone or as part of a team. The salient feature was that they devalued human life and exploited their victims to satisfy personal needs. They would keep going until someone stopped them, because they never had enough.

And people were indeed trying to detect and stop them. In 1940, Hugh Macdonald of the Los Angeles Police Department devised the Identi-KIT system, eventually patented by gun manufacturer Smith & Wesson. The earliest kits used transparencies on which separate features such as a nose, eye, or ear were drawn in varying shapes and sizes. These could be stacked on top of one another as witnesses picked them out, until the composite image resembled the person seen. During that same year, Karl Landsteiner, Phillip Levine, and Alex Wiener described Rh blood groups, which would offer better matching criteria for this biological evidence to reduce a suspect pool.

In addition, Bell Labs in the U.S. used L. G. Kersta's work to develop voiceprint identification. The company's sound spectrograph analyzed the frequency and intensity of sound waves to produce on a graph a visual record of distinct voice patterns. During the war, acoustic scientists used the technology to attempt to identify enemy voices on telephones and radios, and later it proved useful for criminal investigation.

War Psychosis

As British crime writer Colin Wilson notes, war seems to incubate sex crimes. Notable among them was a case involving murders that occurred during a four-day blackout, as Hitler's *Luftwaffe* flew over London. On February 9, Evelyn Hamilton was strangled with her own silk scarf in an air-raid shelter. Soon thereafter, Evelyn Oatley was killed and left nude on her bed in her apartment. Next to her was a bloodstained tin opener, used to slash her lower body. A thumbprint turned up on a mirror from her purse that did not match hers, as did several prints on the opener. Both murders indicated a left-handed killer, ac-

cording to a police report. On February 13, two dead
women were found, one of whom had been strangled with
a silk stocking. Dr. Bernard Spilsbury, a renowned British
pathologist, labeled the murders sex crimes.

Recalling the days of Jack the Ripper, London panicked, especially when four more women reported being
accosted by a man who had tried to strangle them. He
seemed to move quickly from one crime to another, apparently without pause. Exacerbating this fear of an unknown strangler was the news that Singapore had fallen
to the enemy. Some people believed the Blackout Strangler was linked to two other unsolved murders from four
months before. Fortunately, the perpetrator was soon apprehended, thanks to his carelessness and some outstanding detective work. On February 16, Gordon Frederick
Cummins, an air cadet, was arrested and charged with
four murders and four assaults. Although he proved to be
a "sexual maniac," he also said he had killed for gain. His
conviction was based on a combination of physical and
behavioral factors: fingerprints, trace evidence, his left-
hand orientation, items in his possession belonging to the
victims, and the similarity of one crime to another. And
he was not the only serviceman to become a killer.

Australia was threatened by the Axis powers about
midway through the war, after the attack on Pearl Harbor. The people there felt exposed and vulnerable, certain that like other countries, they would soon be
bombed. They had no real army, so foreign servicemen
were posted there, mostly Americans. The country's anx-

iety manifested in Melbourne in wild parties, with here-tofore respectable women available at every turn. It was inevitable that murder would visit as well.

In three weeks' time, three different women were found strangled, bruised, and lying on the streets. Their clothing was disheveled or torn to shreds. A sentry on the U.S. Army base noticed a returning GI who appeared disturbed and was covered in yellow mud. That was a good clue, for one victim had been found near a pit of yellow mud. The GI's name was Edward Joseph Leonski. He was a tall, blond, good-looking young man from Texas with an engaging smile. He also cried on many occasions, and admitted to killing the women—but for a rather unique reason. He said he had killed them to "get" their voices. He missed his mother and when they had talked with him they had reminded him of her. In fact, when he drank, he talked like a girl himself and went a little crazy. He said that one victim had sung a song to him, and it drove him mad. He could not bear to leave her without taking her voice with him. Although his family had a history of insanity, the "Singing Strangler" failed to convince a judge that he was not responsible for his misdeeds, and he was summarily hanged in November 1942.

With the study of modus operandi, behavioral analysis gained some ground, so the U.S. Office of Strategic Services (OSS) sought a specific kind of report on Adolf Hitler in 1942, specifically to attempt to predict what he would do under certain conditions. The OSS wanted a psychological assessment that would help it to make plans, so Dr. Walter C. Langer, a psychoanalyst based in New York, offered a 135-page "long-range" evaluation. He utilized speeches, a lengthy biography, Hitler's book *Mein Kampf*, and interviews with people who had known Hitler to discuss his possible future behaviors.

The character profile noted that Hitler was meticulous, conventional, and prudish. He was also robust and viewed himself as a trendsetter. Though he had manic phases, he rarely exercised. He was in good health, so it was unlikely he would die from natural causes, but he was deteriorating mentally. Hitler always walked diagonally from one corner to another when crossing a room, whistling a marching tune. He feared syphilis, germs, and moonlight, and loved severed heads. He detested the learned and the privileged, but enjoyed classical music, vaudeville, and Richard Wagner's operas. He also liked circus acts that endangered people. Since he appeared to be delusional, it was possible that in the face of imminent defeat, his psychological structures would collapse. The most likely scenario was that he would end his own life, although he might get one of his henchmen to end it for him. Given this general picture, it was clear that a good strategy would be to step up the pressure, because he would not try to merely escape to some neutral country.

While the war raged on, some found it easy to get away with murder. Police forces were stretched to the limit as men were conscripted into armies. One man, Bruno Ludke, had been arrested for sexual assault and sterilized. But that had failed to stop him, and he'd turned to strangling women. When he was questioned after one such

Albert Howard Fish, escorted to Sing Sing prison in 1935.

Dennis Nilsen, after he appeared in court in 1983.

Wayne Williams, convicted of two murders during the 1979–81 rash of killings in Atlanta, Georgia.

Saeed Hanaei, before being hanged in Iran on April 17, 2002, after strangling sixteen women.

William Heirens in his cell on September 5, 1946, in Illinois after he was sentenced for three murders.

Waushara County Sheriff Art Schley escorts Ed Gein of Plainfield, Wisconsin, to the Central State Hospital for the Criminally Insane, on November 23, 1957, for examination.

Anatoly Onopriyenko, thirty-six, from Ukrainian police file, taken April 23, 1996, after he admitted to killing fifty-two people.

File photo of Moses Sithole, after his 1995 arrest in South Africa.

Police booking photo in 1990 of Arthur Shawcross, convicted in Rochester, New York, of several murders.

John Wayne Gacy, convicted in the murders of thirty-three young men in Illinois.

FBI photos taken in the 1980s of James J. Bulger, wanted in connection with eighteen murders. He was spotted in London after his photo was seen in *Hannibal*, a film about serial killer Hannibal Lecter.

Albert DeSalvo claimed to be the Boston Strangler but was never tried or convicted for those crimes. Imprisoned on other charges, he was murdered in 1973, and his status as the Strangler is now in question.

Charles Manson sticks his tongue out at reporters as he appears in a Santa Monica, California, courtroom on June 25, 1970.

Undated police photo of Harrison Marty Graham, who was arrested in 1987 after seven decomposing corpses were found in his Philadelphia apartment.

"Green River Killer" Gary Leon Ridgway appears at a pretrial hearing in King County Superior Court on March 27, 2003, in Seattle. He pleaded guilty to killing forty-eight women.

Juan Corona leaves the Solano County Hall of Justice after being sentenced to twenty-five consecutive life turns for the mass slaying of itinerant farm workers in Yuba City, California.

Richard Ramirez, known as the Night Stalker, responds to reporters after his guilty verdict was rendered on September 20, 1989.

Admitted health-care serial killer Charles Cullen listens to the prosecution present its case at a hearing in Belvidere, New Jersey, on May 19, 2004.

Theodore Robert Bundy is led into the Pitken County courthouse for a hearing in Aspen, Colorado, on June 8, 1977.

Javed Iqbal, second from left, listens in a court in Pakistan on March 16, 2000, as he is sentenced for the murders of one hundred children.

Confessed serial killer Henry Lee Lucas, center, is escorted to his death row cell in Huntsville, Texas.

David Berkowitz, identified as the Son of Sam .44-Caliber Killer in New York, is taken to police headquarters on August 11, 1977.

Convicted serial killer Aileen Wuornos waits to testify in the Volusia County courthouse on July 20, 2001, about dropping the remaining appeals on her death sentence for the murders of six men.

Charles Sobhraj, know as "the Serpent" and accused of murdering tourists across Asia, is questioned by the Nepalese police on September 19, 2003, after his arrest.

Coral Eugene Watts, during a break in his preliminary examination in Ferndale, Michigan, on June 2, 2004, where a judge ruled that there was sufficient evidence for a trial in a 1979 slaying. He was convicted.

Jeffrey Dahmer, who confessed to cannibalism and serial murder, walks into the Milwaukee County courthouse on August 6, 1991.

killing, near Berlin in 1943, he physically attacked his interrogator. He insisted that he was mentally defective and therefore could not be indicted, though he went on to enumerate eighty-five rape-murders that he had committed, stabbing or strangling his victims. The Kriminal Kommissar investigated Ludke's claims and found them to be true—or at least verified that the murders had occurred and that Ludke had been suspected of them. But innocent men had been arrested for many of them and sent to prison. Rather than execute Ludke and thereby make these errors public, the Nazi regime sent him to Vienna to be a human guinea pig. There, an experiment finally killed him.

It was not only men who turned to murder. Even as servicemen went off to war, a femme fatale was nabbed in Denver, a string of dead lovers in her wake. Two husbands had committed suicide over Louise Peete's infidelity, and she had shot an acquaintance in "self-defense." She also shot a third husband and buried him in the basement. For that, Peete was convicted of murder in 1921—after she had already married her fourth husband. He, too, committed suicide when she ignored him while serving her time in prison. Paroled in 1933, she was suspected in the death of one elderly woman and the disappearance of another, Margaret Logan, whose home she took over. Married again, she finally chose unwisely. Her husband, Lee Judson, saw a suspicious mound of earth in the garden and let the police know about it. They dug up the remains of Margaret Logan in 1944, but "the Duchess of Death" threw the blame on Margaret's now-deceased husband.

No one bought it. Judson was charged as an accessory, and although he was acquitted, he became another suicide in the long list of Peete's husbands. Louise, while pleased with his reaction, found herself saddled with a death sentence for Logan's murder, and she was executed in 1947.

Just before Peete was caught in the States, in Paris in March 1944 police investigating a noxious fire discovered in the basement of a building at 21 Rue Lesueuer a stack of twenty-seven mutilated and dismembered corpses. One was still smoldering inside a furnace. "This is not job for us," the next day's *Matin* quoted the police. "The place is full of corpses!" One body had been split in two, and numerous heads lay around the place.

Investigators identified Dr. Marcel Petiot as the building's owner, and he explained that the corpses were the remains of Nazis and their collaborators, killed by Resistance members. Since Paris was under German occupation, with a strong Resistance movement, his statement was credible to Resistance sympathizers. They let him go, and he went on killing. When the Allies liberated Paris in 1944, it became clear that Petiot was lying about his pile of corpses, many of which had been dissected. When he claimed in a newspaper that the victims had been German soldiers, and that he had killed sixty-three of them, he was arrested.

Investigators discovered his long criminal history, including the suspected murder of a patient, and then realized that his victims had been not collaborators or soldiers but wealthy Jews. Forty-seven suitcases were found in

Petiot's possession, and in the building was a specially constructed soundproof death chamber with a peep-hole. It was suspected that he had lured his victims with the promise of smuggling them out of the city, but had instead killed them with an "inoculation," taken their money and goods, and then practiced obscene medical experiments on them. The Gestapo had actually arrested him at one point on suspicion of aiding Jews, but had then released him when they realized what he was doing—something quite similar to Hitler's own "Final Solution" to the "Jewish problem." Since Petiot (like Hitler's henchmen) had incinerated many of his victims, his death toll is unknown. Eighty-six dissected bodies had been removed from the Seine during that period, and there was reason from Petiot's statements to suspect that he may have had as many as 150 victims. The French authorities duly executed him.

The End and the Beginning

By the end of 1944, the Allies had arrived at the Rhine River, with Soviet troops advancing as well, and when Hitler sensed imminent defeat in April 1945, he committed suicide. As the Allies liberated prisoners of war, they came across the extermination camps, a discovery that shocked the world. The images of starving men and women amid masses of corpses shocked even German citizens.

But it wasn't over: There was still Japan to consider. It

refused to surrender, so the U.S. dropped the first atomic bomb on August 6, 1945, devastating Hiroshima's buildings and population. Three days later, Nagasaki took a similar hit, and Japan finally capitulated. But it was not as simple a matter as having found an "ultimate" weapon. The world had now entered the atomic age, and there was no turning back.

Japan, too, had serial killers—two of whom used identical methods. Yoshio Kodaira, a former naval officer, was caught through the blunder of giving his address to a victim, and he confessed to seven of the ten rape-murders that had occurred in Tokyo during 1945 and 1946. Another man, Shizu Koguchi, confessed to the other three. Both men had lured victims to their homes with the promise of black market goods, and both men were sentenced to death.

In Fort Wayne, Indiana, a series of four murders involved a strange turn of events—two different killers confessed to them all, but each insisted he had acted alone. Ralph Lobaugh and Franklin Click each stated that he had murdered four local women between February 1944 and March 1945. Lobaugh said he had dropped a black comb and belt buckle—which indeed were found next to one body. But Click had been turned in by a woman who said he'd attacked her, and there was evidence linking him to one of the victims—at whose funeral he'd served as a pallbearer. He wrote a confession to the four murders that he urged his wife to turn in for the reward money, but then recanted. A jury convicted Click of one of the murders, for which he was executed. The reason he might not have been tried for the other three was because a judge had already sent Lobaugh to death row for these crimes the year before. His sentence was later commuted to life. (He was granted clemency in 1977, given all the confusion with this case, but at Lobaugh's own request, he was back in prison for the criminally insane within two months.)

Around the same time, Alfred Kline, the "Buttermilk Bluebeard," was suspected of murdering nine women in Chicago for money, and a quick succession of other killings in the Windy City involved the police in another desperate investigation, especially when they saw what was left behind. In December 1945, someone broke into an apartment on Chicago's North Side. Frances Brown, 33, was shot and stabbed to death, with a bread knife left in her chest. The perpetrator had attempted to wash her off in the bathtub, and before he exited, he used her lipstick to scrawl on a wall, "For heaven's sake catch me Before I kill more I cannot control myself."

Six months prior to this murder, a man had similarly entered the apartment of Josephine Ross, hit her over the head, cut her throat, and washed her nude body in the tub. Oddly, he then had placed adhesive tape over her wounds before leaving. The crimes were believed to be linked. A month after the Brown murder, a six-year-old girl disappeared from her bed and a ransom note was left in her room, but her head and body parts were found in bags in the sewer. The police increased their vigilance, and in June 1946 an off-duty cop spotted a young man entering another apartment, and chased him down. The seventeen-year-old "burglar" was William Heirens. Under truth serum and a spinal tap, and after being confronted with the similarity between his writing and that of the "Lipstick Killer," he confessed. A psychiatric examination found that entering apartments sexually excited him and made him urinate or defecate. In his defense, Heirens said that his criminal behavior issued from an alter ego. Pleading guilty, he received three life sentences, but recanted his confession in letters to his family.

In the midst of this spree, Texarkana, Texas, experienced its own serial killer. A full moon was out on February 20, 1946, when two teenagers were attacked in their car, and the girl raped. A month later, also under a full moon, another couple was murdered only a mile away. In April, fifteen-year-old Betty Jo Booker and her boyfriend, Paul Martin, were slaughtered, with evidence that Betty Jo had been raped and tortured for hours. The next month saw an elderly couple shot in their home, but the wife managed to escape and raise an alarm. She survived, and matching tire tracks from several of the scenes indicated that the attacks, all perpetrated in the moonlight, had been related. Then the killings stopped, and the murderer was never identified, although police believed that a man who had killed himself and incinerated his car—with special attention paid to the tires—had ended the spree himself.

In Nova Scotia, Lila and William Young ran a babyfarming operation, in which children were starved and badly neglected. The couple actually helped desperate young women give birth, but while they reported a certain percentage of deaths during the process, a handyman later said that he had buried more than one hundred infants on a piece of family-owned property. Reportedly, the Youngs charged a fee to take the child themselves, but once the money was collected, they disposed of the infants. They did adopt out some, charging as much as $5,000 during the war years, and they built their industry into a prosperous business. In the end, just after the war, they were shut down over squalid conditions and fined. The business was closed, and both mercenaries eventually died of cancer.

The war had cost millions of lives, both military and civilian, and many people lost their homes, possessions, and livelihood. A defeated Germany was divided into four zones, to be occupied by the Soviet Union, the United States, France, and Britain. All of Eastern Europe was forced to accept communism, while in 1948, the Jewish state of Israel gained independence—an event with future repercussions for the Middle East. Whole cities had to be rebuilt and economies rescued.

After the bombs devastated Japan, a new awareness was evident that humankind was now capable of wreaking mass destruction. Although the best path toward survival was to settle differences peacefully, world leaders also operated from the fear that another nation led by someone like Hitler—and with nuclear capabilities—could easily gain the upper hand. Both the United States and the Soviet Union emerged stronger than before, but with opposing philosophies of how best to govern. Each wanted its system to spread to other countries and each feared what the other might do to the health of civilization. Only two years after Hitler died, the Cold War began.

The United Nations was formed, with representatives from all the great nations, and for a brief moment, the world seemed poised for peace. But that did not cure the fear that was growing daily about the world's safety. Nor did it repair much of the damage from the war. Plenty of people still exploited the agitated social conditions to commit murder.

On June 20, 1946, a London cabbie saw Margery Gardner in the company of a man, and she ended up dead in a room at the Pembridge Court Hotel, suffocated, bound, and whipped with a metal-tipped implement. Her nipples were bitten off and she'd been brutally raped with a blunt, unnatural object. While she was covered in blood, her face was clean, although there was blood in her nostrils. A man named Neville Heath had signed the register for the room, so police went to find him, but he had escaped to the seaside town of Bournemouth. Checking into a hotel there and posing as a war hero, he encountered Doreen Marshall, twenty-one, and escorted her for an evening stroll on July 4. She then turned up missing. Five days later, her nude body was found in some bushes. She'd been cut up with a knife and sexually violated.

Oddly enough, Heath went to the police to offer his help. When their suspicions were aroused, he feigned innocence in the case of Doreen Marshall and said that his name was not Neville Heath, but the police detained him to search his belongings. They found a braided whip that matched the patterns left on the first murdered woman.

Heath, twenty-nine, also had in his possession a blood-soaked scarf that matched Margery Gardner's blood type, and there was speculation that he had licked the blood from her face. Another handkerchief, tied into a gag, turned up in his drawer at the seaside hotel. Hair from it was matched to Doreen Marshall. Further investigation into Heath's military record and personal history indicated that he'd participated in several incidents of sadistic behavior toward women.

Arrested and tried for murder, Heath hoped to use an insanity defense, but while psychiatrists believed he was sadistic and perverted, they could not say that the "Gentleman Vampire" was legally insane. Found guilty, he was sentenced to be executed.

Even as West Germany was putting together an entirely new government and social order, another lust killer was caught. A man found axed to death led to the arrest of a twenty-three-year-old thief, Rudolf Pleil, and while in prison, he wrote a memoir detailing some fifty murders during the two prior years. The diary, authored by the self-described "retired death-dealer," was a tribute to Hitler, in whose army Pleil had served. He recalled that watching the Nazis haul corpses around had been wonderfully erotic. As a security guard, Pleil had been posted at the East-West border, where he had committed most of his offenses. As women passed through into the western zone, he would beat them senseless and rape them, often finishing them off with strangulation, bludgeoning, or an ax. In fact, he was so determined to gain notoriety for this accomplishment that when he was charged with only nine murders, he protested that the number was much higher, and he wanted the record to show that. He apparently had two accomplices as well, and they were arrested. His final victim was himself.

Another ax killer showed up in the States. Bertha Kludt, fifty-three, and her daughter, Beverly, were found in their home in Washington, D.C., in October 1947, hacked to death with their own ax. A black man was arrested after a fight with police. Under interrogation, Jake Bird admitted to the double homicide, and added a long list of similar slayings across eight states. All of his victims had been white women and all had been attacked with hatchets or axes. Eleven were confirmed as Bird's handiwork, but he was suspected in as many as forty-four such deaths.

That same year, in England, Dr. Robert George Clements committed suicide after the death of his fourth wife. Whenever his previous wives would die, he would suggest a diagnosis to the attending physicians, and then cash in on the woman's wealth. An autopsy on his fourth wife indicated morphine poisoning. When questions were asked, the good doctor overdosed himself.

In Los Angeles, a homicide became one of the country's most sensational cases. The nude body of a young woman was found early on the morning of January 15, 1947. She had been severed neatly in half, she'd been bathed, and her hair was washed before she was left in a spot where she would likely be discovered. The coroner found that the letters BD had recently been carved on one thigh, and she was soon identified as Elizabeth Short, twenty-two, an aspiring actress from the East Coast known as the "Black Dahlia." Confessions came fast, but no one was satisfactorily linked to the crime. It would be decades before both George Hodel and Janice Knowlton would separately accuse their late fathers of being serial killers, with the Black Dahlia one of their victims.

During the war, women had flooded the workforce and found their collective strength in making a living. To get them back into the home to take care of family, social propaganda dictated what it meant to be a "good woman." This had the effect of cementing into the minds of some men both that women were a threat to their earnings and that women needed to be kept in their place. That double whammy would inspire killers for decades to come with the idea that men were superior and women were no more than objects for their domination and gratification.

On July 1, 1948, a man broke into an apartment in Tulsa, attacking a woman and her two teenage daughters. The mother was raped, but they all survived, thanks to a neighbor's interruption. But down the street, the man cut a hole into the door of another home and bludgeoned a woman to death before raping her. A witness who saw him outside described him to police, and they traced him to a trucking company. Charles Floyd was known to have a passion for red hair, and each victim had been a red-head. Once caught, he admitted that redheaded women excited an overwhelming lust in him. In fact, he had killed before. In 1942, he'd murdered the redheaded pregnant wife of a fellow truck driver, followed later that year with the rape and murder of a mother and daughter, both redheads. Two and a half years later, he killed a redhead whom he had seen undressing in her apartment.

In a sense, the quest for stimulation involved in such lust murders may have worked in a similar manner at a larger level. With the excitement of war ebbing and the Cold War settling in, paranoid agitation influenced art forms such as science fiction novels and films about alien invaders. Americans took up the attitude that to effectively eliminate danger, one had to destroy it. Yet no matter what strides America made in nuclear weaponry, within a year the Soviet Union had matched them. Nuclear arsenals that could destroy the world increased as America sought to "contain" the spread of the evil ideals of communism. Americans indulged in fears about spies and killers in the guise of ordinary people. War veteran Howard Unruh, worried about what his neighbors were saying, went out into his Camden, New Jersey, neighborhood on September 6, 1949 and in twelve minutes fatally shot thirteen people. Diagnosed with paranoid schizophrenia, he was assumed to be just another man whom the war had traumatized.

In 1947, a strange couple teamed up to swindle and kill women. Overweight Martha Beck met Raymond Fernandez at a lonely hearts club and fell for his charm. Married three times, Beck had an appetite for bizarre sex. She persuaded Fernandez, who believed in black magic and who had conned over one hundred women out of money, to let her in on his schemes. Their grifting soon turned to murder. One victim was strangled into unconsciousness before Beck drowned her child in a bathtub. Arrested,

Beck and Fernandez boasted of other murders, and were extradited to New York to stand trial for one: Beck had hit Janet Fay with a hammer and Fernandez had finished off the job with strangulation. After a sensational proceeding that involved Beck's descriptions of her strange sexual practices (a failed grab for an insanity defense), they were convicted of murder. Despite Beck's attempt to appear to have fallen under a con man's spell, the two were sent to their executions on the same day in 1951. Beck proclaimed her love for Fernandez all the way to the chair. Although officially tied to only three killings, they were suspected in as many as a dozen.

Another con artist in England was arrested in 1949 in the disappearance of a wealthy woman, Mrs. Olive Durrand-Deacon, who supposedly had gone with him one afternoon to make an investment. The man was John George Haigh, and his first question to the authorities was about Broadmoor, a mental institution. Thereafter, whatever he had to say bore the tinge of malingering.

Haigh, thirty-nine, knew the power of the monstrous image to incite horror in people's minds. He launched into a detailed confession that involved killing six people in order to drink their blood. He said that he had lured them into a storage area and bludgeoned them to death. Then he had cut open arteries in their throats and filled a cup with blood to drink it, because imbibing fresh blood revived him. His final act was to dissolve the corpses in large drums filled with acid. He couldn't help himself, he claimed. He had terrible dreams about bloody crucifixes and had acquired a taste for blood.

Yet he clearly knew what he was doing and that he had to cover it up. "The Acid Bath Murderer" had a criminal record for fraud and theft. Despite his claims of mental illness, the deaths of his victims, as early as 1944, always coincided with his need for money, and he'd always gained access to their funds through forgery, ultimately making a fortune. With the help of his descriptions, investigators managed to find twenty-eight pounds of sludge at his workshop that they identified as human remains, along with part of a left foot, intact dentures, and the handle of the missing woman's purse. Haigh had also left a diary behind with the identities of his victims—people who were all in fact deceased.

Twelve physicians examined him, and only one thought he had an aberrant mental condition—egocentric paranoia. The others believed that he was malingering to avoid the death penalty. In prior incidents, whenever it had suited his purposes, he had posed variously as a doctor, a lawyer, and an engineer. In this case, he posed as a psychotic person who drank blood. He'd even studied up on how to play the part. But Haigh's role-playing failed to work this time. He was found guilty and executed.

As the decade closed, most war-torn countries were recovering, some at a rapid pace. Yet into the 1950s, several incidents would confirm a widespread unease beneath the superficial prosperity. During that decade, women were well represented as killers, perhaps because the rigid expectations placed on them provoked some to reject their roles and others simply to exploit them for personal

advantage. Among the males was a killer who would become famous throughout the world, for decades to come,
for his bizarre behavior. Indeed, his acts, and the way they
would be depicted, would reflect a fragmented culture
that had lost its self-awareness and its bearings.

CHAPTER NINE

Poised for More

Wary Recovery

By 1950, communist governments controlled land from Czechoslovakia to China, where Mao Tse-tung took over. Approximately a third of the world's population was under such regimes, although China and the U.S.S.R. disagreed over how to practice the philosophy. The Western nations, including Japan, formed the capitalist bloc, but not all were democracies and some had socialist leanings. Many colonies, especially in Asia and Africa, took advantage of the chaos to shed European control. Due to greater industrial progress, Western Europe was much wealthier than Eastern Europe, which put an edge on the West's recovery, but the U.S. was recognized as the dominant world power with the highest standard of living.

Nevertheless, during the early 1950s, a sense of lawlessness pervaded the youth culture as an ominous backlash against the mainstream emphasis on clean, orderly, and disciplined families in perfect homes pursuing the American dream. As Americans struggled to restore a sense of innocence, television came into the home to help families to follow prescribed roles: Fathers were providers and mothers contented homemakers. But bucking this idealistic trend were those who rebelled, and some did so with hatred and urgency. Ex-convict William Cook, in his black leather jacket and "Hard Luck" tattoos, a man who'd been abandoned as a child by his father, went on a murder spree, forcing people to become his hostages before killing them. First was a family of five, whom he shot in their car. He drove around with their corpses before depositing them in an abandoned mine shaft in Missouri. Then he headed to California, where he killed a salesman. From there, he took two men hostage in Mexico, but the authorities grabbed him before he could harm them, and California executed him.

As the century entered its midpoint, President Harry S. Truman emphasized the U.S. mission to defend free countries from the spread of communism. Eisenhower took over in 1953, and while the U.S. had a balanced economy and substantial industrial growth, racial issues fed another avenue of unrest. It was as if, in seeking the perfect world, America sought to plug all the holes but inevitably overlooked weak spots in its structure. Its killers would reveal them.

Mutual suspicion between the East and West heightened. On both sides of the Iron Curtain that divided Europe, armies increased. Offers of economic relief were leveraged in needy countries for political control, and in some instances a contained show of force seemed necessary. Those on each side of the communist question viewed the other as the aggressor. In Indochina, French troops fought to contain communism's spread southward, while a political conflict in Korea provoked the newly formed United Nations to assist the South against the communist North. Eventually boundaries were defined between democracy and totalitarianism, and each side set about developing the most powerful weaponry possible. Advanced technology ushered in the age of military secrets, clandestine missions, and espionage. The imminent threat of a third world war, which could be impossibly devastating, kept aggression under wraps, but the idea of world peace was only nominal. With the development of the unprecedented destructive hydrogen bomb, which could kill everything within a radius of thirty miles, peril was always present—especially if the bombs were in the "wrong" hands.

In terms of repetitive killers, England and Germany vied with the U.S. for which country's conditions spawned the worst of them, although the Eastern bloc countries kept their crimes to themselves, so the contest was difficult to call. England took an early lead that decade with the psychotic murders of two young girls by John Thomas Straffen, just released from a mental institution in Bristol, England, in 1951. Found unfit to stand trial, he went to Broadmoor but soon escaped. At large only four hours, he killed a third girl and seemed proud of himself that the act of strangulation was so easily accomplished, taking him "less than two minutes." This time he was prosecuted, found guilty, and sentenced to life.

Stretching back to the immediate postwar years, another man caught in 1953 had been busy burying or walling up female corpses in his home at London's 10 Rillington Place. When he sublet the flat in 1953 and wandered off, he signed his death warrant. The new renter, Beresford Brown, tore wallpaper from a malodorous alcove and saw the nude decomposing back of a woman. He ran for the police, who found three molding bodies stuffed together. One had been placed head down and another was tied by the neck to a third dead woman. All had been sexually molested, oddly diapered, and strangled. That sent police on a chase after John Reginald Halliday Christie, even as they found more victims. Christie's dead wife, Ethel, lay beneath the floorboards and the skeletons of two more females were unearthed in the garden—the thighbone of one propping up a trellis.

The papers posted one headline after another about this "house of horrors" and the Notting Hill Murders. Christie's whereabouts were unknown, which inspired scary stories about how a seemingly ordinary neighbor might actually be a monster, since he was so nondescript a middle-aged man that he could pass right by anyone on the streets without being noticed. And in fact, that's just what he did.

As the police investigated his background, they realized that Christie had been a temporary security officer during the Second World War who had once been accused of murdering the wife and daughter of Timothy Evans, the resident of the flat upstairs. Christie had protested that charge so convincingly that the police released him. Now they wondered. Once they grabbed him, he confessed to using a homemade contraption on women he brought home that dispensed a poisonous coal gas. As they passed out, he raped them while strangling them and then collected their pubic hair in a tin. As repulsive as his necrophilic behavior was, the worst moment came when the police realized they had wrongly hanged Timothy Evans for the murder of his wife and daughter—that Christie had in fact committed these homicides. Evans had told them the truth when he said that Christie had posed as a doctor and performed an illegal abortion that had gone wrong. Christie's manipulative façade had sent an innocent man to the gallows, raising debate all over England about the merit of capital punishment. But Christie was unmoved, selling his tale to the *Sunday Pictorial.*

It was a unique case for forensic science, as the police considered consulting biologists to determine how long the bodies had been in the cupboard, based on what might be expected about the growth of mold in a typical London cupboard. In the end, their work was not necessary, since Christie confessed. But the idea of creating a time line based on a scientific analysis of plant life took root for forensic analysis in other cases. Toxicologists proved that Ethel Christie's alleged "overdose" of phenobarbitone was a fabrication and showed the presence of carbon monoxide in the bodies of the three victims from the closet. In addition, this case demonstrated for medi-

cal professionals a heretofore unknown fact—that sper-
matozoa could be preserved for weeks in a corpse. Yet
even with these positive discoveries for science, it took
London quite a while to shake off the gruesome horror of
the Christie case.

In Australia that year, Caroline "Aunt Thally" Grills,
named for the thallium she used to kill four people and
to attempt to kill two others, stood trial. Grills was one
of several grandmotherly women during the 1950s who
turned out to be unscrupulous killers. At the time of
her trial, she was sixty-three. Her apparent motive was
simply the thrill of having the power to kill someone—a
difficult idea for many to accept about a female, let alone
such a nice elderly woman. But she would not be entirely
unique. Rhonda Bell Martin ended up being executed in
the electric chair in Alabama in 1957 for the fatal poisoning of her husband. She had also confessed to killing another husband, her five children, and her mother.

Similarly, Christa Lehman had been poisoning family
and friends for some time in Worms, Germany, before a
piece of candy gave her away in 1954. This case posed an
interesting challenge to forensic toxicology.

On Monday, February 15, seventy-five-year-old Eva
Ruh left a cream-filled chocolate truffle for her daughter,
Annie Hamann. Annie bit into it, but finding it bitter,
spat it out. The family dog lapped it up. Annie spotted her
mother across the room and was about to say something
when a sudden blindness seized her. She got to her bedroom before she lost consciousness. Her mother sent for
help, but within moments Annie died. So did the dog.

The arriving doctor called the police, who in turn contacted Professor Kurt Wagner, director of the Institute of Forensic Medicine. During an autopsy, he focused on the convulsions as a symptom of poisoning.

In the meantime, detectives had traced the poisoned truffle to Annie's friend Christa Lehman, a widow and mother of three. She'd recently handed out truffles, giving one to Eva Ruh, who had decided to save it. When interrogated, Lehman insisted that the candies had to have been poisoned in the store where she bought them. Those truffles still at the store were sent for toxicological analysis and came back negative. The police looked to Wagner's analysis for answers, but he had a difficult time pinpointing just which poison had been used. Then he read a publication about an insecticide, E 605, and its description of symptoms matched Annie's and the dog's. It was the first known time this substance had been used in a homicide. None of the candies from the store tested positive for it, so investigators looked for its source in Lehman's home.

But they found much more. Christa Lehman was associated with a string of deaths—her husband, mother-in-law, and father-in-law had also died in ways that might have been attributable to poison. Exhumations and autopsies confirmed that all of them had been murdered. Confronted, Lehman confessed to the four murders, saying that she had first tried the poison on a dog and had then used it on her husband and his parents. She had intended the truffle that killed Annie for Eva Ruh, because she did not like the woman. At her trial, her psychiatrist described her as a "moral primitive." In fact, after her conviction, she offered statements to reporters to the effect that her victims had deserved to die, and that besides, she "liked to go to funerals." Unfortunately, the publicity her case received inspired a high number of homicides and suicides throughout Germany with the use of E 605—dubbed the "Worms poison" by the press. For forensic scientists, it was a grim victory, because now they would have to use the test more often, but they were at least satisfied that science had assured correct results.

Terror

The U.S. continued to be overwhelmed by fears of communism's creeping into society, and even ordinary people were alert for spies. Starting in 1950, a senator named Joseph McCarthy led a campaign against "card-carrying Communists" who he claimed had infiltrated the government and the country's communications systems. The House Un-American Activities Committee, founded in 1938, provided a good venue for his paranoia. Many entertainers were ruined during this shameful and contagious exhibition of irrational fear, labeled as communist sympathizers and blackmailed into giving up other names. Aside from a few voices of protest, even the press colluded.

During the "red scare," government employees had to go through loyalty tests, and illegal measures were tolerated in the name of "national security." The FBI kept records on people considered "subversive" and allowed sources to be kept secret. Any reasonable doubt was sufficient cause to fire someone. Finally, in 1954, McCarthy was discredited by a Senate censure when he attempted to investigate the U.S. Army. During this time, Ethel and Julius Rosenberg were tried and executed for giving nuclear secrets to the Soviets. The only evidence such convictions required was the word of informants. But as the advent of television made the hearings visible to the public, the press began to call for real evidence. Eventually, the idea that people must conform to a specific set of political beliefs in order to ensure the nation's safety lost favor.

Nevertheless, the threat of communism was taken seriously, so when France lost colonies in Indochina, U.S. military advisers helped French forces to resist the spread of communism there. The attitude that the U.S. had a mission in such conflicts was firm, although the government's secretive actions would eventually cause a backlash. In other parts of the world, Germany was rebuilding fast, but other countries in which there were few resources continued to struggle.

Things were roughest in Poland after the war, which provided advantages to criminal offenders. In 1954, Wladyslaw Mazurkiewicz, a former black marketer and thief, was caught and charged with the murder of six people. His motive was money, while male nurse Fritz Rudloff sought only revenge when he killed four patients in an East German hospital. He disliked his supervisor, so he sacrificed people via arsenic to ruin the man's reputation.

Another older woman convicted of fatally poisoning people, this time for fun, was Nannie Doss, the "Giggling Grandma" from Tulsa. During the 1940s and 1950s, she rid herself of four husbands, but at her trial she claimed that she had done it for love—"the real romance of life"—not money. An avid reader of romance novels, she had sought the perfect mate, but each man she married had failed to measure up. It was easy enough to slip them rat poison and move on to the next prospect—while also collecting the insurance money. She told reporters, who duly printed it, that she had enjoyed killing so much that she had also poisoned her mother, two sisters, two children, a grandson, and a nephew. She was sentenced to life, and died in prison shortly thereafter.

Men killed spouses as well. George Sack had murdered two wives in Chicago during the 1920s and claimed the insurance money. He hired Clarence Darrow to win an insanity acquittal for him, and when he got out of a hospital for the criminally insane, he proceeded to kill again. A business partner, a tenant, and a third wife all died mysteriously between 1939 and 1954. For these murders Sack was found guilty, and in prison he committed suicide.

The "*Tokoloshe* [Bogeyman] Murders" in South Africa claimed fifteen people over a period of two years during the mid-1950s, supposedly as sacrifices to boost the failing practice of witch doctor Elifasi Msomi. Most often, he took children from their families and stabbed them to death to procure fresh blood. Twice the police took him into custody, but each time he was released. When he was finally caught with incriminating evidence, his claim that the *tokoloshe* was responsible was rejected by the court, and he was executed.

Just as Msomi's body was laid out for village elders to inspect, in South Africa's Atteridgeville, six boys were castrated and murdered. This series of homicides was never solved, and the same was true of three murdered teenage girls found in Chicago. However, in West Germany, a pair of killers was caught for a series of "doubles" killings. Werner Boost had long exploited people's desperation to cross from East to West Germany, and he had killed people on his own for a while before he took a partner to hold up and murder people in their cars. The "Düsseldorf Doubles Killer" managed three double homicides between 1953 and 1956. A fourth attempt was foiled and Boost was arrested. His partner, Franz Lorbach, confessed to his part, claiming that Boost had hypnotized him. Boost was sentenced to life in prison, while Lorbach received six years.

For most of this decade, murders were fairly routine, although law enforcement was disturbed by the increase in multiple homicides. No one was prepared for the psychosis and brutality that arose during the second half of the 1950s.

Ghouls and Beasts

When the police went to the Plainfield, Wisconsin, farm of an eccentric loner named Ed Gein on suspicion of robbery, he appeared not to be at home. They snooped around and then entered a darkened building. There they saw that he'd been hunting, as they viewed a dressed carcass hanging from the rafters. But it did not look like a deer. On closer inspection, they realized that the corpse was human. Hung up feetfirst was the headless body of a woman, slit from her genitals to her neck, washed cleaned, her legs splayed wide apart. They wondered if she might be a missing storekeeper named Bernice Worden. It was quite a shock to find her thus, but that was only the beginning. Next the police entered Gein's house.

It was difficult to believe that this man who claimed he was too squeamish to hunt for deer could be as ghoulish as the evidence indicated he was. During their search they found chair seats made of human skin, a box of preserved female genitalia, a heart in a frying pan, a box of women's noses, several sawed-off skulls, refrigerated intestines, death masks made from skin, a skin vest with breasts, a female scalp with black hair, and a pair of lips on a string.

Taken in for questioning, Gein admitted to stealing parts from freshly dead bodies in the cemetery. He had also killed both Bernice Worden and another missing woman, Mary Hogan. He seemed unaware that what he had done was wrong. The bizarre case drew international attention, especially among those who studied criminal psychology, who made much of the fact that Gein had been raised by a puritanical, domineering mother, now dead, after his father and brother had died years earlier. She had taught him that sex was perverse and wicked, "causing" a mental imbalance, and he had apparently developed a thorough self-hatred for himself as a male. Alone and socially inept, Gein had devoured books on human anatomy and Nazi experiments, sending away for shrunken heads to decorate his home.

Then, when he spotted a newspaper report about a recently buried woman, he decided to dig her up so he could have a look at a female body. He continued with this sinister habit, usually under a full moon, for around ten years. Sometimes he took the entire corpse and sometimes just certain parts. He later claimed that he had dug up nine separate graves in three different cemeteries. (The police did not believe him until they went out to exhume the dead. Some weren't there.)

Storing the organs in the refrigerator, Gein made things out of the bones and skin. He apparently hoped to transform into a woman, i.e., to become his mother, whom he eventually dug up as well. Indeed, in locked rooms he had created a shrine to her, leaving things exactly as they had been when she was alive. Rather than get a sex-change operation, which was possible during that time, he simply made himself a female bodysuit and mask out of the skin taken from his grave thefts, and he wore this as he danced in the moonlight or excavated other graves. Then he decided to get bodies that were more pliable. That meant killing someone. In 1954 and 1957, Gein shot two older women who resembled his mother and brought them to his farm.

No one was surprised that he was found insane and incarcerated in an institution. Gein's miserable goods were offered at an auction, and reportedly thousands of people showed up to bid. Entrepreneurs sought macabre souvenirs that they could display for money or sell to collectors. One person hoped to turn the farmhouse into a tourist museum, but as with the Holmes castle half a century before, a mysterious fire leveled it before any such plans could be put into effect. Still, the Gein legacy would hang over the culture like a viral infection that could not be cured. He may have been a loner, but he was clearly one of us.

That same year, Ajette Lyles, a voodoo practitioner in Macon, Georgia, was arrested for poisoning four family members for funds for her practice, and also found to be insane. Mary Elizabeth Wilson was yet another elderly poisoner who dispatched three husbands and a lover in England in 1957, all for paltry gain. She was sixty-six when she went to trial. What made her case stand out was the argument offered by her solicitor that forensic toxicology had never before had a case of phosphorus poisoning, so the rate of the oxidation of phosphorus was unknown and could not be used to convict her. Indeed, at the time, sexual stimulants contained phosphorus, and it was feasible that the deceased, given their advanced ages, might have been taking such medication. A renowned doctor was on hand to support this contention, but the judge made it clear to the jury that he did not buy the argument, and Wilson was found guilty of murder.

People were puzzled by the fact that so many killers did not "look" the type: They were witnessing elderly women and frail middle-aged men going about the bad business of murder, and this was contrary to what they were watching in movies. Then in Scotland came another surprise: a handsome, cultivated killer.

In early January 1956, the body of seventeen-year-old Ann Kneilands was discovered in the woods near Glasgow. She had been sexually assaulted and battered about the head. Nine months later, an intruder killed Mrs. Marion Watt, her sister, and her daughter. William Watt was on a fishing expedition, but since he had not been far enough away for a clear alibi, the police questioned him. Oddly, a man brought in on charges of burglary while Watt was detained in a cell said that he could provide evidence to exonerate Watt. Watt's attorney believed from the information that this handsome burglar, Peter Manuel, gave him about the Watts' home that Manuel had to be either the perpetrator or an accomplice, but there was no evidence with which to charge him. Nevertheless, Watt was let go. But then another adolescent girl was assaulted and murdered, as was a family of three during a robbery. When Manuel spent a traceable five-pound note, he was caught. After items related to the murders were found in his father's home, Manuel confessed, but then insisted that he had been coerced. Still, he revealed where his fifth victim had been buried. Despite his impressive comportment at trial, where he believed his striking figure would win the day, he was convicted of seven murders. The police also suspected him in the shooting death of a Newcastle cabdriver, but did not bring charges.

Canada had to deal with the serial murders of three children in 1957 and 1958 by seventeen-year-old Peter Woodcock. Declared insane, he went into treatment at a psychiatric facility. When after three decades he seemed to have become a model citizen, he was granted privileges that gave him the freedom to murder once more. He was used as the example in a documentary about psychopathy that treatment does not necessarily produce a cure.

A case in Los Angeles would eventually shift the tide for law enforcement. In September 1957, the police came across a woman along a roadside struggling with a man, and stopped. She had been shot in the thigh. Her name was Lorraine Vigil and she claimed that the man, Harvey Glatman, had told her he was a photographer. The police arrested Glatman and searched his apartment, where they found photographs of three women who had disappeared. All had been posed bound, gagged, and looking terrified. Glatman confessed that he had killed them and showed the police where he had buried two of the women.

Over the previous two months, he admitted, he had made artistic expression part of his MO. In August, he had pretended to be a photographer from a detective magazine, and once he had his "model," Judy Dull, bound and gagged, he raped her. But since he was already a convicted felon, he decided he'd have to kill her to remove her as a witness. He strangled her with a cord and left her in the desert. Then he used a lonely hearts club to find his next victim, Shirley Ann Bridgeford. He pretended to be a plumber as he arranged a date, and took her out to the desert. He persuaded her to pose for bondage pictures and then completed his deadly ritual, burying her there. The next victim he picked up from a nude modeling agency. He bound and raped her, and then took her on a "picnic" to a spot near where he had left his second victim. He raped her repeatedly, photographed her, and then killed her with a length of cord. In short order, Glatman was convicted and executed.

His crime spree was to inspire a Los Angeles detective, Pierce Brooks, to consider the viability of a nationwide computerized databank on violent crimes. As he studied the crime, he came to believe that the offender had killed before. Then he was assigned to an unrelated case that struck him the same way. Brooks spent off-hours and weekends in the library looking for similar incidents as a way to link these crimes to a repeat offender. He started in Los Angeles and then began to go through articles from other major cities. The tedious task initially seemed hopeless, but then he uncovered a murder that seemed similar. He made a fingerprint match between the two cases and found a good suspect. But the process had consumed a lot of time, so he went to his chief to ask about purchasing a computer. The chief scoffed at the idea, because at that time computers were extremely expensive, not to mention rather large; such a machine would require a building to house. The request seemed ludicrous. It would take two more decades before the FBI took Brooks's idea seriously, and by then technology would be more manageable. It helped that with the U.S.S.R.'s launch of *Sputnik* in 1957, the U.S. decided to strive for the lead in technology and science, especially in the race to the moon. Computers were needed for that.

At the same time, psychology was penetrating further

into criminal investigation. More than three dozen explosions had occurred during the 1940s and 1950s in places like Radio City Music Hall and Grand Central Station in New York City, and the perpetrator had sent angry letters to area newspapers, politicians, and utility companies. Psychiatrist James Brussel was asked to offer an analysis to help catch the perpetrator. Believing there was a "method to his madness," Brussel studied the crime-related material and provided details about the man's ethnicity, motivation, approximate age, personal presentation, living situation, level of paranoia, religious affiliation, employment status, and typical manner of dress—a double-breasted suit. The man was a skilled mechanic, Brussel said, and contemptuous. He had once worked for Con Edison, the utility company to whom letters had been sent, and his resentment was given no relief. He would probably live with a maiden sister or aunt in a New England state.

When the police finally tracked down George Metesky in 1957 in Waterbury, Connecticut (thanks to an open letter Brussel had published in the newspaper that drew a veiled response from Metesky), he was in his robe. He lived with two unmarried sisters, and was of the correct age, ethnicity, and religion. The police told him to get dressed and he returned (according to Brussel's memoir) buttoning up a double-breasted suit.

Around then, another criminal deviation occurred in the form of a killing couple who had absorbed the youth culture's identification with nihilistic philosophies. The

Beats were getting attention and a movie star named James Dean epitomized the feeling of alienated youth in a popular film, *Rebel Without a Cause*. Charles Starkweather, nineteen, saw Dean as his role model, and with his fourteen-year-old girlfriend, Caril Ann Fugate, he cut a murderous swath through Nebraska in early 1958, killing family, friends, and strangers.

"I had hated and been hated," Starkweather once said. "I had my little world to keep alive as long as possible and my gun. That was my answer." With everything going against him, he finally acted out to punish society. On December 1, 1957, Starkweather held up a gas station and killed the attendant. Then seven weeks passed, and on January 21, Starkweather killed Caril Ann's family. By the time the bodies were discovered a week later, the two lovers were on the move. They killed a man, his dog, and a young couple who had helped them out. Then they murdered a wealthy man, his wife, and his maid, and a salesman asleep in his car. During this tussle a cop appeared, and after a high-speed chase, Starkweather was caught. For his senseless spree, he was executed, while Caril Ann went to prison.

But America was shaken. This young man had been a roving stranger, killing people senselessly, and so was the next perpetrator of multiple murder. These killers were striking at good families, as if to undermine the very foundation of America.

A missing family led police in 1959 to a grisly discovery in Virginia. It had been two months since Carroll

Jackson and his wife and children had abandoned their car near their home in Apple Grove, and Jackson's bound body, shot in the back of the head, turned up in a ditch not far from Fredericksburg. As detectives removed him, they found the corpse of his infant daughter beneath him, apparently smothered to death from having his weight on top of her. But Jackson's wife and five-year-old daughter were still missing.

A few weeks later, the bodies of Mildred and Susan Jackson were found deeper in the woods. Both had been raped, and Mildred, the mother, had apparently been forced into other sexual acts, as well as tortured before she was bludgeoned to death. Investigators found a cinder-block building not far away filled with pornography, morgue photos of dead females, and torture implements. They also noticed the photograph of a young woman.

The police wondered if there was a connection between this mass murder and the sexual violation and shooting death of a young woman in 1957 not far from the same area. A man had come up beside Margaret Harold and her boyfriend in their parked car near Annapolis, Maryland. He'd demanded money and then shot Margaret. Her boyfriend had escaped to get help, but when police arrived, Margaret was dead. She had been stripped and raped.

An anonymous letter to the police that described a twenty-six-year-old self-styled existential philosopher and jazz musician named Melvin Davis Rees Jr. provided a lead. When investigators checked Rees's background, they discovered that he had once dated a coed from the

University of Maryland, and a check of the school yearbook showed that she was the girl whose photo they had found taped inside the cinder-block structure. That was a good lead, although she denied knowing him.

The trail went cold for a year, until the author of the anonymous letter went to the police in person to inform them of Rees's new address in Arkansas. The FBI entered the case and searched Rees's home, where inside a saxophone case they found the evidence they needed. Rees had penned a private journal in which he described the Jackson family murder, indicating how he had come upon them and shot the man so he could have the woman and girl to himself. Newspapers dubbed him the "Sex Beast," and while he was suspected in the 1956 murders of four adolescent girls in Maryland, he was tried and convicted for only the other five killings. He was sentenced to death in Maryland. Although he was supposed to be executed, his sentence was commuted to life. In 1985, he confessed to the murders of sixteen-year-old Shelby Venable and eighteen-year-old Mary Fellers, two of the four Maryland victims. The same reporter to whom he confessed said that he had acknowledged guilt in seven or eight murders. Rees died in prison at age sixty-six, from heart failure.

Another such deviant showed up in 1959 in West Germany: the "Beast of the Black Forest." In a dark alley in Karlsruhe, the body of a woman was discovered. She had been raped and her throat was slit with a razor. Another woman had reported that on the night of the murder, she had been accosted by a man who had run off when a taxi drove by. There were no clues to assist police in tracking the offender.

But several more dead women turned up over the next few months, and there were a series of complaints about sexual assaults. One woman had apparently been thrown off a train before being raped and murdered. Still, there were no particularly helpful clues.

Then, during the summer of 1960, a young man entered a tailor's shop to drop off a suit, leaving his briefcase behind while he went on an errand. The tailor noticed something odd about it, so he opened it and found a rifle modified with a sawed-off barrel. He alerted the police, who arrested the man, Heinrich Pommerencke. They suspected him in a robbery the day before in a nearby town, and he admitted that he had done it. As a ruse, they told him that they had found bloodstains on the suit he'd left at the tailor's shop, which matched the blood of several murder victims in the Black Forest area. Pommerencke fell for it.

He explained how he had watched a showing of Cecil B. DeMille's *The Ten Commandments,* seen the licentious women dancing around the golden calf, and decided that he "would have to kill." This twenty-three-year-old had already participated in numerous sexual assaults, but had recently decided it was his mission to kill. Among other felony charges, he was convicted of four murders, a dozen attempted murders, and twenty-one rapes. He was also suspected in six other murders. What he had done would be repeated a lot by other killers during the decade to come.

Science and the Serial Killer

Even as science was being used more often in criminal investigation, there were setbacks. A famous case involving poisons was that of Marie Besnard, known as the "Black Widow of Loudun." Besnard, fifty-two, was accused of killing twelve people with arsenic, including her husband and mother. The string of deaths stretched across two decades, from 1929 until 1949. Marie benefited in some manner from each of the murders, thus providing the prosecution with a motive. All of the bodies were exhumed, and high levels of arsenic were found in each one. However, even with the poison, the prosecution had only circumstantial evidence.

When the case went to trial, the defense attorney attacked the lab technique of toxicologist Georges Beroud as careless. This caused sufficient doubt that a second analysis by a group of four toxicologists was requested. While this investigation was under way, the defense counsel learned about a new theory that arsenic could enter the hair of a corpse from the ground through anaerobic bacteria. So the prosecution's experts also had to prove that the arsenic in the bodies had not been introduced after burial.

Once completed, the second investigation found significant levels of arsenic in the corpses, but one of the experts had been careless. The procedure required that the hair be subjected to radioactivity for twenty-six and a half hours, but he had cut that short by ten hours. So a third analysis was performed, by another group of toxi-cologists, but when they could not disprove the defense's new theory about surrounding arsenic in the earth, Marie Besnard was acquitted. It had been a long process, but she was free and science was left to ponder its mistakes. Some people believed that a multiple killer had gotten away with her crimes, and she is included on many Internet serial killer lists.

As people learned more about such killers in the news, they began to fear the random attack. Free love and greater mobility were increasingly decorating the cultural landscape, and as a result people were feeling even more vulnerable, and killers took advantage. America was not only the dominant world power, as well as a nation to be reckoned with in terms of production and technology, but it was to become the playground of more multiple murderers than any country had ever seen. The brutality about to occur over the next twenty-five years would inspire an entirely new approach to such crimes.

CHAPTER TEN

Serial Killers Come of Age

Restless Arena

In 1960, Alfred Hitchcock released *Psycho,* a grainy black-and-white film based loosely on the story of Ed Gein, showing a demented, mother-dominated nerd, Norman Bates, who could present a personable front while harboring a compulsion to fatally stab women who aroused him—in effect, killing an unacceptable part of himself. Along with his taxidermy hobby, indicative of death and rigidity, his condition of multiple personality disorder shocked the nation, especially with its creepy cross-gendered manifestation. The film transitioned viewers from the blind naïveté of the 1950s and foreshadowed what lay ahead. During the next decade, Americans witnessed a host of other multiple killers, many of whom had psychiatric problems. Psychologists and law enforcement alike mobilized to focus on the phenomenon even as they dealt with the violence of disaffected youth and livid African-Americans. A decade that opened with creepy Norman Bates would close with one of the most shocking crimes on record. The public had failed to see its own dark shadow.

After World War II, the U.S. population had boomed, while technological advances offered easy credit and a variety of goods to people ready to spend. Consumer confidence had propelled the economy, encouraging entrepreneurs to set up hotel chains, fast-food restaurants, and mass-produced houses. Workers demanded improved wages and working conditions, and women sought better opportunities.

In 1960, John F. Kennedy employed the venue of television to debate his political opponent, Richard Nixon: It was the first time TV had been used for this purpose. After becoming the youngest president to date, Kennedy launched the space race to compete with the Soviet's orbiting cosmonaut in 1961, and everyone aimed toward the moon. That same year, the Berlin Wall went up and South Africa left the British Commonwealth. By '62, the U.S. Military Council was established in Vietnam. It was an ominous development, and college kids across America and Europe protested what they perceived as manipulative "establishment" propaganda. They were hungry for raw experience and new identities. Inspired by the rebels of the 1950s, who eschewed the material values of the previous generation, many roamed the country in search of answers to the cosmic riddles, settling together as comrades in West Coast enclaves. Feeling unmoored, they created their own identities, yet failed to recognize how they, too, contributed to social and personal disintegration.

South America came into its own as a place of multiple murder, due in part to extended political violence. Although Colombia had only three reported cases, in reality its victims of multiple murders totaled in the hundreds. England and Germany remained on an equal footing with each other, while the U.S. outpaced all other countries in how often multiple murders occurred, with an average of more than one series per month. With the media's increasing coverage of such crimes, including bestselling books and movies, cases such as those of the Boston Strangler, the Co-ed Killer, the Manson massacres, and the Zodiac enigma drew international attention.

American killers made a mark early in the decade—Leonard Mill killed three in California and Julian Harvey five on a Miami boat trip—but other countries took the earliest hits. On June 12, 1960, a shoeless man was found bludgeoned to death on an isolated moor near Baslow, England. His shoes were found in a bloodstained car that had crashed into a lamppost. After a witness report, the police questioned Michael Copeland, a twenty-year-old soldier who at the time of the killing had been on leave from the British Army, and was now stationed in Germany. They let him go, and later that year a young man was stabbed to death in Germany. Copeland was also questioned in this case, but was again released. He returned to England, where another male corpse turned up in the spring. The body's dump location and head injury linked him tentatively with the first victim. Copeland was suspected, but without evidence the police could do nothing. Two years later, he called and confessed. They were hate crimes, Copeland admitted. He had believed the men to be homosexuals. At trial, he recanted his confession, but he was convicted and sentenced to be executed. His sentence was subsequently commuted to life.

In Australia, another killer also sought out males. Over the course of eighteen months, starting in June 1961, the "Sydney Mutilator" viciously stabbed four vagrants, especially around the genitals. When one victim was identified as Allan Brennan, it turned out that William MacDonald, posing as Brennan, had attempted to "murder" himself. In custody, he claimed that he had once been sexually assaulted in the army, so he was taking revenge on easy targets. Why he had masqueraded as one of the victims remained a mystery. At his trial, he claimed insanity but was convicted.

A night of terror in Perth, Australia, occurred in January 1963 when a couple was shot in their car, two men in their beds, and another man at his front door. Two of the victims died. Law enforcement tracked down .22-caliber rifles to run ballistics tests, but nothing turned up. Then the gunman struck again in August, using a different rifle to shoot a woman in the head. This weapon was discarded, so the police staked it out and grabbed Eric Cooke, thirty-two, who quickly confessed and turned over both weapons. He also confessed to a 1959 shooting, stating simply that he "wanted to hurt someone."

Similar motives drove a succession of multiple murderers in Colombia, South America. During that country's prolonged political upheaval, known as La Violencia, as many as three hundred thousand people lost their lives, and bandits like Teofilo Rojas killed a fair share of them, with estimates of from five hundred to over three thousand. A fatal ambush in 1963 terminated his violence, but in Cali between October 1963 and February 1964, ten adolescent boys were found drained of blood and dumped in vacant lots. The police suspected that a "blood ring" was grabbing children to sell their blood. No perpetrator was ever identified.

During that period, another killer slaughtered children in Colombia, Peru, and Ecuador. Pedro Lopez, the "Monster of the Andes," kidnapped, raped, and murdered young girls throughout two decades until he was stopped in 1980. He claimed he had killed more than three hundred. He also murdered three men who had raped him when he was eighteen. As he grabbed a nine-year-old girl from a tribe in Peru one day, he was caught but allowed to leave the country. Then, in Ecuador, after a river disgorged the remains of four girls, Lopez was arrested as he was leading another girl away. In his confession, he claimed that he was paying others back for what had been done to him. He searched for the innocent ones, he admitted, and as he strangled them while raping them, he enjoyed looking into their eyes. His claims seemed extravagant, but after the police unearthed fifty-three of his victims, they believed him. At one point, he stated, "I am the man of the century."

Then, in Mexico, a confession was gained that revealed the source of disappearances of many young women over the past decade from Guadalajara. Josephina Guttiériez offered details about girls taken to a brothel run by two sisters, Maria and Delfina de Jesus Gonzales. Both women had fled by the time police arrived, but on the property the authorities discovered a veritable cemetery. More than eighty girls had been killed and buried there, along with aborted fetuses. A few men had been murdered and deposited, too, presumably for their money. The sisters were eventually arrested, tried, and convicted.

Focus on America

To that point no such crime bender had touched the U.S., but President John F. Kennedy faced his own crisis. During the Cold War, as a containment measure, the U.S. had set up military bases around the Soviet perimeter, but when both sides gained the capability to deploy ballistic nuclear missiles from subs and silos, each became much more vulnerable to the other. In 1962, after the U.S. failed to overthrow the communist regime in Cuba, the U.S.S.R. tried to establish nuclear missile sites there. Kennedy put a blockade around the island, threatening retaliation that could lead to massive destruction for all parties, so the Russians removed their missiles. After that near-disaster, many countries with nuclear capability agreed to a partial test ban treaty. But not everyone agreed, so countries stockpiled nuclear armaments, just in case. Cold War tensions continued.

The press soon found another story brewing, in

Boston. On the evening of June 14, 1962, Anna Slesers' son found her murdered, with the cord from her bathrobe wrapped around her neck and her legs positioned for shock effect. She had been sexually assaulted with a hard object, possibly a bottle. Two weeks later, sixty-eight-year-old Nina Nichols was assaulted and strangled in her apartment with two of her nylon stockings, the ends tied into a bow. On the same day, fifteen miles north of the city, Helen Blake, sixty-five, met a similar death, assaulted and strangled with two stockings. Then two more elderly women were strangled in their homes. An unknown killer was terrorizing Boston, somehow getting easily into apartments.

Then the pattern shifted to young women. On December 5, 1962, Sophie Clark, twenty, an African-American student at the Carnegie Institute of Medical Technology, was found dead by one of her roommates. A neighbor reported that a man wearing a dark jacket and green trousers had been knocking on doors, falsely stating that the superintendent had sent him and commenting inappropriately about women's bodies.

Then, on December 31, Patricia Bissette, twenty-three, was discovered murdered when her boss arrived to pick her up for work. Her apartment building was near where Anna Slesers and Sophie Clark had lived. Three months went by and then, on March 6, 1963, sixty-eight-year-old Mary Brown was found beaten to death, having been strangled and raped. This murder was followed by that of graduate student Beverly Samans on May 8. A friend found her nude on a sofa bed, her hands bound behind her and two nylon stockings and a white scarf knotted around her neck.

Some twenty-three hundred police would eventually become involved in the urgent investigation, interviewing thirty-six thousand people. Hundreds of suspects were fingerprinted and more than three dozen given lie-detector tests. Every known sex offender was tracked down and patient leaves from mental institutions were checked, but the police remained stymied.

A quiet period ensued that summer, but on September 8, in Salem, Evelyn Corbin, a fifty-eight-year-old divorcée, was found strangled with two of her nylon stockings. Then, on November 24, as the Boston area grieved the shocking assassination in Texas of President John F. Kennedy by Lee Harvey Oswald, Joann Graff was raped and murdered in her ransacked apartment. Two brown nylon stockings and the leg of a black leotard were tied in an elaborate bow around her neck.

The new year arrived with President Lyndon Johnson at America's helm—and with nineteen-year-old Mary Sullivan being found murdered in her Boston apartment. Like the other victims, she had been strangled: first with a dark stocking and then, over the stocking, with a pink silk scarf tied in a huge bow under her chin. A broomstick handle had been forced into her vagina, and a card propped against her foot that said, "Happy New Year." The Massachusetts attorney general, Edward Brooke, had set up a "Strangler Bureau" to collect, organize, and assimilate over thirty-seven thousand documents. In a forensic first, a Concord company donated a computer to help keep track of it all. Psychiatrists, including Dr. Brussel from the Mad Bomber case, offered opinions on the nature of the person who would commit such crimes. But the conflicting expert opinions made it clear that no one really knew. Some said there had been one perpetrator, others believed there were more.

On November 5, 1964, Albert DeSalvo, known as the "Green Man" for his green work clothes, was arrested for rape. He turned out to be the infamous Measuring Man as well—a sexual deviant arrested earlier for entering women's apartments to molest them. He soon confessed to being the Boston Strangler, and his attorney, F. Lee Bailey, worked out a deal that sent him to prison for other crimes, so he was never prosecuted for the murders. He would eventually recant his confession and put into doubt not only that he was the Strangler but also that a single man was responsible for all of the crimes. Still, for America, he became part of the cultural mythology.

Upon his confession, the country breathed a sigh of collective relief. Little did they know that this spate of crimes had ushered in America's age of the sequential killer. Something shifted as ordinary decent people realized how vulnerable they were. Yet what they feared also attracted them. A book on the case became a best-seller, spawning a movie. As with *Psycho*, viewers found a new source of titillating dread. And they wanted more.

The phrase "series killer" had been used in Britain for some of its notorious cases, but it was not yet in the American crime lexicon. One criminologist had written about "chain killers" and others mentioned "pattern crimes," but investigators in the United States still lumped together as a mass or multiple murderer all those who killed more than one person. Given the Boston case, law enforcement officials realized that if this type of murder continued they would need better resources for coping with it.

And the next such case overlapped the Strangler investigation. In 1965, *Life* magazine did a shocking spread about Charles Schmid, twenty-three, the "Pied Piper of Tucson," which offered some intriguing content. Self-conscious about his short stature, he strutted around in boots stuffed with newspapers and tin cans, wore makeup, and adopted an Elvis Presley persona. Yet girls were enamored of him. First he raped and killed Alleen Rowe in the desert, burying her in the sand. He was arrested following the double homicide of two more adolescent girls, after he showed a trusted friend where he had buried them. Schmid was tried and convicted.

These incidents stunned Americans, but the pervasive moral atmosphere placed blame on the victims, pointing to miniskirts, rock music, promiscuity, hitchhiking, and drugs as evil influences. Conservative Americans believed that society was eroding, and in an effort to retain the status quo in the South, the Ku Klux Klan murdered three civil rights activists, while black assassins killed Black Muslim leader Malcolm X. And then there were the serial killers—in one case, two brothers. Larry Lee Ranes was only nineteen years old in 1964 when he confessed to murdering five men in three states. His last victim was a schoolteacher, whom he had shot in his car. He then drove with the body through several states, even getting through a police roadblock. The other men he killed while robbing gas stations or accepting rides. Less than eight years later, Danny Ranes would rape and strangle four young women in Michigan, making them the first brothers who independently became serial killers (unlike the Harps, who did it together), albeit with entirely different motives, MOs, and victim types.

Then there was Sharon Kinne, caught in Mexico City with a .22 pistol after shooting a man who had accompanied her there. She shot the hotel proprietor as well, but he was not badly wounded and managed to hold her for the police. She claimed self-defense in both shootings, but she had used the same pistol in a murder in Kansas City of a woman whose husband had been attracted to Kinne—and for whose death Kinne had been acquitted. In addition, Kinne had been tried four times for shooting her husband to death that same year, resulting in mistrials (she'd laid the blame on their two-year-old daughter, and police had accepted that). She was convicted, and remained in prison in Mexico.

International Predators

Across the ocean, another "Jack" showed up in London in 1964, as young prostitutes were found unclothed and asphyxiated. Most had been strangled, but a few appeared to have died from forcible fellatio. The press dubbed this killer "Jack the Stripper," and by some theories, he had started as early as 1959. His victim count was between six and eight, and he was never caught, although when a key suspect committed suicide, these murders stopped.

Then England got another nasty surprise. In Manchester, seventeen-year-old David Smith reported to the police that he knew of a murder, opening up a Pandora's box. Smith's sister-in-law, Myra Hindley, had a boyfriend, Ian Brady, who had smashed open a man's head with an ax and asked David to help hide the body. After Smith went to the police, they searched the home in question—where an elderly woman lived—and found the victim's body in an upstairs room. They arrested Brady and Hindley on the spot.

The search of the home resolved another mystery: what had happened to ten-year-old Lesley Ann Downey, who had disappeared in December 1964. The police found pictures of her and a tape-recording of her voice on which she begged to go home. In addition, they turned up plans for the murder of a twelve-year-old boy, also missing. It seemed that Hindley would lure children to the moors for picnics, where Brady would kill and bury them. Police suspected them in several other disappearances of children in the area, but they refused to confess.

Brady was a true postmodern nihilist. Inspired by Dostoevsky, the Marquis de Sade, and Nietzsche, he believed that certain men can rise above society's moral standards and do as they pleased. A loner with a criminal record, he had enlisted eighteen-year-old Myra in his plan to commit the perfect murder. Their first victim, in 1963, had been a sixteen-year-old girl. Brady would later publish a book, *The Gates of Janus,* to express his philosophies. For him, killing was an exciting venture for the solitary explorer "consciously thirsting to experience that which the majority have not and dare not." Killers like himself, he wrote, are "unavoidably a failure in many normal walks of life," lack patience, and eschew the boredom that others accept. "The serial killer has chosen to live a day as a lion, rather than decades as a sheep." Once he has committed homicide, Brady continued, he accepts his acts as "normal" and views the rest of humanity as "subnormal."

Before meeting him, Hindley had been a simple girl, an easy mark for a man like Brady. According to her diary, he convinced her that morality was relative, and she was soon expressing the same sentiments of hatred that he did. He proposed that they enrich themselves through a life of crime, to which she acceded. And for which she paid the price. In 1966, both were sentenced to life in prison, and each would eventually accuse the other as the instigator. Their case renewed the demand for capital punishment.

In Germany, the "Midday Murderer" was at large for some four years, killing sporadically in parts of Nuremburg during the middle of the day. Then, in 1965, Klaus Gosman was caught after shooting to death someone in a shop, and his diary detailed his involvement in eight other fatal shootings since 1960, when he was only nineteen. He planned each incident meticulously, but finally slipped up.

Starting in 1962, four boys were murdered in brutal fashion in Bonn, West Germany. They were beaten or bludgeoned, strangled, and sometimes dismembered, and had their eyes plucked out. Then Peter Frese, age five, escaped his kidnapper in 1966 and alerted police to nine-teen-year-old Jurgen Bartsch, who had been keeping him restrained. They arrested Bartsch for attempted murder and he was tried and convicted. Then details about his life came out. He had been abandoned by his mother and adopted into a family who forbid him to play with other children. He revealed that at school, a priest had raped him when he was twelve, and two years later he started to abuse other boys—and committed his first murder. Offered psychiatric care, he eventually requested castration, but died during surgery from an accidental overdose of anesthesia.

Unrest

In 1965, rioting in Los Angeles over civil rights took thirty-four lives and caused massive damage. Dr. Martin Luther King Jr. organized the black suffrage movement even as people in Cleveland adamantly resisted the integration of schools. It was a time of great fear among whites and blacks. Violence continued in various cities over the next two years. At the same time, American involvement in the Vietnam War escalated, and the reckless prosperity of the 1950s took its toll in runaway inflation. The government was helpless to do much except put down riots, often with force. Police became "pigs."

And it seemed that the Boston Strangler was at it

again, only this time in Cincinnati. In October 1965, a man tried to rape and beat a sixty-five-year-old woman, but failed to kill her with the clothesline he placed around her neck. Two months later, he made sure. Then four months passed and he raped and strangled a fifty-eight-year-old woman in her apartment. Now the papers were calling him the Cincinnati Strangler, and demanding that police arrest someone. But in June and October, two fiftyish women were similarly killed, and within eight days, an eighty-one-year-old was killed in her home with the cord of a heating pad wrapped around her neck. All of the victims had been sexually assaulted. In December 1966, after an elderly woman was found strangled in an elevator, Posteal Laskey was arrested and charged in her death, at which point the murders ceased, prompting officials to assume that he had been responsible for the others as well. He was sentenced to life in prison.

In New Jersey, from 1965 to 1966, nine patients were killed with curare injections in Oradell, but the perpetrator was not identified, while in Ocean County during that same period, six people of both genders were sexually assaulted and murdered. Again, no one was caught, but the crimes ceased.

By the end of 1966, America had also seen three shocking mass murders that made international headlines. Richard Speck entered the home of a group of nursing students and killed eight of them. Charles Whitman climbed up the University of Texas tower in Austin, picked off forty-five people with a rifle, killing fourteen (as well, it turned out, as his mother and wife, hours earlier), and kept shooting until police killed him. Then eighteen-year-old Robert Smith, who worshiped both Whitman and Speck, went to a beauty school in Phoenix with his birthday gun and shot five women and two children. His stated motive: "I wanted to get known."

That year and into 1967, Janice Gibbs poisoned her husband and five children in Georgia, escaping suspicion because she donated some of the insurance money to her church, but when she was finally arrested she claimed that she thought the world was too terrible for her husband and children to live in. Considered unfit to plead, she was committed until 1976, when she finally stood trial, was convicted, and received five life terms.

Then William Dale Archerd was arrested in Los Angeles on the suspicion that he had murdered a nephew and two of his seven wives. He became the first American to be convicted for using an insulin injection as a murder weapon. He was also suspected in the deaths of three others, going back as far as 1947.

Several other countries had problems with multiple killers as well. Hans van Zon came to the attention of the Holland police in 1967 when his wife accused him of trying to murder her, but he was not convicted (even though, in fact, he had already killed several people). One woman he slaughtered with a bread knife when she refused to have sex, and another victim was a male film director. Two women and a man fell to his signature bludgeoning before an elderly woman shouted loudly enough to save herself. This time, the police put him away.

In Poland, a more prolific murder spree occurred

during the same period. Young blond women were being disemboweled, mostly during public holidays, and "The Red Spider" was writing cryptic letters in spidery red ink to the police, revealing where bodies could be found and challenging them to catch him. They did, thanks to an analysis of the ink on his notes, which turned out to be artist's paint, and the fact that two victims—sisters—had been members of an art club. The Polish Ripper turned out to be Lucien Staniak, twenty-six, a government translator and an artist who had once depicted a mutilated woman, mostly in red. After another murder, he was arrested. He said that he had started killing as the result of the government's not prosecuting a blond woman who had unintentionally killed his parents and sister in a car accident. He claimed twenty victims, but was convicted of only six murders and committed to an asylum.

Then, as James Earl Ray, who had assassinated Martin Luther King Jr. in Tennessee on April 4, 1968, was being returned from England to the U.S. for trial, Martin Brown, four, and Brian Howes, three, were found murdered in Newcastle, England. Brian had been mutilated with a sharp instrument, and the killer had carved an M in the flesh of his stomach. It was an atrocity past all imagining, and neighborhood residents feared a predator. In fact, a series of scribbled notes claiming responsibility for the first killing, two signed by "Fanny and Faggot," that indicated the killer was not finished, had been left at a nursery school: "I murder so that I may come back." No one knew what to think, and certainly no one was prepared for what happened next.

A neighborhood child came to the door of Martin's family to ask if she could see him. When his mother informed her that he was dead, she smiled and said, "Oh, I know he's dead. I want to see him in his coffin." A gruesome request, to be sure, but dismissed at the time as childish immaturity.

Then, when the second boy was buried, Chief Inspector James Dobson observed the same young girl waiting outside the family's house to watch the coffin being carried out. She rubbed her hands together and laughed. With a chill, he realized that he might have a child murderer on his hands—a girl. And she was only eleven. It seemed impossible, but he had to investigate. He found out her name was Mary Bell. To stop her from acting again, he arrested her for questioning, along with her thirteen-year-old chum Norma Bell (no relation).

Each immediately accused the other, and both were held for trial. Mary gave a detailed statement to the police that was unsettling in its nonchalant, self-serving delivery. When the girls were brought to the courtroom, the press had a field day with the notion of a "bad seed," or a child born evil—she had been only ten when she'd committed the first murder. Mary, with her indifferent expression, fit the bill, both for the press and the prosecutor. "In Norma," he said, "you have a simple, backward girl of subnormal intelligence. In Mary you have a most abnormal child, aggressive, vicious, cruel, incapable of remorse, a girl moreover possessed of a dominating personality, with a somewhat unusual intelligence and a degree of cunning that is almost terrifying."

Norma was acquitted, but Mary was convicted of manslaughter. She was thought to be the mastermind of the duo, if such a young child can even form criminal intent, and she was sentenced to an all-boys' institution, because she was considered quite dangerous. The press called her a bully, a liar, and a callous murderess, capable of acting on her own. "This pretty little girl," said one newspaper, "is evil incarnate." In 1980, Bell was released and in 2003, granted lifelong anonymity.

Developments

From 1965 to 1967, forensic science gained from technological inventions: the first high-resolution electron microscope, the immunelectrophoretic technique, and the FBI's National Crime Information Center (NCIC). This computerized index permitted state and local jurisdictions access to FBI archives on such items as license plate numbers and recovered guns, and enabled them as well to post notices about wanted or missing persons. In other words, it was a way to coordinate certain types of national investigations.

It was the summer of love; it was the summer of hate. During the long, hot days of 1967, Timothy Leary urged those of free mind and heart to come to Berkeley to "Tune in, turn on, and drop out," even as buildings burned and thirty-eight died in Detroit's race riots. In Ontario in 1967, five women were found dead, but the perpetrator was not caught. Across the bridge from Canada, in the Ann Arbor/Ypsilanti area of Michigan, the body of a coed was found in a farmer's field. The following spring, another body turned up nearby with forty-seven stab wounds. But no one had yet linked these killings.

Americans had not yet recovered from the John F. Kennedy assassination before a second one wounded them in 1968: that of Robert Kennedy, as he campaigned to become the next president. The Chicago Seven spat demands at the Democratic National Convention and Ted Kennedy survived a car accident at Chappaquid-dick that resulted in the drowning death of Mary Jo Kopechne. It was a time of upheaval, self-awareness, and venturing forth. Young people affirmed the excesses of the rock musicians Jim Morrison and Janis Joplin and embraced the disturbing undertones of the Beatles' *Sergeant Pepper's Lonely Hearts Club Band*. Inspired by Tom Wolfe's book *The Electric Kool-Aid Acid Test,* a whole subculture experimented with drugs and the occult. Student revolt spread into Europe, even as the Soviets invaded Czechoslovakia.

Then, in Michigan in 1969, there were five more murders of young women, the youngest of whom was thirteen. The earlier two Michigan murders were linked to these. Several of the victims had lived on or near the Eastern Michigan University campus. All had been sexu-ally mutilated, but killed in a variety of ways—shot, stabbed, strangled. It was possible that one person had committed the crimes, but no one was sure.

The perpetrator left most of the bodies in the open

where they would be easily discovered. And he played games. While the police searched a burned-out barn foundation for evidence, someone placed flower blossoms outside that corresponded to the number of victims thus far. Then, when a citizens' group imported nightclub psychic Peter Hurkos, who predicted another murder, the body of eighteen-year-old Karen Sue Beineman was left within a mile of the psychic's hotel.

Just as American men walked on the moon and Woodstock neared its August 1969 opening as a great lovefest, the Beineman murder was traced to a handsome young elementary education student named John Norman Collins. He had picked up girls on his motorcycle at a time when hitchhiking and motorcycles were considered fashionable. Suspected in the second murder, he had been let go, but the Beineman evidence was compelling. It indicated that he had kept her body for a while in the basement of his uncle's—a state trooper. He was arrested and held for trial.

The investigation relied on a controversial forensic technique called neutron activation analysis, in which a specimen was placed in a nuclear reactor and irradiated with a stream of neutrons. This treatment allowed scientists to measure and identify the sample's smallest constituent particles. Hair samples from the victim's clothing and clippings from the floor of the crime scene were subjected to this technique, which influenced Collins's conviction for Beineman's murder. The state of California suspected him in an eighth murder, for which there was strong physical evidence from a trip he'd made there, but decided against extraditing him. He got life in prison in Michigan.

Just after his arrest, the nation came in for another shock. On Saturday, August 9, at the home of film director Roman Polanski, a massacre occurred that made instant headlines around the world. Five people were slaughtered in a blood-drenched spree, including Polanski's eight-months-pregnant wife, Sharon Tate, twenty-six, an actress.

The first victim, Steve Parent, eighteen, turned out to have just been in the wrong place at the wrong time. He'd visited an acquaintance having nothing to do with the other victims and was just leaving the property. Inside the Polanski home were two blood-covered bodies. Sharon Tate, stabbed sixteen times, had a nylon rope tied loosely around her neck. A long end had been tossed over an overhead rafter and then tied around the neck of her friend, hairstylist Jay Sebring. He had been shot once and stabbed seven times. On a door, the word "PIG" was written in blood. Outside on the lawn lay Voytek Frykowski, bleeding profusely from his many wounds. He had been shot five times and stabbed fifty-one, as well as bludgeoned thirteen times in the head. Nearby was coffee heiress Abigail Folger, stabbed twenty-eight times.

Oddly, the investigators did not believe the crime had any association with a July 31 murder of a musician in which a message about "pigs" was written in blood on a wall. Nor was the incident that followed the next night thought to be related. Leno and Rosemary LaBianca were stabbed to death in their home, and the killer or killers had carved "War" into Leno's chest and used his blood to write "Death to Pigs," "Rise," and "Healter [sic] Skelter" on the walls.

Then, in October, a young woman named Susan Atkins, in jail for unrelated crimes, revealed to a cellmate that she had been involved in these massacres. That led the police to her associates, an odd collection of unemployed hippies living on the Spahn ranch outside the city, led by a skinny man named Charles Manson. Eventually they arrested three of the women—Susan Atkins, Leslie Van Houten, and Patricia Krenwinkel—along with Manson and a drifter called "Tex." As the story was pieced together, it became clear that Manson had urged several of the cult members to go on a killing spree, telling them to make it look like the work of black militants. He'd formed this group from down-and-out "hippie" kids in the Haight-Ashbury district of San Francisco. Some claimed to believe his notion that he was Christ. His disciples were known as "The Family," and his vision of "Helter Skelter" (taken from the Beatles' *White Album*) meant that blacks would rise up to massacre whites and reclaim the earth.

Prosecutor Vince Bugliosi made the case in the 1970 trial that since Manson was the group mastermind, he was culpable. President Richard M. Nixon nearly caused a mistrial when he publicly declared Manson guilty. Finally it was done, despite one defense attorney's going missing, and the jury convicted Manson, Susan Atkins, and Patricia Krenwinkel of seven counts of first-degree murder. Leslie Van Houten was convicted on two counts. In a separate trial, "Tex" Watson was convicted for his part.

For the sentencing phase, Manson shaved his head, trimmed his beard into a fork, and announced, "I am the Devil and the Devil always has a bald head." Experts took the stand to discuss the effects of LSD on the brain, but that proved to have no mitigating effect: All were ultimately sentenced to death, although none was ever executed. They were suspected in as many as thirty-seven murders altogether, including Manson Family members who had disappeared.

While that case was being investigated, four women and a man were murdered in their homes by a killer in Memphis. The spree began on August 14, 1969, with the double homicide of Roy Dumas and his wife (whose sexual organs were cut with scissors) and lasted a month before George Howard Putt was finally apprehended. Since the murders seemed to be sexually motivated, the police wondered if the Boston Strangler case had inspired someone, so they examined names of people who had taken a copy of the book from the local library. But before long, witnesses caught the killer in the act and chased him into the police's arms. Everyone was surprised. Putt had seemed like a nice young man with a wife and a decent middle-class life.

By 1968, for psychiatrists, the term "sociopath," used to describe people like Manson and Putt, had officially yielded to "personality disorder, antisocial type." America was waking up to more episodes of random violence and asking hard questions about social conditions. While theorists looked for causes, few noted how the media fed the public's appetite for increasingly dramatic details. Journalists and news anchors may even have encouraged the development of some predators. Serial killers were transformed in the media from *nobodies* into *somebodies,* and international coverage added to their gratification. More than one said later that he wanted to be known as the world's most notorious killer.

Then California again became the focus of a multiple murder investigation. In December 1968 and July 1969, a man shot two couples in Vallejo, California; only one young man survived. Then the editors of three San Francisco papers each received part of a strange letter claiming to be from the Vallejo killer. He had used too much postage and his message consisted of a printed cryptogram composed of symbols and signed with a crossed-circle symbol. A teacher cracked the code, which said:

I LIKE KILLING PEOPLE BECAUSE IT IS SO MUCH FUN IT IS MORE FUN THAN KILLING WILD GAME IN THE FORREST BECAUSE MAN IS THE MOST DAN-GEROUS ANAMAL OF ALL TO KILL SOMETIMES GIVES ME THE MOST THRILLING EXPERIENCE IT IS EVEN BETTER THAN GETTING YOUR ROCKS OFF WITH A GIRL THE BEST PART OF IT IS THAE WHEN I DIE I WILL BE REBORN IN PARADICE AND ALL THE I HAVE KILLED WILL BECOME MY SLAVES I WILL NOT GIVE YOU MY NAME BECAUSE YOU WILL TRY TO

SLOI DOWN OR STOP MY COLLECTING OF SLAVES
FOR AFTERLIFE.

Thus began a cat-and-mouse game devised by a man who called himself the Zodiac. He wasn't finished. On September 27, 1969, Cecelia Ann Shepard and her friend Bryan Hartnell were picnicking at Lake Berryessa when a man wearing a black executioner's hood approached them. He stabbed them, attacking the girl repeatedly, and afterward called the police to report the crime. He struck again two weeks later, killing cabdriver Paul Stine and leaving two fingerprints in blood. Soon after, the *Chronicle* received a letter with a torn piece of Stine's shirt. Yet no leads proved productive. Until 1984, the Zodiac kept in contact with the SFPD and the *Chronicle,* but his killing seemed to end with seven victims. His identity continues to be a mystery.

That year, when three women were strangled to death in Scotland in the same area, a man who acquired the moniker "Bible John" became the key suspect. He had shared a cab with his third victim and her sister, who was able to describe the encounter. He had said his name was John and he had talked about scripture and prayer. All three victims had left a ballroom just prior to their murders, and all were having their periods. Their killer was never identified.

Back on the West Coast, three women going missing over six months had officials alarmed at Oregon State University in Corvalis. Then decomposing remains were found by the river, bound and weighted down. Some girls

had complained of getting strange calls from a man trying to lure them out of their rooms, and there were reports of a suspicious man loitering around campus, so
when he showed up again, they picked him up. His name
was Jerry Brudos, and under questioning, he admitted to
having killed and mutilated four women, then throwing
their bodies into a river after he cut the parts he wanted
from them. His first victim was minus her left foot (he
had a shoe fetish), and two others had their breasts removed (one was preserved and turned into a paperweight).
He also photographed them while under his power, had
sex with their bodies, and put the body parts into a
freezer. Despite an insanity plea, several psychiatrists indicated that while he had a personality disorder, he knew
what he was doing and that it was wrong. He pled guilty
to three murders and was sentenced to life imprisonment.

Across the country, another mentally disordered man,
Antone Costa, left a trail of murders from Massachusetts
to California, inviting his victims first to do drugs with
him. After killing them, he would have sex with their
corpses. Diagnosed with schizophrenia, he was nevertheless convicted, and later he hanged himself in his cell.

Even Canada did not escape the upsurge of lust murders during this time. A young schoolteacher, Norma
Vaillancourt, was found murdered in 1968 in her apartment in Montreal. She'd been strangled, raped, and bitten
all over her breasts. The crime was sadistic, but among her
many boyfriends, there were no good suspects.

Only a day later, another victim was found in that town
in the same condition, and the bite marks were matched,

which linked the cases. Both women appeared not to have struggled, so it was assumed that they not only knew their attacker but may also have been engaged in something they wanted to do. Then Marielle Archambault told coworkers that she felt entranced by a man she'd recently met. She, too, turned up dead . . . and similarly bitten.

There were two more victims, one of them in Calgary, before the "vampire" was stopped in 1971. The police arrested Wayne Boden, and an odontologist took an impression of his teeth to show how they matched the wounds on each victim. Boden admitted that he had indeed killed these women while having rough sex. He would strangle them and then become frenzied with the need to feast on their breasts.

There were a number of similar killers at large during this time around the world who would not be caught until years, even decades, later. The sixties proved to be a moment of flux in world culture, a time of upheaval, excess, and paradox. While growth and change took positive directions, there was also a reaction in negative directions. Opportunity undeniably bred progress, but it also sparked danger—and the violence of the sixties was soon to multiply. As college campuses in the U.S. erupted in hostility over the escalating war in Vietnam, the Students for a Democratic Society (SDS), with over one hundred thousand student members, yielded to a revolutionary group called the Weathermen. They advised the government that they would be planting bombs in public buildings to protest the Vietnam War; these would represent the first acts of organized terrorism on American soil. They declared war and claimed that the U.S. was murdering millions of people. During the October 1969 "Days of Rage," in which three hundred students rampaged down a street in a wealthy Chicago neighborhood to protest the trial of the Chicago Seven, President Nixon referred to them as "thugs" and "hoodlums."

As the last notes of the peace-loving Woodstock performances from 1969 transformed into the violence at the Rolling Stones' San Francisco–based Altamont concert, with the Hell's Angels beating a black man to death in front of the stage, *Life* magazine ran shocking photos of the 1968 My Lai massacre of women, children, and old men by American troops in a village in Vietnam. The Weathermen exploited this atrocity to cultivate what they hoped would be critical mass movement toward a significant social conversion into something more humane. Believing this could only be achieved through violence, they planted bombs at the Capitol, Pentagon, and other government buildings. The sixties were definitely over, but the seventies would be another era of enormous cultural stress, from the fall of a presidency to recession to a failure of the American vision on an international scale.

With social unrest, increased mobility, and unprepared law enforcement, it grew easier for skilled predators to pick off the vulnerable. At the same time, a few agents at the FBI pondered a radical new approach.

CHAPTER ELEVEN

The Profilers Respond

Keeping Up

Just as the sixties ended with California seemingly a center for multiple murder, so the seventies began with similar incidents in several parts of the world before descending again dead center on California. The rate of stranger homicides picked up dramatically, as if keeping pace with a prickly mood that issued forth in more campus violence, political dissension, and public disillusionment. America's Age of Innocence was truly over. So were the days of the sporadic multiple murderer. There would now be regular incidents, and many offenders teamed up.

The Los Angeles police learned about the six-year crime spree of Mack Ray Edwards when he brought in a loaded gun in 1970 and said he felt guilty. Since the 1950s, he told them, he had murdered half a dozen children, all of whom had in fact disappeared. To prove it, he showed police two graves. He was convicted and sentenced to death, but when he could not short-circuit the appeals process he hanged himself in his cell.

Not so remorseful was "toxicomaniac" Graham Frederick Young, an Englishman infatuated with poisons. Since the age of eleven, he'd been obsessed with gaining power over others through chemical substances. He killed his stepmother with antimony when he was fourteen, which earned him nine years in an asylum. Emerging "cured," he found employment that put him close to thallium, with which he then experimented on people. When two died, he exhibited so much knowledge of their conditions that he was arrested and convicted of their murders. It was clear from a list he'd made that he had targeted many others.

In Japan, Kau Kobayashi went to the gallows for three murders that she had plotted and perpetrated during the previous two decades. Her plan was nearly ingenious. She would get a lover involved and mastermind a plot to end another person's life via poisoning, strangling, or stabbing. In 1952, her husband was her and her lover's first victim. Eight years later she and another lover plotted the death of that man's wife, and for this they paid a homeless man in money and sexual favors. The homeless man became Kobayashi's new lover, and together they killed the second lover and coconspirator. It wasn't long before she found yet another accomplice to help her dispatch the third guy, but before they could accomplish this, they were arrested.

In Holland, when Sjef Rijke's third wife left him she

saved her life and brought his career as a series murderer to an end. His first two wives had died, and when his girlfriend began to suffer severe stomach pains, the by-then-estranged wife told police enough to get the man arrested. He confessed that he took great pleasure in watching women suffer. He didn't mean to kill them, he insisted; he just wanted them to get terribly ill.

Americans witnessed the highest known murder count yet by one person. In Yuba City, California, in 1970, two bodies were discovered hacked up and buried on a ranch, one of them sexually assaulted. This launched an intensive two-week investigation into two orchards near Yuba City that turned up the fresh graves of twenty-five men, all of them migrant workers. They had been stabbed or shot and their heads had been badly mutilated with what seemed like a machete. Labor contractor Juan Corona, who was considered a solid family man, was convicted on evidence that included an apparent ledger of victims, a machete found in his home, and witnesses who placed him with some of the victims. There were also blood-stains in his car, and he had a history of mental illness. In two separate trials, he was convicted both times of more murder counts than anyone in America to date.

While these bodies were being uncovered, the Vietnam War spread to Laos and Cambodia. But the country's focus then shifted to a strange incident in Washington, D.C. In 1972, a group of burglars broke into the Demo-cratic campaign headquarters at the Watergate hotel complex. Democrats believed that the Republicans were behind it, though President Nixon denied it. Despite his reassurance, taped conversations revealed that he knew about the burglary, which had been planned by members of the committee to reelect him. Even as he insisted he was "not a crook," he felt pressured, and resigned in 1973. Many other government officials were convicted in the conspiracy.

At the same time, things were shifting in the FBI in a manner that would have a dramatic effect on investigations. Back in 1935, Hoover had set up the FBI Training Academy in Washington, D.C., and it eventually spread onto the marine base at Quantico, Virginia. As murder rates had risen during the 1950s and 1960s, the FBI had received expanded jurisdiction. The Ten Most Wanted program and the National Crime Information Center had provided better focus, but over the decades the Bureau had noticed that more criminals were committing repeat violent offenses and realized it needed a more radical approach to investigations. At the Academy, a handful of agents wanted to introduce ideas from psychology and sociology. Law enforcement to that point had distrusted these disciplines, believing that mental health professionals forged "excuses" for murder, but it knew that the field also had good insights gleaned from research and experience to offer.

Special Agent Howard Teten met with psychiatrist James Brussel, who had accurately profiled the Mad Bomber in New York, and learned his method for analyzing unknown offenders based on behavioral manifestations at a crime scene, especially when there was evidence of an aberrant mental disorder. Teten introduced the method into his course at Quantico in psychopathology, and with Special Agent Patrick Mullany, who held an advanced degree in psychology, Teten refined the approach for law enforcement. Eventually, word spread about his analysis of specific crimes, and he found himself in demand, so he trained other agents to become crime consultants. That was the start of the Behavioral Science Unit (BSU), now known as the Behavioral Analysis Unit.

The BSU was initially formed with eleven agents, and Jack Kirsch was its first official chief. While the agents offered advice to local law enforcement on different types of crimes, pattern violence quickly became their forte. The unit's approach was intended as a teaching program for agents and police officers, but it expanded to field agents, developing an identity as the Crime Analysis and Criminal Personality Profiling Program. The idea was to use rational means against an irrational foe, to show people that they could feel safe once these killers were figured out. The public was reassured that experts were working hard to delete such dangers from their midst—and just in time, as many more offenders were killing randomly, aggressively, and repetitively.

Killers Across America

For three years in a row in Rochester, New York, young girls whose first and last names began with the same initials were raped and murdered. The first was Carmen Colon, eleven, in 1971. Then came Wanda Walkowicz and Michelle Maenza. Several hundred suspects were questioned, but no one was ever arrested for the "Alphabet Murders." A suspect whose car was identified near one crime scene was to figure later in the decade as one of the most notorious serial killers to date. But by that time, Kenneth Bianchi, a member of the team that would be known as the Hillside Stranglers, had moved to Los Angeles. Whether he may have been involved in the Alphabet Murders has never been established.

But even in the early seventies, California was already commanding headlines. Santa Cruz, California, had become a hub of homicidal activity. Near the end of 1970, John Linley Frazier murdered five people—the Ohta family and a secretary—to defy the spread of progress that he said was ruining the environment. An extremist in the hippie lifestyle, he was diagnosed with paranoid schizophrenia but nevertheless convicted.

Then in 1972, across a period of four months, another series of murders centered on Santa Cruz. Among the victims were a priest, four campers, a man digging in his garden, a girl, and a mother and her two sons. The police finally arrested Herbert Mullen, twenty-five, who had just completed his goal of thirteen "sacrifices." He had been institutionalized and evaluated as a danger to others, but had become an outpatient. Down on his luck, he stopped taking his medication and heard a voice urging him to kill someone. In order to save people in California from earthquakes, it was time to "sing the die song," which he believed would persuade people to either kill themselves or allow themselves to become human sacrifices (which he said they communicated to him telepathically). Using a knife, gun, or baseball bat to slay those he selected for the cause, he killed without remorse again and again until the police picked him up. Diagnosed with paranoid schizophrenia, he was nevertheless considered legally sane and was convicted on ten counts of murder.

But it was the next arrested murderer in Santa Cruz whose case really shocked people. The juvenile court system had long been based on the idea that wayward children could be rehabilitated. So when a boy named Edmund Kemper shot his grandparents to death at the age of fifteen, he was placed into that system, where he had only to stay in a secure training school until he was twenty-one. He was then freed with a clear record in 1969. It was not long before Kemper killed again.

He picked up hitchhiking coeds and killed six of them, sometimes two at a time. Then he shoved them into the trunk of his car to take home. At his apartment or his mother's house, Kemper brought the bodies inside to behead and dismember. He later admitted that he also had sex with the parts. After killing six young women, the six-foot-nine giant murdered his mother and her best friend, and then fled to Colorado, where he called the police to turn himself in. The police went to his home and found his mother's decapitated body in a closet, battered and used for dart practice. Her tongue and larynx were chopped up beside the garbage disposal. Her friend was there as well, beheaded and stuffed into a closet. Although Kemper hoped to receive the death penalty and even tried killing himself, he was convicted during a time when the

Supreme Court had placed a moratorium on capital punishment and all death sentences were commuted to life. He had admitted to cannibalism but recanted that later, claiming his statements were intended as part of an insanity defense.

Another phone call to police, this one in Texas on August 8, 1972, alerted law enforcement to another killer—or actually, three of them. Seventeen-year-old Elmer Wayne Henley told officials he had just killed Dean Corll, thirty-three, known locally as the "Candy Man." As Henley showed the police one buried boy after another, he implicated David Brooks in the scheme to lure victims to a boathouse, where Corll tortured, raped, and murdered them. Sometimes, Henley added, Corll even chewed off their genitals or castrated them. Henley claimed that he had shot Corll in "self-defense." By the time the exhumations and confessions were over, the Texas trio had broken Juan Corona's record, with twenty-seven victims. Brooks and Henley both received life sentences.

A gang of five, known as the "McCrary Family," rampaged from Florida to California, grabbing young women from stores to rape and shoot them, after which they dumped them from the car. They were stopped during a shoot-out with the police and convicted of ten of twenty-two cross-country murders in which they were suspects.

Gerard Schaefer was convicted around that time of a 1972 double homicide of two teenage girls in Florida, although he was actually suspected in thirty-four murders. Not content with that paltry sum, he confessed in several separate letters to having killed between 80 and

110 over a period of eight years, but later recanted. Years later, he published a collection of "fiction" that detailed crimes suspected by police to have been memories rather than his imagination.

Also during the early 1970s, on the otherwise tranquil island of Bermuda, two black men shot and killed Police Commissioner George Duckett after luring him to the back door of his home. They also wounded his daughter, who'd run to help him. The next incident was a double murder of even greater proportions. On March 10, 1973, the island's governor, Sir Richard Sharples, and his captain, Hugh Sayers, were shot on the terrace of Government House. Sir Richard's dog was also shot and killed. Two black men were seen running from the area. Then, on April 6, Mark Doe and Victor Rego were bound in their supermarket and shot with a .32 revolver, although .22 bullets found at the scene linked this incident with the previous shootings. Two black men were seen leaving this scene as well, and a witness identified Larry Tacklyn. Police arrested him, but his partner went on to rob the Bank of Bermuda. Then Erskine Burrows, the bank robber, was arrested, and officials felt they had their killing team. Burrows was found guilty on all charges, but Tacklyn was convicted only of the shopkeeper murders. Both were hanged.

Another team, who chanced to meet while drifting aimlessly around the country, were Doug Gretzler, twenty-two, and William Luther Steelman, twenty-eight. Steelman had once been committed to a mental institution, and his encounter with Gretzler set the stage for a

spree unlike any the American Southwest had seen before. It started on October 28, 1973, when they entered
a house trailer in Mesa, Arizona, and shot to death the
adolescent couple who lived there. Then they went to
Tucson and killed a young man, leaving his body in the
desert before returning to Tucson to murder another
couple in their apartment. As they drove from there into
the desert, they killed a man in a sleeping bag. In Phoenix, they grabbed two more young men, then stripped
and killed them, leaving their bodies in California.

Arizona authorities knew who they were looking for
and quickly issued warrants. On November 6, this spree-
killing team hit again, but this time with nine victims all
at once. They had gone to a house where an eighteen-
year-old girl was babysitting Walter and Joanne Parkin's
two children. The sitter's parents had dropped by, along
with her brother and fiancé, and then the Parkins came
home. The killers shot them all, leaving the Parkin couple in their bed and stuffing the rest of the bodies into
a closet. Collectively, these nine people had been shot
twenty-five times.

Two days later, the killers were apprehended at a motel.
Gretzler cracked, describing where all the bodies had
been left. Convicted in trials in two states, they were sentenced to die in Arizona. Steelman died in prison, while
Gretzler was executed in 1998.

Back East, young black boys in Harlem were being
murdered. All had been mutilated, and the penises had
been removed from four and sliced open on one, who
had also been stabbed thirty-eight times. Erno Soto con-

fessed and said that God had wanted him to make boys into girls, but controversy about his mental state surrounded his confession, so the "Charlie Chop-off" murders may not have actually ever been solved. Soto was committed to a mental institution.

Not far away, elderly women were being sexually assaulted and stabbed to death at the Park Plaza Hotel. A man seen carrying a television was arrested. It turned out that Calvin Jackson, a convicted burglar, had killed nine women to steal from them. To try to prove insanity, his attorney told the court that after each murder, he would make a sandwich and watch his victim for up to an hour to ensure that she was dead. He received eighteen life sentences.

Back in California, a group of black males seeking initiation into the "Death Angels" randomly killed as many as fourteen white people and wounded eight others over a period of six months. One might have believed that this was Manson's prophesied "Helter Skelter," and the police believed that more than a hundred murders were associated with this frightening cult. The public was panicking over the "Zebra Killings." One man, Anthony Harris, finally confessed and turned in several of his alleged fellow killers. The shocking trial lasted over a year, and Manuel Moore, Larry Green, Jesse Cooks, and J. C. Simon were convicted. Five were arrested later but freed for lack of evidence.

By that time, the U.S. had admitted defeat in Vietnam and was withdrawing troops. They returned without fanfare, as people still remembered how the National Guard had shot into a crowd of protesting students in May 1972 at Kent State University, killing four. The entire agenda overseas now seemed a costly mistake, and coupled with the Watergate fiasco, citizens were viewing politics with a jaundiced eye. On the home front, people were seeking spiritual growth through encounter groups, sexual liberation, and pharmaceutical experimentation. To many, the inner world seemed one's best bet.

But there was no way to hide from the increased violence. Throughout the early seventies, there was a rash of unsolved pattern killings. In 1971, ten gay men were stabbed in their homes in Washington, D.C., just as gay men around the country were demanding their rights, and within the next four years, there were seven such murders in New York City. Four women were murdered in San Francisco between May and June 1973. "The Babysitter" killed half a dozen children in Michigan, where twenty prostitutes had also been murdered in 1973, and in northern California, fourteen females between the ages of twelve and twenty-two were killed.

In 1974, the FBI went hunting for a man who appeared to be leaving a string of murders across the country. The suspect was Paul John Knowles, released from prison in Florida thanks to the efforts of the attorney of one of Knowles's female correspondents—now his fiancée. Soon after his release, they met for the first time in San Francisco, but she felt skittish about him and broke off the engagement. This so enraged him that he went out (he said later), selected three people at random, and slaughtered them. During the next month, in Florida, three more people died, and over the next few weeks, he murdered five. From Connecticut to Georgia, he continued to kill, sometimes robbing victims along the way. One man he bound and stabbed repeatedly with scissors. He also enjoyed wearing his victims' clothing or driving their cars afterward, as if absorbing their lives. He met a British journalist, Sandy Fawkes, hinting to her what he had done and telling her he would be dead within a year. He killed two more people before he was finally captured. For posterity, it seems, or in the hope that the journalist would write about him (she did), he gave his attorney a taped confession of his crimes. Attempting escape in Georgia during a prison transfer, the good-looking "Casanova Killer" grabbed for a gun and was shot dead by law enforcement officers. He claimed to have killed thirty-five people, but "only" eighteen murders, committed over four months, are officially attributed to him.

Pressure Building

An energy crisis loomed, and as the failed war in Vietnam ended, American atrocities in Cambodia came to light. The voices from the sixties channeled society's repressed anger, erupting in diverse collective demands for greater freedom. One was the Women's Liberation Movement, placing more power into the hands of women, and another was the removal of bans from pornography, encouraging its publication and widespread distribution. The sexual revolution had inspired people to pursue pleasure in whatever manner they wanted, and many sought to explore the forbidden. Sexual imagery became increasingly explicit in novels and film, and even the depictions of death-drenched orgies by the Marquis de Sade enjoyed some popularity. The easy availability of erotic materials that treated women as sexual—even expendable—objects influenced the types of violence that arose. In fact, many serial murders appeared to be scripted by S&M literature.

BSU agents made such murders a special area of study, coming to understand just how often they were driven by violent fantasy. The first-generation BSU agents seemed to have a knack for behavioral analysis, and as they went out to local jurisdictions to teach, they helped to solve many puzzling cases. Among these was one in Montana in 1973–74. The kidnapping of a seven-year-old girl yielded a viable suspect, David Meirhofer. Yet he was well-groomed, courteous, and educated, and had passed a polygraph. Although they eventually got him for killing a young woman in the area, he would not confess to the girl's murder. The local police who had consulted the profilers were ready to pass on him, but the BSU team remained convinced that Meirhofer was the man they were after. He finally confessed to having killed a child whom he'd imprisoned for a period of time, and added the murder of two boys, before committing suicide.

Despite the emphasis in crime fiction and film on thuggish villains, it was becoming clear that handsome, articulate men with charm could be deadly as well. Some were even married, had families, and held down jobs. Popular culture clung to Lombrosian ideas, but people were more vulnerable than they realized to the random stranger killer who resembled them. At the same time, psychologists were refining the idea of a psychopath. Since the word had lost its value, thanks in part to the generic slang, "psycho," professionals had gone through various labels for this disorder, from "sociopath" to "antisocial personality disorder" (APD), which was defined by a set of behaviors that emphasized the violation of social norms. However, this psychiatric label fell short of Hervey Cleckley's concept of psychopathy from 1941, and many researchers were dissatisfied. Dr. Robert Hare, a leader in this area, determined that in forensic populations, diagnoses of APD had little utility for treatment outcome, institutional adjustment, or predictions of postrelease behavior.

So Hare and his associates clarified a new set of diagnostic criteria, based on Cleckley's work, for *The Psychopathy Checklist (PCL)*. Hare listed twenty-two items (twenty in the revised *PCL-R*) to be evaluated by clinicians working with potential psychopaths, and including both personality traits and antisocial behaviors. He defined psychopathy as a disorder characterized by such traits as lack of remorse or empathy, shallow emotions, deception, egocentricity, glibness, low frustration tolerance, episodic relationships, parasitic lifestyle, and the persistent violation of social norms.

Around the same time in 1976, psychiatrist Donald Lunde published *Murder and Madness,* based on cases in California in which he had been involved for assessment, analysis, and court appearances. Lunde made a distinction between mass murder and what he referred to as serial killing. A mass murderer, he said, was like John Linley Frazier, who killed a number of people in a single incident, while serial murder referred to "a number of murders by a single person over a period of months, or occasionally, years." Each murder was a discrete episode, such as the manner in which Edmund Kemper had operated, and there was usually a common motive, method, or victim type. Within a couple of years, the FBI would be using the term "serial killer" to describe a pattern killer.

Thus did America have its hands full during this decade. But other areas of the world had cases of repeat predators as well. A night watchman in Hamburg, Germany, named Fritz Honka was revealed as a killer in 1975 when a blaze forced firemen to make a hole in his apartment and they found the odiferous, dismembered remains of four missing women. One was mummified and two were mere torsos, while the forth was cut into parts that had been placed into a pile. Honka was known to choose as companions women with no teeth, the better to facilitate oral sex. Initially, he pretended to have lost his memory—a common ploy for killers during this era—but he finally confessed and was convicted.

In Liverpool, England, police captured Patrick Mackay after a two-year crime frenzy that claimed the lives of eleven people. It was learned that as a fifteen-year-old, he had been committed to an institution as a certified psychopath, "without mania," or compulsive behavior. Five years later, in 1972, against psychiatric advice, he'd been released. A disciple of Nazism, he began to kill people at random, throwing one man from a bridge, stabbing an elderly woman with her grandson, and axing a woman who ran a café. When a priest befriended him, Mackay bludgeoned him with his bare hands, stabbed him, and then finished him off with an ax. The man died touching his own exposed brain, which Mackay reportedly found highly erotic. In all, Mackay took the lives of eleven people over a period of two years. He was captured in 1975, halting his one-man reign of terror. In a prison journal, he wrote that his original diagnosis had been in error: He believed he had psychopathic mania and had been unable to control himself. He'd walked into the world with the best intentions, "but unfortunately one cannot always foresee the certain type of stigmas that can form . . . in such an imperfect world as this."

In 1976, the West German police in Duisburg received a report that a four-year-old girl was missing. An elderly man told them that a tenant in his building had warned him not to use the common toilet because it was clogged with "guts." Indeed, it contained human offal, which turned out to have been removed from the missing girl. That led to the apartment of balding, fortyish Joachim Kroll. In his refrigerator were bags of human flesh, and on the stove they found a child's hand inside a simmering stew. They realized they'd come upon the area murderer, active over the past two decades and known as the "Ruhr Hunter."

Kroll had started to rape and kill in 1955, when he was twenty-two. At one point, on a whim, he'd tasted the flesh of a murdered woman, and had found that he liked it. Thereafter, he'd stalked women or girls who he thought would yield tender meat and left their bodies to be discovered, sans pieces of flesh. His victim count was fourteen, including one male he'd stabbed to death. Kroll believed that the police would order the surgical removal of his need to kill and consume flesh, but instead he was sentenced to life in prison.

After killing a boy in Johannesburg, South Africa, Ronald Frank Cooper was followed by a prior victim who had survived his attack, and was arrested. In his possession police discovered a careful plan to become a serial child murderer. In fact, he had made his first attempt thirteen years earlier, when he was eleven. He aspired to rape and kill young boys, some by stabbing, some by suffocation, some by strangulation. He had determined that he would kill thirty and then shift to girls, but his arrest in 1976 prevented him from making anyone else a victim. The evidence in his diaries helped to convict him.

Back in the USA

While a veterans' hospital in Ann Arbor, Michigan, was experiencing a rash of unsolved murders and Vaughn Greenwood was arrested as the "Skid Row Slasher" in Los Angeles, Donald "Pee Wee" Gaskins was describing 1975 as his "killingest year." His autobiography, *Final Truth*, depicted his life as a tough, pint-size rapist and killer in

South Carolina and along the Southeastern coast. He divided his murders between his anonymous "coastal kills," which helped him to relieve tension, and his slaughter of associates and relatives. Spoiled as a child, with no restrictions or discipline imposed, he soon got a stepfather who beat him, and began acting out against animals and girls. His petty crimes resulted in prison time, which fed his hatred until it felt red-hot. "I have a special kind of mind," he said, "that allows me to give myself permission to kill." He claimed to have had over a hundred victims. The police arrested him on the suspicion of his involvement in five murders, and one of Gaskins's associates led them to the burial site of six bodies, with two others not far away—a woman and baby. Interrogated under the influence of truth serum, Gaskins confessed to thirteen more killings. Then he killed a man in prison, and from that point he began to brag about his other murders—perhaps to prove how tough he was.

Just as brutal was Harvey Louis Carignan, who had avoided the hangman's noose in Alaska in 1949 only to kill again. In 1973 in Washington State, he used a hammer to bludgeon to death Kathy Miller after she answered an ad for employment at his service station. He went to California, where more women turned up dead, and then moved to the Midwest. He assaulted and raped a number of other females, including two girls who were hitchhiking to Minneapolis, and his next murder victim was someone with whom he was romantically involved. When she tried to end the relationship, she disappeared.

Her body was found over a month later, with her skull crushed by a hammer. When several states coordinated their efforts, Carignan was arrested. Among his possessions was a map with 180 locations circled in red, and some were associated with unsolved murders or assaults. Carignan said that he was acting as God's instrument, killing "whores." He was nevertheless convicted on numerous charges from rape to murder.

Philadelphia had the spotlight in 1975 with Joseph Kalinger, who killed one of his sons for insurance money, as well as murdering a woman during a burglary. When caught and convicted, he attempted to prove that he was deranged, asking an author to document his psychotic state of mind and turn it into a best-seller. He too insisted that he was God's instrument, sent to eliminate humankind, but then blamed it all on "Charlie," one of his personalities. It's likely that he was responsible for a third murder as well—a young boy found on a construction site in 1974 and thought to have died by accident. Convicted and sent to prison, Kalinger eventually went to a hospital for the criminally insane.

In the general Chicago area in the early to middle 1970s, Richard Otto Macek, the "Mad Biter," was thought to have killed half a dozen women and girls, leaving teeth marks on several. He also cut slits into the eyelids of one victim. He claimed he could not remember what he had done, yet he had persuaded a dentist to pull out all his teeth, which prevented an odontologist from making an accurate analysis for court. Still, he was sentenced to life for two murders and two attempted murders, and in 1987 he committed suicide.

New York came under siege in 1976 and 1977 from the ".44-Caliber Killer," who randomly shot couples in parked cars. Attacking thirteen people in just over a year, he killed six. He also wrote letters to the newspapers, calling himself the "Son of Sam" and creating an aura of terror throughout the city, because it seemed that he could strike at any time after dark, anywhere in the city, and then just melt away. Two women were shot while sitting on their porches. Special Agent Robert Ressler, from the BSU, said that this case was the first time in America in which the term "serial killer" was used by law enforcement, fashioned from the British term "series killer." After David Berkowitz, twenty-four, was caught for the crimes, thanks to a parking ticket that led police to him, he raised insanity issues by claiming that a neighbor's dog had commanded him to kill. When he tried to sell his story, the city blocked him with what it called the "Son of Sam Law," which prohibited offenders from making money on their crimes. Later he admitted that the dog-and-devil story was a hoax.

In the Los Angeles area, the remains of a dismembered, naked man were discovered off a highway near San Juan Capistrano. Eight more such victims were found over the next two years, and all were similarly cut up and packaged. Those who were identified turned out to have been gay. In 1977, one victim was traced to Patrick Kearny's roommate, who went with Kearny to the police. Kearny took the rap for the "Trash Bag Murders" and claimed to have killed twenty-eight young men because it made him feel dominant. He offered the police evidence from his home and led them to several burial sites. Without resistance, he pled guilty to all charges.

At about this time, Australia discovered a pair of team murderers. James William Miller was arrested for the murders of several women during a seven-week spree, and he insisted he had participated only because he was in love with Christopher Robin Worrell. According to Miller's story, Worrell would have him pick up girls, and after Worrell had sex with them and killed them, he'd make Miller help him dump the bodies. Miller claimed complete innocence in the murders, although it was clear that, at least in most instances, he knew what Worrell planned to do. Seven women died and one was buried alive before Worrell was killed in a car accident. Miller led the police to three of the bodies that had not yet been found, claiming that his love for the man had made him unable to turn Worrell in. Helpless or not, he still got six life sentences.

Canada, too, turned up a serial killer when three women were found assaulted and strangled in their apartments in Ontario in 1977. The police looked up sexual offenders and linked the murders to Russell Johnson, a tenant in the apartment complex where two of the victims were found. Since Johnson had been diagnosed a compulsive sex attacker, he was found not guilty by reason of insanity, but he confessed to four more murders in 1973 and 1974 that had been attributed to natural causes.

Forensic Psychology Gains Ground

By 1977, the BSU had a three-pronged purpose: crime scene analysis, profiling, and analysis of threatening letters. The agents who entered the unit during its "golden age" knew they were pioneering a program that would require a careful introduction to law enforcement agencies. The right personalities came together to produce an important contribution to understanding the most brutal and extreme human behaviors. Unlike technicians, who could unambiguously compare fibers or fingerprints, the profilers were evaluating the indirect results of elusive and sometimes clever minds.

To devise a multidimensional profile, psychological investigators examined such aspects of the crime and crime scene (usually murder but other crimes as well) as the weapon used, the type of killing and body dump sites, details about the victim, the method of transportation, the time of day at which the crime was committed, and the relative position of items at the scene. The basic idea was to acquire a body of information that revealed common patterns for producing a general description of an UNSUB (unknown subject) in terms of habit, possible employment, marital status, mental state, and personality traits.

Special Agents John Douglas and Roy Hazelwood devised a typology based on what they called "organized" and "disorganized homicides." Some cases seemed carefully planned, with awareness of investigative methods, while others were spontaneous and even sloppy, which was often evidence of a specific kind of psychopathology. Profilers also observed whether the offender used a vehicle and whether he or she was criminally sophisticated or appeared to be enslaved to a sexual fantasy. They examined the type of wounds inflicted, the risks an offender took, and his or her method of committing the crime and controlling the victim, and looked for any evidence that the incident might have been staged to look like something else. Many killers left a "signature"—a behavioral manifestation of an individualizing personality quirk, such as positioning the corpse for humiliating exposure or tying ligatures with a complicated knot. This helped to link crime scenes to one another and point toward the types of behavior to look for.

One of the early success stories, in 1978, involved a serial killer dubbed the "Vampire of Sacramento." He had murdered a woman in her home, eviscerating her and drinking her blood. It was so brutal that the FBI was called in, and it gave the profilers a chance to apply their method, at least on paper as a test case. Agents Robert Ressler and Russ Vorpagel developed independent profiles, as did Lieutenant Ray Biondi, the lead investigator. From a psychiatric study of body type and mental temperament that Ressler had read, he thought the offender was scrawny. Given the disorder at the scene, it was likely that the UNSUB had no career and little education—nothing that required organized concentration. Vorpagel's profile was similar, as was Biondi's.

They figured the UNSUB for a disorganized killer, with clues pointing toward the possibility of paranoid psychosis. He clearly had not planned the crime and did little to hide or destroy evidence. He left footprints and fingerprints, and had probably walked away with blood on his clothing. In other words, he gave little thought to consequences. His domicile would be sloppy and his mental capacity was likely limited. That meant he probably did not drive a car, so he would have to live in the vicinity of the crimes. He was white, between twenty-five and twenty-seven, thin, undernourished, lived alone, and probably had evidence that pointed to the crime in his home. He was likely unemployed and the recipient of disability money. All of this was derived from known information that the type of crime they were investigating tended to be intraracial, specific to a certain age range, and committed by someone with a paranoia-based mental illness. From what Ressler knew, it was likely that this offender would kill again. They had to work fast.

Three days after the first murder, the killer struck again, this time slaughtering three people in a home, including a man and child. He grabbed a baby and stole the family car, but then abandoned it. Ressler and Vorpagel were sure he lived close to both scenes, and after a massive manhunt that involved the media, profiles, and neighborhood canvassing, the police found Richard Trenton Chase, twenty-seven, living less than a block from the abandoned car. His appearance was just as anticipated and he suffered from paranoid delusions. Body parts, empty pet collars, and a bloodstained food blender were found in his apartment. He lived alone, was unemployed, and had a history of psychiatric incarceration. He had been released only months before he began to kill. His arrest stopped a string of murders that apparently, from marks on his calendar, was to include some forty-four more victims that year alone.

Vorpagel faced this man in the interrogation room, and Chase admitted he had committed the murders, but added that he had done nothing wrong. He was saving his own life, because his blood was "turning to sand" and he needed someone else's to prevent that. Talking to someone like Chase helped to confirm the profile, and it was cases such as this that gave Ressler an idea.

While on the road teaching local police jurisdictions this method of behavioral analysis, Ressler decided it would be productive to visit some of the prisons they were near to gain access to dangerous criminals. Although they were profiling unknown offenders, they could actually talk to known offenders to learn more about their motives and their crimes. If the BSU could devise a consistent protocol of questions to ask, and could get detailed responses, they could start a database of information about traits and behaviors that these men shared in common.

Initially, they contacted different types of offenders, from mass murderers to assassins to serial killers, and also collected data on 118 victims, including some who had survived an attempted murder. Finally the team devised a questioning routine that covered the most significant aspects of the offenses. The goal was to gather information about how the murders were planned and committed, what the killers did and thought about afterward, what fantasies they had, and what they did before the next incident.

Criminals willing to talk included Edmund Kemper, the Coed Killer of San Jose; Jerry Brudos, the Oregon killer with a shoe fetish; and Richard Speck, who had slaughtered eight nurses in Chicago. Other offenders who were not killers were interviewed as well, such as Gary Trapnell, who had hijacked airplanes and committed armed robbery, but the database was primarily for gathering information about serial murder.

The initial study, meant to include one hundred convicted offenders, compiled data from only thirty-six. But when all was said and done, the researchers had gained statistical information that proved highly useful for developing profiles. A third of the offenders were white, nearly half had a parent missing from the home growing up (usually the father), three-fourths reported having had a cold or negligent parent, a majority had a psychiatric history as well as a history of unsteady employment, the mean IQ was bright normal, three-fourths had sexual fetishes, and the same percentage reported enduring some form of physical or psychological abuse.

The development of the BSU, with its initial database, came just in time for the tsunami of serial crime that would hit the country over the next decade. Other countries would take note, giving the FBI's specialized serial killer experts an international reputation.

CHAPTER TWELVE

Creative Derangement

Forensic Advances

The gas chromatograph-mass spectrometer (GC-MS) was first evaluated in the U.K. for forensic use in 1976. Chromatography is a method by which compounds can be separated into their purest elements, as inert gas propels a heated substance through a glass tube where a detector charts each element's unique speed for a composite profile. The mass spectrometer, linked to it, then affirms the identifications via patterns of spectra. With this equipment, forensic scientists could analyze such items as hair samples for drugs or poison, charred remains for accelerants, and the composition of explosives.

The following year, 1977, Fuseo Matsumur at the Saga Prefectural Crime Laboratory at the National Police Agency of Japan observed his fingerprint on a glass slide and mentioned it to colleague Masato Soba. A few months later, Soba developed latent prints on smooth surfaces with superglue fuming. (A story is also told of how a British police officer, repairing a broken tank, discovered several fingerprints illuminated on its side. He then tried the glue in other areas, with success, and scientists realized that superglue fumes adhere to amino acids.)

In England, Bob Freeman and Doug Foster invented the electrostatic detection apparatus. The device was initially intended for detecting fingerprints on paper, but indentations from writing corrupted the readings. Then the duo realized that the invention could be used for document analysis. This involved placing a sheet of writing-indented paper over a glass plate and under a sheet of Mylar. This was then placed on a machine with a brass plate and a lid charged with high voltage. A fine electrostatic substance was sprinkled onto the paper, and those particles moved toward the brass plate, filling in the paper's indentations to reveal a clear presentation of the handwriting, which could then be photographed.

But perhaps the most unique idea of that time was proposed by Dr. William Bass III, a forensic anthropologist at the University of Tennessee at Knoxville. Called by law enforcement into numerous cases, he realized during a 1977 investigation of a set of bones that were difficult to accurately analyze that someone needed to do a scientific study of human remains under a variety of conditions and time periods. Persuading his university to give him a three-acre parcel of land for the project, in 1980 he broke ground for the Anthropology Research Facility. It would eventually be dubbed the Body Farm.

Bass laid out the first body, an unclaimed cadaver, in 1981. As with others that would follow, the conditions for its decomposition were meticulously documented. Corpses were placed in open air, water, shallow graves, buildings, and cars. As they lay out, they provided information about what happens to decomposing bodies under different conditions. The researchers expanded in number and specialization, and the Body Farm became a center for training and consultation in difficult cases.

Malignant Narcissism

On November 18, 1978, members of the Peoples' Temple at Jonestown in Guyana, South America, killed Congressman Leo Ryan and his fact-finding party at an airstrip. That deed signaled an end to the Utopian experiment called Jonestown. Jim Jones had led a thousand disciples to this area, promising peace but warning of persecution. To prepare for that, he had trained them for the "White Night"—a mass suicide. The congressman's visit was the trigger, and his murder was immediately followed by the deaths of the residents of Jonestown. When it was over, there were 909 corpses of men, women, and children, black and white, lying in rows or atop one another.

The end of the seventies, highlighted by this spectacular event, appeared to signal not only a surge in religious ideologies threaded with death but also increasingly strange and brutal stories of serial murder. While the Skid Row Stabber (not to be confused with the Skid Row

Slasher a few years earlier), killer of eleven men in Los Angeles, was identified from a palm print as Bobby Joe Maxwell (later linked to a cabdriver murder in New York), two different but strangely linked series of murders in 1977 and 1978 occurred simultaneously in Columbus, Georgia. It began with the rape and murder by strangulation of seven elderly women by a man dubbed the "Stocking Strangler." From witness reports, there was reason to suspect that the perpetrator was black.

About a month after the seventh murder, in March 1978, the chief of police received a strange handwritten letter on military stationery from the "Chairman of the Forces of Evil," who said he represented a group of white men. He then made a dire threat: They intended to kill black women on a regular schedule until the Stocking Strangler case was resolved. They had already abducted the first victim, he said, but the police could purchase her release with $10,000. The letter set a June 1 deadline. BSU Special Agent Robert Ressler was convinced a black soldier had written the letter and had already killed the hostage. And indeed, her body was found before the deadline, decomposed and badly mutilated—killed before the letter was written.

Thanks to an anonymous phone call, another black woman was found bludgeoned and decomposing in a shallow grave near a barracks at Fort Benning. An investigation turned up a description of a man seen with this woman, a black soldier named William Henry Hance. Allegedly, he had been a pimp for both victims. An army Criminal Investigation Department officer listened to tapes of the calls and recognized Hance's voice. He was arrested and confessed to both crimes, adding a third from the year before, a white woman. He was convicted of all three murders and given a death sentence.

Not long afterward, the police identified Carlton Gary, a black man seen jogging in the neighborhood of one victim, as the Stocking Strangler. Once convicted of rape in New York, he was eventually captured and convicted of the seven murders.

But the most spectacular arrest of 1978 occurred in Florida. It spelled the end to a long string of suspected murders by a nomadic serial killer who had twice escaped prison and had traveled to Florida from as far away as the West Coast. The murders had first been noticed in 1974 in the Pacific Northwest, when a number of attractive young women went missing in quick succession around Seattle and Olympia, Washington, and then from Oregon. By the time two women disappeared from Lake Sammamish on the same summer day, there were already half a dozen such reports in other places. Witnesses offered descriptions for a drawing of a man named "Ted" who had driven a tan Volkswagen Beetle. Several months later, the remains of the two Lake Sammamish women were found. But then no more murders occurred in the area.

In Utah, four women were missing, and when their bodies were found, one had been bludgeoned so badly about the face it was difficult to identify her. Then there were four victims in Colorado, but a woman named Carol Da Ronch had survived an assault to finger Theodore

Robert Bundy, a former law student from Washington State. The police picked him up. While he was in prison, investigators considered his possible link to the missing girls from the other states. Colorado prepared to try him for the murder of Caryn Campbell, but he escaped. Caught, he ran again, landing in Tallahassee, Florida.

On January 15, 1978, Lisa Levy and Martha Bowman were raped and clubbed to death one night in their sorority house at Florida State University, after which a witness had seen the perpetrator fleeing. Less than a month later, twelve-year-old Kimberly Leach disappeared from her schoolyard and was discovered in the woods, murdered. The police arrested a man driving a stolen Volkswagen and before long realized they had Ted Bundy in their jail. In fact, he began to brag about his notoriety.

He went through two trials, identified by both the sorority house witness and the bite mark he had left on one of the victims. The impression was a match to a dental impression of Bundy's teeth. He attempted to defend himself but inadvertently admitted to his involvement with self-incriminatingly phrased questions. Found guilty, he was also tried and convicted for the murder of Kimberly Leach. Once Bundy had been sentenced to death three times, he confessed to thirty murders in six separate states, dating back to May 1973, although experts believe there were more. Bundy described his sexual compulsions, claiming that the violence was inspired by the need to possess his victims totally, especially after death. Theories were spun that he had picked dark-haired women who parted their hair in the middle (a common fashion those days) because he was once spurned by a woman with a similar appearance. Thanks in part to that, a myth arose that serial predators invariably attack victims of similar appearance.

Bundy had lured women with his good looks and charm, and with an added touch of feigned neediness. He said of himself that during these encounters some malignant portion of his personality took over. By all accounts, he looked and acted normal. Yet as he said to his mother just before his 1989 execution, "Part of me was hidden all the time." Many experts referred to the work of Robert Louis Stevenson to try to understand his Jekyll/Hyde transition.

Bundy bargained with law enforcement to keep him alive for "study" and then for clearing up more murders not yet assigned to him. They declined, but through him criminologists did learn about the way such killers can compartmentalize different facets of their personality. Bundy was a remorseless psychopath, and his articulate confessions spurred experts to develop better ways to assess such people. He had been a suspect in Washington State, but he had been considered too decent and likable to be seriously considered, so no one had followed through on his arrest. If ever a man defied Lombrosian thinking, he was it.

While in prison, Bundy received an abundance of fan mail from adoring women. Then, during the proceedings, girls crowded into the front rows of the courtroom to show their support. Many adopted the appearance of his supposed victim type, and a former acquaintance, Carole

Ann Boone, became his steady girlfriend. During the penalty phase of his final trial in 1980, she testified as a way to make it possible for him to legally marry her. In court, they mutually declared their desire to marry and, based on an archaic law and the presence of a notary public, were legally bound. Boone even bore him a child

In part due to Bundy's appeal, serial killers became more interesting to the media and the public. Journalists were quick to exploit the fear that people who seemed normal, even sociable, could be deadly predators. The FBI contributed its share to this growing unease by releasing inflated figures about the number of serial killers operating at any given time around the country.

Bundy met other serial killers as well. One report says that he used to steal cookies from Arthur Frederick Goode, a nearly retarded man who had killed several young boys. Jimmy Rode was in the same prison as Bundy and guards saw Rode attempting to strike up conversations with him. At one point, Bundy slipped him a newspaper from Washington, with personal ads circled, and Rode used one of them to start up a correspondence from his cell. When he later got out of prison during the 1980s, he went to the Pacific Northwest, leaving a trail of victims, raped, molested, and sometimes murdered. Many were elderly women. Rode, alias Cesar Barone, was convicted of four murders and given the death penalty.

Even before Bundy got through his two trials, a killer in Des Plaines, Illinois, near Chicago, shocked the world with his own manner of luring and controlling his victims—but even more so with what he did afterward.

Near the end of 1978, Chicago police watched a man they believed had abducted a missing boy and quickly learned that prominent businessman John Wayne Gacy had secrets to hide: While he played as a clown for children in the hospital, he was associated with numerous reports of missing boys and young men, many of whom he had hired for his construction company.

As he eluded police, one officer entered his home and smelled decomposition. Soon forensic investigators were exploring the crawl space beneath Gacy's house and finding human remains—lots of them. The final victim toll on the property was twenty-eight, but Gacy confessed to having thrown the corpses of five more young men in the Des Plaines River. He had picked the men up, taken them home, tricked them into allowing themselves to be handcuffed, and then raped and strangled them.

Gacy offered an insanity defense, claiming that he had blacked out before each killing and that an alter ego named Jack Handy had then done the deed. But his ability to draw an accurate map of where he had placed each body and his preparation for some of his fatal encounters convinced the jury that, contrary to his defense, he had hardly suffered from an irresistible impulse on each of these thirty-three separate occasions. Gacy was convicted and sentenced to death.

At the same time that Gacy was being investigated, on New Year's Eve in 1978, train conductor William Gulak, flagman Robert Blake, and fireman Charles Burton were all shot to death while waiting in a depot in Jackson, Michigan. Two years earlier, an engineer had been shot to death in Indiana, and eight years before that, in the same train yard, another engineer was shot. All were thought to be linked to the "Railway Sniper," as were a pair of 1963 murders in which two men were shot in the cab of a freight train. Police tracked down James Bladel, an ex-employee of the rail line who had been laid off in 1959, when operations were relocated to the Indiana site where two of the victims had died. But a trial was able to prove only that Bladel had wounded a fellow rail man, for which he was imprisoned. Then hikers found the buried rifle, which proved through ballistics comparisons to be the weapon used in the New Year's Eve shootings. It was traced to Bladel, who confessed and then recanted, but was convicted of the final three murders.

Also in 1978, three people were shot multiple times in their homes in Columbus, Ohio, with a .22 rifle. Ballistics tests implicated the same gun in four more shootings (including victims' pets), and then the police matched it to bullets found in Newark, Ohio, the year before in two women who were shot while leaving work and then left to freeze to death in a snowbank. Another man was shot before Gary Lewington was finally arrested, for credit card fraud. Since he possessed items that belonged to one of the victims, he was interrogated, and while he admitted his part in the killings he claimed that his brother Thaddeus had initiated them. Thaddeus was arrested, and he made a full confession but implicated Gary as the trigger-happy one. Both were convicted of multiple counts of first-degree murder and given multiple life sentences.

Overseas

A con man and burglar engaged in a series of predatory murders in Scotland and London between 1975 and 1978. Archibald Hall had posed as a butler to Lady Margaret Hudson, but the entrance of a former lover of his, David Wright, foiled his plans when Wright stole a diamond ring from her. For that Wright received a fatal shot in the head. With a partner, Hall bludgeoned another employer and smothered the man's wife. Hall then battered a girlfriend to death with a poker and drowned his half brother in a tub. The "Mad Butler" received two life sentences. His motive in each murder, save one, had been to conceal his crimes; his half brother he had simply disliked.

In Yugoslavia over the course of two years, young girls began to disappear from the village of Dolenja Vas. After the third one went missing, the frightened population wondered if a vampire was visiting them. Then two neighboring villages reported a missing girl each, bringing the total to five. When a tourist reported an assault to police, the description sounded like Metod Torinus, a farmer. Checking in his oven, they found charred human remains, identified as female. Dental work helped to match the remains to some of the missing girls, and Torinus broke down and confessed to torturing, raping, and strangling them. It was his only means, he said, for achieving sexual gratification. Within four days of his conviction, he was executed.

Shortly thereafter, Kampatimar Shankariya was arrested in India and convicted of killing as many as seventy people with a hammer, which he said in his confession had brought him great pleasure. He was hanged.

But the majority of pattern predators during the next decade crept around in the U.S.

Becoming an Item

Robert Joseph Zani murdered six people in Texas, Oklahoma, and Mexico, including his mother and real estate agents, while a spate of murders began in Los Angeles during the fall of 1977 with a nineteen-year-old girl. The first three victims were prostitutes who were dumped naked by the roadside. After nine murders, they stopped abruptly. The police waited through the holidays, and then on February 17, 1978, a highway helicopter patrol spotted an orange car crashed off a highway. Locked inside the trunk was victim number ten: Cindy Hudspeth, twenty.

Almost a year later, in Bellingham, Washington, college roommates Diane Wilder and Karen Mandic were reported missing. On January 12, 1979, a security officer said that one of them had indicated they were going to do a security job for Ken Bianchi, a good-looking man with a girlfriend and infant son who was a captain at the company. The girls were found, murdered, and the evidence against Bianchi was good enough for an arrest. It didn't take long to connect him with his cousin, Angelo Buono, who ran a car upholstery shop in Los Angeles near many of the body dump sites there.

Bianchi's attorney hired psychiatrist Dr. John Watkins to examine him. Watkins hypnotized Bianchi, got him to admit to several of the murders, and then declared that he had multiple personality disorder (MPD). This was a first in such legal proceedings, despite the fictional interpretations of Ed Gein more than two decades earlier of someone suffering from MPD. But Bianchi had studied psychology and read *Sybil,* a 1976 best-seller about a woman with sixteen personalities. Supposedly, Bianchi had killed as "Steve Walker" and thus was not competent to stand trial. His role-playing convinced three more experts, but the prosecution's psychiatrist tricked him into admitting his fakery. To avoid a death penalty for himself, he agreed to turn state's evidence in his cousin's trial. On Halloween 1983, a jury convicted Buono of nine of the ten murders and gave him nine life sentences. Bianchi, who had pled guilty to five of the murders, was given five life sentences on top of the two he had in Washington.

During the trial there was an interesting twist. Buono's defense attorney had brought playwright Veronica Lynn Compton to the stand, and she testified that she had conspired with Bianchi to kill women in the manner of the Hillside Stranglers so as to bring reasonable doubt to his case: If he was in prison, he could not be committing these crimes. They had intended to then frame Angelo Buono and make him take the heat. Bianchi had given her some smuggled semen to place in a victim and make it look like an authentic rape-murder by a man.

Compton had then traveled to Bellingham and lured a woman to her motel. When she tried to strangle her, the intended victim escaped, and Compton was subsequently convicted of attempted murder. But she was not the only woman to assist a serial killer.

Claudine Eggers, seventy-eight, became a pen pal to Joseph Fischer, in prison for the murder of a sixteen-year-old boy. After twenty-five years, he was paroled in 1978 and moved in with Eggers in her New York home. She then financed a thirteen-month cross-country "trip" for him on which he killed several people. He was soon indulging in a pursuit that media coverage was beginning to inspire: the distinction of being the most notorious serial killer. Claudine Eggers became one of his victims, stabbed to death, and Fischer surrendered to police and confessed to her murder. In fact, he went on to confess to more murders, saying he had decided on twenty-six but had accomplished only nineteen. Various murders from around the country were attributed to him, and soon his total went over thirty. However, he was tried only for the killing of Eggers, for which he was convicted of second-degree murder. He then granted interviews to the media, including tabloid-style talk shows, and soon he was claiming a victim total of up to one hundred fifty. Like Pee Wee Gaskins, he thrived on the notoriety. Many believed him, but it would not be long before members of law enforcement who went along with such psychopaths realized they were being duped. In the meantime, they had other concerns.

In Wichita, Kansas, someone had killed a family of

four early in 1974, singling out the daughter for torture and strangulation by hanging. Six months later, a young woman in the area was murdered in her home. The local newspaper then received a letter with crime scene details of the family massacre, and while arrests were made, no one was identified as the killer. Then two women were murdered in the area in 1977, followed by a poem sent to the press referring to the first woman. The killer had also called from one crime scene to direct police to it. FBI profilers had suggested downplaying the murders and dispensing with all the glitzy media. Apparently that made the UNSUB angry. He sent a letter to a local television station claiming responsibility for the murders and explaining that he was among the elite serial killers. He enumerated a list of them and said that all serial killers were motivated by "Factor X" and could not help but murder. He referred to himself as B.T.K., for "Bind them, torture them, kill them." He indicated that he had not gotten the media attention he deserved so he was now stalking victim number eight. And indeed, he did enter a home, but left before the woman arrived. How many people had to die, he asked, before his work would be recognized? (In 1986, another woman would be killed in the area, but investigators did not think she was linked to the earlier murders. It would be nearly twenty years before they found out they were wrong.)

The phenomenon of serial killing had created a "type," and this man clearly aspired to be known as one. The city of Wichita felt terrorized, wondering who he might kill next. Profilers suggested planting a subliminal message into a news program, as well as placing a classified ad aimed at this person. Neither strategy generated a response, and eventually BTK stopped communicating. But he would be heard from again.

Another angry man attacked several women in the greater New York area. Maryann Carr, a radiologist, was asphyxiated and dumped outside a New Jersey motel on December 15, 1977. Two years later, two women were discovered together in a burning motel, their heads and hands removed. One was a prostitute, as was the next victim, found five months later in a hotel in Times Square. Her breasts were severed and her body had been set on fire. Then Richard Cottingham was arrested at the motel where Maryann Carr had been dumped—and where another murdered woman had been found two weeks before. His intended victim that night had screamed loudly enough to get attention, but only after she had been bitten and assaulted. In three trials in different jurisdictions, Cottingham received several life sentences. His profile defied the typical ideas about such killers: He was married, was the father of three children, had been an athlete, and held down a responsible job. His arrest and convictions surprised everyone who knew him.

When Gerald Eugene Stano was arrested in Florida in 1980, he offered a detailed confession of so many past murders, mostly of hitchhikers and prostitutes, that he astounded the police. Leading them to twenty-six graves, he claimed forty-one victims in New Jersey, Pennsylvania, and Florida. His methods included shooting, strangling, and frenzied stabbing. He did not molest his victims, but merely enjoyed the act of killing. Convicted on several murder charges, he was given the death penalty.

Another killer who confessed that year was Carroll Edward Cole, in Texas, and he claimed thirteen victims. Convicted, the "Bàrfly Strangler" then admitted to murders in Nevada so that he could be extradited there and executed. When his sentence was announced, he thanked the judge. Between childhood abuse, mental illness, and alcoholism, he'd apparently decided that he wanted neither release on parole or life in prison: He wanted out. It was his feeling that he was killing his mother over and over again for her terrible treatment of him. Psychological tests had diagnosed him as antisocial but harmless, failing to appreciate his repetitive fantasies of rape and murder (indeed, he often preferred most of all to have sex with a corpse). Once, he had even cut flesh from a woman and consumed it. He believed that he had killed as many as thirty-five women, and it was ultimately his own act of turning himself in that brought his compulsive killing under control.

Several couples of mixed race were shot in 1977 and 1979, and the suspect was right-wing Nazi supporter and Ku Klux Klansman Joseph Paul Franklin. He was also suspected in the murders of four young black men; in each incident, he was in the area—Wisconsin, Oklahoma, Ohio. Then, in Salt Lake City in 1980, after two black men were shot for jogging with a white woman, Franklin was caught and sent to trial in several different states, for bombings, murder, and civil rights violations. He received six life sentences. Also suspected in a dozen other murders in the South, as well as nearly a dozen nonfatal shootings, he was said to have changed his name eighteen times, altered his appearance, and carried out murder for sport for at least three years. He also confessed to shooting *Hustler* magazine publisher Larry Flynt in 1978, crippling him.

Women, too, turned to serial murder, and in 1978 the spate of deaths attributed to Velma Barfield in North Carolina defied any stereotype. Her first husband had died while drunk and smoking in bed. Because he was abusive, there were those who believed that this "Death Row Granny" did him in, but she actually preferred poison and seemed to like to watch her victims die in writhing pain. Starting her killing career in her late thirties, she got rid of her second husband in 1971, followed by her mother. Both deaths were attributed to natural causes and both netted Barfield money, which she desperately needed to feed her growing addiction to tranquilizers. In fact, it was this addiction that became her defense years later for committing four murders: She'd been in a fog and didn't know what she was doing when she fed arsenic to her victims. The jury convicted her and in 1984 she died by lethal injection in North Carolina.

Another case seemed to involve an altered personality as well. Audrey Hilley claimed that she often blacked out and became her twin sister, whereupon she would do things like poison coffee to serve to relatives and neighbors. Three people died. She was judged insane and released, then continued her behavior, so by 1979 she was finally concluded to be a danger to others and was sentenced to life.

Tag Teams

For a period of three or four years, mostly in California, serial murders were committed by two people working together. Sometimes they were male, but often they were male and female. Usually each person sparked something in the other that fed the murder impulse.

Roy Norris and Lawrence Bittaker met in prison and discovered a common taste for sadistic sexual torture. Once released, they bought a van in Los Angeles, which they dubbed "Murder Mac," and used it to troll for young female victims. They grabbed Cindy Schaeffer, sixteen, on June 24, 1979, and repeatedly raped her before strangling her with a coat hanger. Their next victim got an ice pick through the brain, and following that attack, the duo tortured and murdered two teenage girls at once before dumping their bodies over a cliff. They killed another girl on Halloween and left her on someone's front lawn. Then a pickup whom they raped but released turned them in. In custody, Norris confessed and implicated Bittaker as the ringleader, showing the police the body dump sites. Both men were charged with five counts of murder. Norris was sentenced to forty-five years, while Bittaker went on California's death row.

Over a period of six years, southern California accumulated the bodies of forty-four young men who'd been dumped along highways. The "Freeway Killer" apparently picked off homosexuals, torturing and strangling them or stabbing them to death. Not all of the murders seemed linked to the same offender, but investigators figured that at least half were. The victims were adolescents, the youngest twelve, and during the first five months of 1980 alone, the police found a dozen mutilated corpses.

William Ray Pugh offered information about truck driver William George Bonin, thirty-two, who turned out to be a convicted sex offender living in Downey. The police picked him up, along with accomplice Vernon Butts, and charged Bonin with fourteen counts of murder. Butts offered a deal: more offender names in exchange for leniency. Three more men were arrested and charged in one or more of the murders. All of them turned on Bonin, offering information in exchange for life rather than the death penalty (Butts, however, committed suicide). Bonin was charged with eight more counts of murder. He apparently admitted to a reporter that he had killed twenty-one young men and could not control himself. The jury convicted him of ten of the killings and sentenced him to death.

Then there were the killing couples. From 1978 to 1980, Gerald and Charlene Gallego engaged in a series of sex crimes together in California and Nevada. Charlene (Gerald's seventh wife) would entice girls into their car for Gerald to rape, abuse, and murder. Often kidnapping two girls together, they killed ten people. A witness linked the last dead couple (a male and female) to the Gallegos, and they were quickly captured. Charlene turned against her husband, getting a lenient sentence for her testimony. Gerald received the death penalty in California and Nevada.

Not long after this spree, in the early 1980s, Doug Clark and Carol Bundy were responsible for the "Sunset Strip Slayings" in Hollywood. Bundy enticed women into the car so that Clark could force them into sexual acts and shoot them. After one murder and decapitation, Bundy applied makeup to the face, which she later said that Clark had used for sexual pleasure. When arrested, they were charged with six counts of murder—five females and one male (a former lover of Bundy's whom she had killed, cut up, and beheaded).

While in jail awaiting trial, Clark learned that Veronica Lynn Compton (who had helped Ken Bianchi) was in the same prison as Bundy, so he tried to seduce her into saying that Bundy had confessed to her. When a Washington jury convicted her of attempted murder, he sent her a rose. Compton enthusiastically responded to Clark's descriptions of necrophilia with her own but failed to help him with Bundy. On January 28, 1982, after ineptly trying to defend himself, Clark was found guilty of six counts of murder and one count of attempted murder, for which he received six death sentences.

In the South, Judith Ann Neelley persuaded her husband, Alvin Neelley, to participate in a series of brutal crimes. In 1980, she robbed a woman at gunpoint and then began a fatal rampage. The two viewed themselves as outlaws, "Boney and Claude." One day they lured a thirteen-year-old girl into their car and molested her. Judith injected her with liquid drain cleaner and then shot her. She also shot a man, but he survived and fingered her for killing his girlfriend. When this team was arrested and put through separate trials, Alvin pleaded guilty to one murder and was given two life sentences for murder and aggravated assault. He claimed that Judith had instigated the crimes, being responsible for at least eight murders, and that he had just gone along. She quickly blamed Alvin and said she was a victim of domestic abuse. An insanity defense failed and the jury convicted her. She received death, but her sentence was later commuted to life.

Investigative Analysis

In August 1979, outside San Francisco, a lone hiker, Edda Kane, was found murdered and left naked in a kneeling position. She had been shot, but there was no evidence of sexual assault. Another female hiker was found in the area six months later, stabbed while kneeling. Then a dead woman was found in October 1980, shot but fully clothed. A .44-caliber and a .38-caliber weapon had been used. Two female corpses were found near one another off a different trail, both shot in the head. Then two more bodies were discovered that same day, a man and his fiancée. The "Trailside Killer" was picking up steam, and some people wondered if the Zodiac Killer, never identified, was active again. But there were no communications. A pair of bifocals near one crime scene was the only lead.

FBI profiler and then–BSU chief John Douglas looked at the crime scene data and said the killer would be shy, reclusive, and have a speech impediment. He would be familiar with the area, but unsure of himself in social situations. He chose victims of opportunity rather than preferring a certain victim type. He was white, intelligent, and had spent time in jail.

After Douglas left, the Trailside Killer shot a young couple in a park near Santa Cruz, but the young man survived to give a description. It did not stop the next murder, but on the day she was killed that victim had told someone that she would be with teacher David Carpenter. He drove a car like the one described by the surviving victim, had the same optometrist as another of the victims, and had a record for sex crimes. He also had a severe stutter. In two trials, he was convicted in several of the murders. This had been a successful case for the BSU, but the agents still sought a truly sensational one with which to make their mark—and it wasn't far off.

International Scene

In Britain, a six-year investigation of the murders attributed to the Yorkshire Ripper, which ended early in 1981, by some accounts involved twenty-two tons of evidence and documentation—an indication of how the information age was affecting investigations. The killings started with prostitutes, similar to the crime spree in London a century before involving another Ripper—Jack. In fact, letters signed "Jack the Ripper" came to the police during this time, with taunts similar to the earlier Jack's. But these murders were more brutal and less frequent. A woman discovered in Leeds in 1975 had been battered to death with a hammer, as well as stabbed fourteen times. Another victim was found three months later, but then a year went by before there were seven murders in the course of fifteen months. All the victims had been bludgeoned and slashed. In some cases, the killer mutilated their genitals, and while the initial victims were prostitutes, the pool soon included working girls and college students. The Ripper also switched to a screwdriver, stabbing one victim in the eyes.

When questioned by police on suspicion of picking up prostitutes, Peter Sutcliffe, a former mortuary worker, had a ball-peen hammer and two knives in his possession (which he had tried hiding in the bushes). Under interrogation by the "Ripper Murder Squad," he gave in and confessed over sixteen hours to twenty mutilation assaults and fifteen murders. His insanity defense was based on a claim that God's voice, issuing from a grave he'd been digging, had ordered him to attack the prostitutes. Nevertheless, he was sentenced to life in prison.

Another brutal killer during that time, in the Soviet Republic of Kazakhstan, also hacked up his rape victims with an ax or knife. Nikolai Dzhumagaliev, called "Metal Fang" for his metal false teeth, was arrested and charged with seven murders. He acknowledged his crimes and admitted that he cooked the victims over fires by the river and served the meat to friends. The court deemed

him mentally incompetent to stand trial, so he was institutionalized.

A much more cunning killer, with his wits fully in control, went after children. On Christmas Day in 1980 in
Vancouver, British Columbia, a mutilated twelve-year-old
girl was discovered outside in the cold. Another victim
turned up that spring, and the crime spree continued until
eleven children had been abducted (not all of them were
found). The key suspect was Clifford Olson, an ex-con
who lived in Vancouver with his wife and child. He was
caught picking up two girls, and inside his van was a notebook containing the name of one of the previous victims.
Olson offered a rather shocking deal: He would provide
investigators with locations of the bodies that were still
missing for $10,000 apiece; without that, he would give no
information. The government reluctantly paid $100,000
for ten found graves into a trust fund for Olson's son.
Olson then offered twenty more graves for $100,000, but
this time no one bit. He pleaded guilty to eleven murders
and received life sentences. His horrified wife divorced him
and returned the money to the government.

Later, former detective Kim Rossmo applied his newly
created computerized Criminal Geographic Targeting
program to this case to test its spatial mapping capability. This involved an analysis of a suspect's geographic
patterns: where a victim is selected, where the crime is
actually committed, the travel route for body disposal,
and where and how the body is dumped. Rossmo hoped
it would show something about the suspect's mobility,

method of transportation, area of residence, and ability to traverse barriers. Using the data from the Olson case, he was able to correctly pinpoint, within four blocks, where Olson lived. Geographical profiling eventually received approval to be tested on unsolved cases, both in Canada and the U.S.

Apparently Olson's case also got attention. Marion Pruett probably read about the deal Olson had made, for after he was arrested for the murders of five people in Mississippi, Arkansas, Colorado, and New Mexico, he offered to show journalists where he had buried a female convenience store clerk in exchange for $20,000 and an appearance (for pay) on the talk show *Geraldo*. He received neither. Oddly, he was in the federal witness protection program when he committed his murders, placed there after he testified against a cellmate for a murder that he later confessed to having committed.

In Canada around this time, nine victims were linked to a man named Robert Brown, while the sudden spike in the death rate at the Toronto Hospital for Sick Children indicated the presence of a health-care serial killer. High levels of digoxin were found in twenty-eight dead babies. Suspects were identified, but outright murder was never proved. And in Montreal, James Odo told a courtroom that he had picked up hitchhikers and killed three of them as Satanic sacrifices.

Then, in 1981, Norway was faced with a serial killer when the manager of the Orkdal Valley Nursing Home confessed to his crimes. Arnfinn Nesset, forty-six, said that he had killed twenty-seven patients under his care. But he had also worked elsewhere, and since Nesset could not remember how many he may have killed, officials were left with a list of sixty-two possible victims. Nesset had used the paralyzing drug curacit (from curare) to immobilize them. He claimed that some were mercy killings but also admitted to exercising his morbid curiosity. Then he recanted his confession, which meant that there was little evidence for court. Prosecutors went ahead and charged him with twenty-five murders, along with other crimes such as forgery and theft. He was convicted in twenty-two murders but given only twenty-one years, which in Norway was the maximum term possible.

There were medical deaths in the U.S. as well. In 1980, Dr. Glennon Engleman, a St. Louis dentist, was arrested as a suspect in the murders of seven people. The suspicious wife of a 1958 victim assisted police with tapping incriminating conversations. Engleman pled guilty to three of the murders in exchange for life in prison. Near Los Angeles, a woman called the San Bernardino County coroner in 1981 to report what she believed were nineteen murders in a hospital. The police checked into it and found a dozen sudden deaths. Suspicion fell on male nurse Robert Diaz, who liked to predict which patients were going to die—and was invariably right. He had also been seen administering injections that had not been prescribed. In his home, police found the drug, lidocaine, which had turned up on postmortem examinations of the deceased patients. Diaz was convicted of murdering all twelve of them.

Staggering Numbers

Still stunned about Ted Bundy's being in their midst, residents of Washington and Oregon woke up to the "I-5 Killer" in 1981. A rapist and murderer, he had sometimes claimed two victims at once. Finally an association was made with one victim that led police to Randall Woodfield, a convicted sex offender. A search of his home turned up evidence from some of the attacks. Despite the fact that Woodfield had been a top student and a good-looking athlete with professional football prospects, the thirty-year-old man clearly had troubles. As young as he was, he'd raped over fifty women, and estimates of his murders ranged from four to eighteen.

Across the country, another in-progress investigation was about to be solved. On September 22, 1980, a fourteen-year-old African-American boy was shot in Buffalo, New York, followed the next day by two similar murders. Then a fourth victim was killed in Niagara Falls, not far away. People saw a white youth carrying a bag that they believed contained a gun, for when he had run from the crowd he had dropped a shell casing. Thus, he became the ".22-Caliber Killer." But he was clever. Switching his preferred weapons no fewer than three times, he lay low and then emerged again to kill more black people. He used a screwdriver on one cabbie and a hammer on another, as well as a knife. Both had their hearts removed.

Several weeks passed again before another series of killings began, this time in Manhattan. In just a few hours, five black men and one Hispanic man were attacked by a man wielding a knife. Four of them died. Now Manhattan had the "Slasher," but so did Buffalo. Two more black men were killed and several seriously wounded. Investigators were stymied until a twenty-five-year-old GI in Georgia, Joseph Christopher, told a nurse that he had killed several black people in New York. Forensic evidence piled up against him, and when he confessed, he said, "It was something I had to do." Christopher was convicted of several of the murders in both Manhattan and Buffalo and sentenced to life in prison. Although his behavior seemed racially triggered, all he would say was that something "came over" him. It was not unlike what Ted Bundy had claimed.

In Atlanta, someone was killing black children, and that, too, seemed racially motivated. As the victim count rose to two dozen, the police requested assistance from the FBI, so Special Agents John Douglas and Roy Hazelwood traveled there in 1981. Some of the victims, as young as nine, had been strangled, bludgeoned, or asphyxiated. But all potential leads had turned into dead ends. The only real clue was the presence on several of the bodies of fiber threads. A few also bore strands of what was determined to be dog hair. These specimens were all sent to the Georgia State Crime Laboratory for analysis, and technicians there isolated two distinct fibers: a violet-colored acetate and a coarse yellow-green nylon with the type of trilobed (three-branch) qualities associated with carpets. The fiber discovery was reported in the newspaper and shortly thereafter, bodies were found stripped and thrown into the river.

Douglas and Hazelwood walked around the neighborhoods where the victims had lived and said that this was not a racial crime; they predicted the killer would be black. They also indicated that the next victim would likely be dumped in the Chattahoochee River, since that was the pattern, so the police set up a stakeout. On May 22, 1981, during the early-morning hours, the patrol heard a loud splash. On the James Jackson Parkway Bridge, they saw a white Chevrolet station wagon, and when they stopped it, they were told by driver Wayne Williams, a twenty-three-year-old black photographer and music promoter, that he had dumped some "garbage," so they let him go.

Two days later, the police found the body of twenty-seven-year-old Nathaniel Cater. He'd been asphyxiated, and a single yellow-green carpet fiber was found in his hair. The police got a warrant to search Wayne Williams's home and car, and turned up valuable evidence: Williams had a dog, and the floors of his home were covered with yellow-green carpeting consistent with the samples removed from the victims. Three ensuing polygraph tests indicated deception on Williams's part.

FBI scientists ascertained that the fibers found on the victims came from a Boston-based textile company. Its "Luxaire English Olive" color matched that found in Wayne Williams's home. However, many other homes had this carpeting, too. Thus, the prosecutor had to determine just how likely it was that Williams's carpeting was unique enough to persuade a jury of his connection to the murders. As the prosecution pointed out, company records showed that it had made that type of carpet only over a one-year period, with over sixteen thousand yards of it distributed throughout the South. In comparison with the total amount of carpet distributed across the country, this was a small sample. The prosecution team argued that this made the statistical probability of the carpet's being in any one person's home slight. Thus, fibers on victims that were closely consistent with fibers from Williams's home indicated a high probability that he had transferred the fibers from his residence. Then there were fibers from an automobile carpet.

With Chevrolet's help, the investigators determined that there was a 1-in-3,828 chance that one of the victims, Jimmy Ray Payne, had acquired the fiber found on him via random contact with a car that had this carpeting installed. Williams's car had the right type. They also introduced into evidence the fibers found on the bodies of ten of the other victims, which also matched those in Williams's car or home. In total, there were twenty-eight fiber types linked to Williams (a statistical analysis that was vigorously disputed by the defense and is still disputed by critics of the investigation). In addition, several witnesses had come forward to place him with some of the victims. After only twelve hours, the jury returned a guilty verdict against Williams, with two life sentences. That was good for the FBI's profiling program.

Yet even as law enforcement methods improved, predators grew bolder. To be a serial killer during this time had become a goal for some, a point of attraction. Society had created an identity for them, offering a "profile" of traits and behaviors that could be analyzed and described in newspapers and textbooks. They could read about themselves or find inspiration by reading about others. They wrote to one another in prison, swapping ideas and seeing themselves as members of a special sort of club.

As social roles eroded and class distinctions blurred, serial killers had emerged from all walks of life, from businessmen to law students to unemployed losers. One never knew if one's associate or neighbor might show up on the evening news with a yardful of bodies. In fact, the next decade would explode with such a number and variety of killers that the FBI had to consider a request that had been made back in the 1950s—get a computerized database. In addition, people were beginning to study the neurological data associated with predatory violence. More was learned with each passing year.

CHAPTER THIRTEEN

Social Contagion and the Age of Excess

Groupthink

Around the world during the next decade, a serial killer was caught, suspected, or in clear operation at some point on an average of one every three days. U.S. residents were already accustomed to seeing a new killer almost every month, and since the early sixties, the homicide rate in general had tripled. In 1980, more than twenty-three thousand people were murdered in the USA, including former Beatle John Lennon, and other violent crimes had escalated as well. During that same year, America changed leaders. Ronald Reagan, a former actor, became president, with a pledge to end double-digit inflation, get tough on crime, and make America safer. He freed fifty-two American hostages from 444 days of Iranian captivity, bringing a sense of optimism to the country, but then stumbled upon the surfacing AIDS epidemic. During his time in office he would also propose expensive defensive tactics in outer space and be confronted with political scandals in his administration involving secret illegal arms deals with other countries. The profits from selling arms to Iran for its war with Iraq (a deal made with terrorists) were channeled to the Contra rebels in Nicaragua to help overthrow that country's Marxist government.

The Republican penchant for clear categories of good and evil was grounded in a conservative religious perspective, and it wasn't long before the country was engulfed in waves of psychological hysterias that fed off fundamentalist rigidity. During the 1980s, many day-care workers fell victim to a hysteria that swept the nation in which teachers were accused of performing sexual and Satanic rituals with their charges. Children were subjected to questionable repressed-memory techniques, which ranged from subtle manipulation with genitally-correct dolls to planted suggestions about what they "must" have experienced. To please the adults, many capitulated, although their allegations about things like corpses, Martians, and hidden tunnels were clearly absurd. Nevertheless, their testimony damaged many lives as innocent people went to prison.

During this same period, thanks largely to a book and movie from the 1970s about a woman named Sybil, psychotherapists used hypnosis, dream analysis, and other techniques to persuade large numbers of mostly white, middle-class, female clients to "remember" childhood abuse and to accept a diagnosis of multiple personality disorder. Many fathers, stepfathers, and uncles were subsequently accused, and the courts initially accepted false memories as factual evidence. Some accused people were convicted and imprisoned.

Patients "discovered" dozens, hundreds, even a thousand personalities, known as "alters," some of which weren't even human, and many soon reported Satanic ritual abuse. Whole businesses sprang up to diagnose, treat, and discuss these victims, with publishers, convention promoters, physicians, therapists, and hospitals benefiting. Yet FBI investigators found no evidence to support the allegations, especially about the Satanic activities. This helped to fuel a backlash, and soon former patients won significant damages from therapists. Literature about the condition had filtered into the prisons, giving defendants in murder cases a new excuse. Like Bianchi in California, others found ways to fake this new insanity more convincingly. Occasionally it worked.

At the same time, the residual effects of the "Satanic panics" influenced violent behavior. Many killers adopted Satanic robes, and one killer ringed his victims with a circle of salt. During the decade, Robert Berdella, who ran an occult "Bazaar Bizarre," tortured and killed six men in his Missouri home. Thomas Creech admitted to two dozen supposed Satanic sacrifices in several states, and Leonard Lake, loosely affiliated with a witch coven, teamed up with Charles Ng for a series of torture-murders in a remote California bunker. After strangling or shooting as many as twenty-five victims, they dismembered and burned them in metal drums, in which police found forty-five pounds of bone fragments and teeth. Lake committed suicide and Ng received a death sentence.

Adolescents were equally influenced. In Oklahoma City, Sean Sellers, sixteen, sought to follow the devil, so he murdered a convenience store clerk as "practice" before killing his mother and stepfather in their beds. Six years later he claimed to have been suffering from multiple personality disorder. His schoolmates had voted him the person most likely to become a vampire, because he drank vials of blood and carried the *Satanic Bible*. Sellers indicated that for over two years he had spent hours performing private rituals in his bedroom, using his own blood to write notes to Satan. "Demons were the beings that would do things I wanted done," he wrote in his confession. "They were the keys to the power Satanism promised."

Also during the eighties, a former associate of John Wayne Gacy named Robin Gecht inspired a group of three other men, the "Ripper Crew," to kill an estimated eighteen women. They would murder a victim, according to confessions, sever her breast with a piano wire, use it for sexual gratification, and then cut it into pieces to consume over a Satanic altar.

Supernatural crimes were evident in other countries as well. Adrian Lim used female partners in his murders in Singapore in early 1981. He was a medium with a spiritualist practice who needed victims to sacrifice to Kali, the goddess of destruction. His wife and mistress lured children to him for sexual purposes and then asphyxiated or drowned them.

The person most strongly associated with Satanic trends emerged in California, when in the summer of 1984 a seventy-nine-year-old woman was slain in her home in Glassell Park, near Los Angeles. Within eight months there were two more attacks that bore similarities, and a survivor described the suspect as a lean man dressed in black, with dark stringy hair and bad teeth. In May 1985, two elderly sisters were bludgeoned to death and their attacker left Satanic symbols on the thigh of one in the form of a pentagram. Then he moved into high gear, attacking single females or couples. In one home, he raped a woman next to her husband, whom he had just killed, and forced her to swear allegiance to Satan. He also traveled to San Francisco and shot a couple there. By August he was credited with fourteen murders. A fingerprint pointed to Richard Ramirez, and police discovered that Ramirez was a known Satanist whose favorite song was "Night Prowler." When they rescued him from a group of angry citizens who had recognized him from the newspaper, he claimed to be a minion of Satan sent to commit the Dark One's dirty work.

He continued to use this persona throughout his court hearings and trial. When he was convicted, his lawyers warned him that he could get the death sentence. "I'll be in hell, then," he said, "with Satan." He was ultimately charged with thirteen murders and thirty other criminal counts, including rape and burglary, and sentenced to death. As he was led away, he added for the press, "Big deal. Death always went with the territory. See you in Disneyland."

The Satanic premise appeared to offer killers both the license and the context for viewing their acts as empowered by evil, and therefore more deadly. But less exotic killers were operating around the country as well, and some had a unique twist.

Domestic Terror

Right after the conviction of the Atlanta Child Killer, in 1982 Special Agent John Douglas was involved in a case of domestic terrorism. In the Chicago area, seven people suddenly dropped dead. The police discovered that the victims had all recently purchased and taken capsules of Extra Strength Tylenol, found to be laced with cyanide. It was an insidious killing method, scaring people around the country and forcing a massive recall of the product.

The FBI now faced a problem: the random nature of the tampering. No specific person or store had been targeted and no motive had been clarified via a ransom note. Douglas interpreted it as an act of anger by a person with no specific need to be present at the deaths he or she had caused. But before the FBI had time to adequately profile the case with more evidence, the attacks suddenly stopped, with the perpetrator remaining at large. Copycat crimes in other places were quickly solved as murder under the guise of product-tampering.

The Midwest endured a number of series murders during the 1980s. The "Sunday Morning Slayer" stabbed two women to death in Michigan's Detroit area. A black man named Eugene Coral Watts was suspected, but he quickly migrated to Texas. There he was arrested for burglary and aggravated assault. Pleading guilty, he got sixty years. But Texas law enforcement officers had ten unsolved murders that bore similar circumstances to those in Michigan, and they cast their eye on Watts. He made a deal to confess to those ten, plus the two in Michigan, in exchange for immunity, so to close the cases they agreed—to their regret years later, when Watts's prison term was shortened.

Ohio, too, became a killing ground. Between 1979 and 1982, four couples were shot while out together, and the cases were never solved. Four more murdered couples turned up in Virginia four years later. These cases were also never solved, but a killing couple, Alton Coleman, twenty-eight, and Deborah Brown, twenty-one, were caught in Ohio after making a run through six Midwestern states in 1984. They'd rape and strangle people as they went, and their victims ranged from children to the elderly, both male and female. The FBI had placed Brown and Coleman on their Ten Most Wanted list, and an acquaintance finally turned them in. Convicted on many counts, they were sentenced to death in Ohio.

Gay killer Larry Eyler murdered and mutilated at least eighteen boys in Indiana during the 1980s (he hinted at twenty more), while Nebraska was faced with two unsolved murders of local boys in 1983. The BSU's Robert Ressler thought the killer was a young white male who knew the victims, worked with his hands, and was familiar with the area. There was likely unusual stress in his life and he was prone to deviant fantasies. A witness offered a license plate number that led to enlisted airman John Joubert. He fit the profile perfectly and even had rope in his possession similar to that which had bound the first victim. He confessed to both murders and was also traced to a murder in Maine. Convicted of all three killings, Joubert went to Nebraska's death row.

Not far away in Minnesota, three Native American women who had worked as prostitutes turned up bludgeoned to death and sexually assaulted in 1986 and 1987. The police found drifter Billy Glaze, aka Jesse Sitting Crow, who was known for his hatred of women. He was convicted in all three cases.

Meanwhile, unsolved cluster murders of prostitutes, gay males, young boys, and young girls continued nationwide and in Canada throughout the decade. There was also an increase in suspicious hospital deaths. The "Penn Station Strangler" shot and killed seven men mid-decade, while Satanists were suspected in three murders in Battle Creek, Michigan.

One man in Missouri was freed time and again because of psychological problems, only to keep killing. From 1961 until 1982, Charles Hatcher murdered at least sixteen people and raped many more in several different states, from inmates to children. He practically begged to be stopped, but the legal system's revolving door kept putting him back out. Finally he hanged himself.

But the issue of insanity was about to be reevaluated. John Hinckley Jr. had shot and wounded President Reagan in an attempt to impress actress Jodie Foster, and was acquitted on an insanity defense in 1982. The country erupted in outrage, so several states revised their laws to make insanity criteria more difficult to meet.

Coastal Contagion

"Thrill Killer" Richard Biegenwald was convicted of the murders of three men in New Jersey and Maryland in 1958. Released in 1974, he went to the Jersey Shore to reside and look for potential victims. Arrested again in 1983, he was implicated in several more murders. Biegenwald claimed to have killed three hundred girls with long dark hair (although evidence for this number has never been found). He dismembered and buried two in his mother's garden, and some victims were believed to be contract hits.

Likewise, until he was murdered in 1983, loan shark and Gambino family hit man Roy DeMeo, a onetime butcher's apprentice, seemed to kill for both business and pleasure. He trained a special crew in "the Gemini Method," which amounted to a "disassembly line." The target person would arrive at DeMeo's Gemini Lounge. He'd be shot, wrapped in a towel, and repeatedly stabbed in the heart. Then he would be drained of blood, laid out on a pool liner, and hacked into pieces for packaging, like meat. Finally, the victim would be tossed into a dump. Estimates place the body count between seventy-five and two hundred.

"Ice Man" Richard Kuklinski also murdered people as

a hit man, but on his own lured men into business deals to kill them. Sometimes it was for money, other times for whim or to "off" a cohort who knew too much. Suspected in half a dozen murders in New Jersey and New York, he was trapped by the FBI in 1986. After he went to prison, Kuklinski became the subject of several books and documentaries, and put the number of his murders at just short of two hundred. He claimed he had placed some victims inside caves, leaving the rats to devour them alive as cameras rolled. He watched the films afterward, he said, so he could "feel" something.

On the West Coast, series crimes proliferated at a more rapid pace. Roger Kibbe, the "I-15 Killer" near Sacramento, was linked via microscopic paint chips and fibers to seven rape-murders, while the earlier killer of victims found along the freeways of southern California was finally apprehended. William Bonin and his accomplices had been convicted of ten of the more than forty murders but in May 1983, the police pulled over a car being driven erratically by a man who identified himself as Randolph Kraft, a computer programmer. Inside the car was a corpse. Although he never confessed, he was convicted of sixteen of the remaining unsolved freeway murders, but given his many cross-country trips, was suspected in as many as sixty-seven that fit his pattern of castration, rape, and mutilation.

That same year, a couple was investigated in three murders, one of them occurring in California. New Age–oriented Islamic practitioners Michael and Suzan Carson were engulfed in a spiritual vision involving a paranoid mission to kill witches and psychic vampires. They killed a man in San Francisco, and a year later in Oregon, after writing their manifesto, *Cry for War,* they shot and burned two men to extinguish the demon inside them. Despite their wacky beliefs, they were considered sane and criminally responsible, receiving life in prison.

Another 1983 male-female team, Cynthia Coffman and James Gregory Marlow, robbed and strangled four women as they drifted from one place to another in California and Arizona, while Arthur Gary Bishop, under the name of Roger Downs, confessed to raping and killing four boys in Salt Lake City. Once excommunicated from the Mormon faith, he had taken on an alias and pursued his secret obsessions under the guise of a Big Brother. Blaming Satan for his crimes, he was convicted and sentenced to be executed.

California law enforcement officers were among those officials from twenty states to focus on a pair of parallel predators who were confessing to a number of murders around the country during the 1970s and early 1980s. Henry Lee Lucas, arrested on a weapons possession charge, estimated his body count at somewhere between seventy-five and one hundred—he lost count—but eventually he would raise it as high as six hundred, spread over twenty-seven different states. His partner, Ottis Toole, gleefully added his own tally, and affirmed that he had participated with Lucas in murder, necrophilia, and cannibalism.

In an unprecedented event, lawmen filled an auditorium to talk with Lucas in the hope of closing their open cases, but then Lucas recanted. For a while, no one knew quite what to make of a killer's confessing to so many crimes he did not do—but then he insisted that he'd been forced to recant. His persistent waffling reduced his credibility. While it was eventually agreed upon that he killed at least four people, including his mother, even one of those murders—of a female victim dubbed "Orange Socks"—has come under doubt in recent years. Some criminologists believe he was responsible for between forty to fifty murders, but no one knows for sure. "I set out to break and corrupt any law enforcement officer I could get," Lucas said. "I think I did a pretty good job." He received the death penalty for "Orange Socks," but the sentence was commuted to life, and he eventually died in prison of natural causes.

Ottis Toole claimed to be a cannibal. His voodoo-practicing grandmother, he said, had dubbed him "the devil's child." He committed his first murder at age fourteen when a traveling salesman picked him up and Toole ran him over with the man's own car. He was suspected in four other murders before he met Lucas in 1976. He said he introduced Lucas to a cult called "The Hand of Death" in which they sacrificed children to Satan. While Lucas went off with Toole's niece Becky, Toole allegedly killed nine people out of rage over their various "betrayals." Then, when she grew troublesome, Lucas killed Becky.

Outside the forty-eight continental states, Alaskan police were faced with a strange story in June 1983 from a young prostitute in Anchorage. She claimed that a redheaded john had tortured and raped her, and had planned to fly her to a remote cabin, but she had escaped. She identified the home of local baker Robert Hansen, but he insisted she was lying. Yet the remains of several women had turned up in the wilderness, shot or stabbed, and most had been prostitutes. The police invited the FBI's profiling unit to assist in writing up a warrant and developing a set of questions for Hansen. The warrant turned up a weapon that ballistics matched to bullets removed from the murdered women, as well as missing jewelry and IDs. Hansen finally admitted using his victims as "game." For a sexual thrill, he would drop them off, naked, in the wilderness and hunt them down. Although he confessed to seventeen murders, he only pled to four.

Farther south, a task force had less success. Over a period of two years, from 1982 to 1984, female victims were found strangled or stabbed and discarded around the Green River area in Washington State. Most were prostitutes or runaways, and witnesses had described seeing a white male with a few of them. They were generally left in one of four dump sites, and in a single day, more than one might be discovered. A few had small pyramid-shaped stones pushed into their vaginas and one victim was posed with a wine bottle and a dead fish. FBI profiler John Douglas was on-site to assist. A 1984 letter entitled "whatyouneedtoknowaboutthegreenriverman" and sent to the *Seattle Post-Intelligencer* claimed to be from the killer ("callmefred"). Douglas dismissed it as amateurish and unconnected to the murders, though it contained

facts about cases not released to the press. His profile indicated that the UNSUB would be white, in his twenties
or thirties, and seemingly harmless. He could win trust
easily, despite the number of women known to be turning
up dead, would be a heavy smoker, and hated women.
Since the man was having sexual contact with victims
after they were dead, he was probably returning to crime
scenes and might be expected to communicate with the
press or police. Douglas warned the police not to eliminate suspects based on a polygraph, but they did so
anyway. It was among the many mistakes made in this
investigation.

Ted Bundy wrote from Florida's death row to offer officials an "understanding" of the "Riverman's" mind. He
knew the area intimately and proposed to "figure out"
how the Riverman operated. However, those who questioned Bundy believed his detailed analysis was indicative
of his own modus operandi. They also saw how he was
playing with them to delay his execution, and in the end
his assistance failed to help anyone, including himself.
However, it did close cases still open in Seattle and other
areas. Just before Bundy was executed on January 24,
1989, he hinted that he was responsible for more than his
thirty confessed murders. But by the time he died, the
"Green River Killer" had outpaced him, with over forty
victims and a computerized investigation that had cost
more than $15 million. While DNA samples were taken
from other suspects as well, a few were eliminated via lie-
detector tests and others failed to pan out. The task force

reluctantly disbanded, but several persistent detectives kept those unsolved cases alive. Eventually their efforts would pay off, though not for nearly two decades.

Bundy's keen interest had confirmed for investigators another disturbing notion: Serial killers studied one another. With the plethora of books on such cases now available, and the detailed coverage on television, they could learn from one another, especially from any mistakes made. In prison they talked with one another and sent communications. A piece written for *Vanity Fair* by Mark MacNamara used the bridge game he heard about between serial killers William Bonin, Randy Kraft, Lawrence Bittaker, and Doug Clark as a metaphor for the California death penalty system. The police had to wonder how many young wanna-bes might be watching these men and planning their own careers. They even speculated on competition among them: Had Bundy hoped to stop the Riverman in order to keep his own reputation intact? The media had clearly played a part in creating the cult of the serial killer persona. And although several serial killer wanna-bes would be caught before they could kill many people, their intent to emulate their predecessors was still disturbing.

Southern Comfort

Police in Vero Beach, Florida, received a report in July 1983 that a man had chased down and shot a naked girl in broad daylight. They arrived at the suspect's house to find the body of a seventeen-year-old girl in the trunk of his car. David Alan Gore then surrendered and showed the officers to the attic. There they found a fourteen-year-old girl, still alive, bound to the rafters. In prison, Gore turned on cousin Fred Waterfield, describing their criminal history and alluding to five more murders. They enjoyed hunting down women for violent sexual pleasure. Gore had served as an auxiliary sheriff's deputy, which facilitated their "hobby." Waterfield supposedly offered Gore $1,000 for each pretty girl he brought back, and together they would rape and kill them. Then Gore would dispose of the bodies. Both were convicted of rape and murder.

Around that time, another area in Florida had its own series of sexual murders. A couple of teenage boys walking in a field southeast of Tampa, Florida, on Mother's Day in 1984 discovered the mangled, insect-infested remains of a nude woman. A noose was draped three times around her neck. Soon another female body was found in a similar condition, and investigators found red trilobal fibers on both bodies. The FBI did an analysis, and soon the BSU was called for a profile.

The important factors from both cases were that the victims had been bound, needed transportation, had been left near interstate highways in rural areas, and had carpet fibers on their bodies. The UNSUB probably had a vehicle. The leashlike ropes around the necks of the victims and the brutal beatings that exceeded what was necessary to kill them displayed sexual deviance. The suspect was likely a white male, in his mid-twenties, gregarious, extroverted, and manipulative. He seemed to be what police would classify as "organized." Passing as "normal," he would be argumentative, self-centered, selfish, and exhibit little or no emotion—all common traits for a psychopath. It was probable that he lied easily and had a macho self-image. In all likelihood, he would kill again.

More victims turned up, but then seventeen-year-old Lisa McVey escaped from a man who had raped and tortured her in his home. She led the police back there and they arrested Bobby Joe Long, a distant cousin to Henry Lee Lucas. He confessed not only to nine murders but added a series of rapes. By the time Florida was done with Bobby Joe Long, he had received two death sentences and thirty-four life sentences.

By then, yet another Florida man had committed a cross-country murder spree that got him on the FBI's Ten Most Wanted List. It began with the search for two missing women associated with successful businessman Christopher Wilder, who'd suddenly taken off for California, grabbing pretty young women along the way. He lured them by posing as a photographer who could start them on a modeling career. The "Beauty Queen Killer" tortured and killed most of them, but would use one to lure others. After six weeks on the road, he arrived in New Hampshire, where he murdered his eighth victim and headed to Canada. But a state trooper spotted his car, and in a struggle over a gun, Wilder was shot and killed. Later he was implicated in several rapes and murders in his native Australia.

His case defied the serial killer stereotypes that had

developed to that point. At thirty-eight, he was success-ful, good-looking, sociable, and lived in a beautiful home. He had no trouble meeting and attracting women, although one of his victims had rejected a marriage pro-posal. His case forced criminologists to reexamine ideas that serial killers came from abusive homes and had expe-rienced brain traumas or had substance abuse problems. Some were clearly exceptions, and professionals would have to look for other types of causal factors. A few re-searchers looked at brain processing connections rather than brain damage, but definitive answers eluded them.

A Wider Net

While the U.S. had become the world leader in numbers of serial killers at large or caught, they were active in other countries as well. The eighties was a turbulent time, with terrorist attacks on the rise and some of the stronger world powers facing internal crises. The Iran-Iraq war in the volatile Middle East lasted throughout the eighties, Israel invaded Lebanon, and the U.S. bombed Libya. In the Soviet Union, Mikhail Gorbachev instituted badly needed reforms.

Among the most notorious of the European killers was a man called the "Serpent." Caught in India for two drug-related homicides, Charles Sobhraj had served seven years and was free by 1982 to carry on his profitable ven-tures via charm and fraud. He tended to slither out of situations and escape. A thief and swindler, he once joined a group of bandits who lured in hippies to rob and kill, incinerating some alive. By 1976, Sobhraj was wanted for twenty murders in seven different countries, including Turkey, Nepal, Thailand, and India. Slick and elusive, he became one of Asia's "Most Wanted." Then, in France, he drugged a group of tourists, who collapsed prematurely in a hotel lobby, and police finally caught him. Yet not until 2004, in Nepal, at the age of fifty-nine, would he receive his first actual murder conviction.

Poland had at least two serial killers, including Juan Koltrun, the "Podlaski Vampire," a rapist who drank blood from his two victims. West German poisoner Maria Velten killed five, but it was the "Doorbell Killer" who badly frightened people, because he slipped so easily into the homes of his elderly female victims, all of whom were strangled. From a clothing store receipt dropped at one crime scene, the police identified twenty-two-year-old Waldemar Szcepinski. He confessed to three murders, explaining that he had used a fake FBI badge to gain entry.

Denmark and Austria both produced health-care serial killers who experienced thrills from exercising the power of life and death over their charges. It was a nurse's aide in Vienna who started the bizarre spree at Lainz General Hospital. Waltraud Wagner, twenty-three, had a seventy-seven-year-old patient who supposedly asked Wagner to "end her suffering." Wagner overdosed the woman with morphine and discovered she liked this kind of power. She recruited accomplices Maria Gruber, Ilene Leidolf, and Stephanija Mayer, teaching them the "water cure," which involved holding a patient's nose while forcing him or her to drink. Moving from compassion to sadism, the women took out patients who merely annoyed them. Over drinks, they would relive their escapades, and one day a doctor overheard them. All four were arrested on April 7, 1989. Collectively they confessed to forty-nine murders, and Wagner took credit for giving a "free bed with the good Lord" to thirty-nine of them. However, one of her accomplices believed that Wagner's death count was closer to two hundred. Ultimately, Wagner was convicted of fifteen murders, seventeen attempted murders, and two counts of assault. She got life, as did Leidolf for five murders, while the other two women drew fifteen years for manslaughter and attempted murder.

While it was difficult to know what crimes were perpetrated behind the Iron Curtain, it has since come out that between 1971 and 1985, thirty-six women were found strangled in Russia. The police received a letter indicating that revenge against adulterous women was the motive. A persistent detective made painstaking checks on thousands of passports and car licenses until he finally pressured Gennadiy Mikasevich into a confession. This man, a police volunteer, had involved himself deeply in the investigation. He was convicted and executed.

Two "monsters" showed up in two different countries, and in France, the suspected perpetrator was actually a team. The "Monster of Montmartre" preyed on elderly women in Paris. One was forced to drink bleach and another was stabbed sixty times. The "monster," identified by a surviving victim, turned out to be bleached-blond, black transvestite Thierry Paulin, who often invited his lover, Jean-Thierry Mathurin, on his criminal escapades. They would follow elderly women home from the grocery store and then jump them as they opened their doors. Upon his arrest, Paulin confessed to twenty-one murders, naming Mathurin as an accomplice. Both went to prison.

But in Italy, the "Monster of Florence" stopped killing in 1985 after thirty-two victims over a period of seventeen years had died during full moons. His obsession appeared to be couples in cars making love. The women had often been mutilated, and in some cases their sex organs or breasts were removed: One attorney received strips of skin belonging to one of them. Years later, Pietro Pacciani was caught and convicted of some of these crimes, but he was freed on appeal and died before his retrial.

Italy was also troubled with the murder of seven prostitutes in Turin, linked to truck driver Giancarlo Giudice, but an arrest was not quite so easy with the Ludwig murders. This case began with a man being burned to death in his car and another man being knifed in Padua. The brutality escalated with the ax murder of a prostitute and a fatal hammer attack on two priests (one suffered twenty-six blows, another had nails embedded in his forehead). Then, in Verona, a hitchhiker was burned alive. At nearly every scene, starting in 1980, notes signed by "Ludwig" or "Ludwig Band" were found. Apparently Ludwig viewed himself as the last surviving Nazi, and the victims had "betrayed the true God"—being mostly homosexuals and prostitutes, whom he viewed as society's "inferior people." In 1984, the Ludwig Band burned down a theater in Milan, killing six people, and one person died while forty were injured in a discotheque fire. Then, at the Melamara di Castiglione of the Stivere, where hundreds of people were dancing, Wolfgang Abel, twenty-seven, and Mario Furlan, twenty-six, were arrested before they could burn the place down. Furlan's handwriting matched one of the Ludwig notes, and in Abel's apartment investigators found a book with the name "Ludwig Friar" highlighted. They were found guilty of ten murders, and because they were deemed partially insane, both received sentences of just thirty years. However, after serving only three, they were granted "open custody," living at home and reporting to police on a regular basis.

England produced one of the most notorious killers of the decade. Although the country had seen the arrest of the "Stockwell Strangler," Kiernan Kelly, "Wolf Man" Michael Lupo, and "Railway Killers" John Francis Duffy and David Mulcahy (the first killer to be identified in England with psychological offender profiling), another man was able to move as a quiet predator through London bars for several years.

In 1983, residents of an apartment building complained of a smelly sewer and clogged plumbing. Hunks of human flesh were discovered and led police to Denis Nilsen, who showed them into his apartment. In a closet, police found the dismembered parts of two men. Another torso was found in a tea chest. Nilsen confessed over thirty hours to killing fifteen men he had met in bars over the past five years, partly because he could not bear their leaving him and partly because he simply enjoyed it.

His first murder had occurred near the end of 1978,

and had sexually excited him. He had strangled the man with a necktie and then placed him beneath the floor-boards of his apartment until he could cremate the remains in his garden. He continued to acquire "compan-ions" in this way—strangling them, bathing the corpses, sometimes taking them to bed, and finally butchering them or storing them in various places in his apartment. When he moved and no longer had a garden, he simply flushed the pieces down the toilet, and this had proved to be his undoing. He tried for an insanity plea, but was convicted and sentenced to life in prison.

Serial killers showed up in Pakistan and South Africa as well; one, the "Beast of Atteridgeville," Johannes Mashiane, who threw himself under a bus during a police chase, was believed responsible for twelve fatal stranglings or stonings of boys. But Colombia and Ecuador had the worst spate of known killings during the 1980s. The rape-murders began when convicted rapist and killer Daniel Camargo Barbosa escaped from prison. In one city during a period lasting just over a year, fifty-five female children turned up missing. Barbosa was caught with the photo of one of the girls in his pocket, but he subse-quently confessed to a victim total of seventy-one. He claimed he had grabbed virgins because he liked how they cried when he hurt them. Many of his victims were found, and authorities saw that Barbosa had bludgeoned them to death or used a machete to slash them. One was still hold-ing a candy wrapper, on which Barbosa's fingerprint was found. Nevertheless, he received only sixteen years in an Ecuador prison.

That was better than Angel Diaz Balbin got in Lima, Peru, when a police psychiatrist, overwhelmed by the details of how Balbin had dismembered eight people, strangled the defendant—or so an Internet news site reported.

Across the world in Australia, four young women were murdered in a single month in 1982 in the town of Fremantle. The police learned about it from a hysterical girl who had gotten away from a couple, David and Catherine Birnie, who had held her in their home. Upon being arrested, both confessed and showed the police to the graves of those they had killed. They had spontaneously begun by raping a girl who had come to purchase something, and once she was dead, they went looking for another. This one, a fifteen-year-old, they kept for days, subjecting her to repeated rape and torture. Their trial lasted an hour and they were sentenced to life, which involved a minimum of twenty years.

Toward the end of the 1980s, Jose Antonio Rodriquez Vega murdered sixteen elderly women in Spain, strangling them before sexually assaulting their corpses. When he was arrested in 1988, authorities broadcast a videotape of his home, where he had a collection of items that the families of victims recognized.

Nevertheless, even with all this activity around the world, by the end of the decade the U.S. had to admit to having spawned over two-thirds of the world's known serial killers. That had to say something about its culture, and many blamed permissive standards, the failed family structure, and increased sex and violence on television.

But at the same time, the U.S. was also a leader in developing crime investigation methods.

Forensic Advances

Crime investigation took several large steps in the middle of this decade in terms of linkage analysis and criminal identification. Two developments occurred simultaneously.

The FBI put a national computer database into place. This had been the dream of L.A. Detective Pierce Brooks in the late 1950s during several murder investigations, and he had pushed for it for nearly three decades. It was called the Violent Criminal Apprehension Program (VICAP), and was slated to become the most comprehensive computerized database for homicides nationwide. Police departments around the country would be invited to record solved, unsolved, and attempted homicides; unidentified bodies in which the manner of death was suspect; and missing-persons cases involving suspected foul play. (Canada later introduced VICLAS—the Violent Criminal Linkage Analysis System—which was multilinguistic and applicable in other countries.)

At a Senate subcommittee meeting, Brooks and others argued for funding such a system. John Walsh was among the group, testifying about his murdered son, Adam (who may have been killed by Ottis Toole). True crime writer Ann Rule also testified, pointing to mobile serial killers who had traveled from state to state, including Ted Bundy, Kenneth Bianchi, and Harvey Louis Carignan. She said that in Bundy's case, a system like VICAP might have saved as many as fifteen lives. Brooks bemoaned the fact that his own painstaking method of researching linked crimes had remained the same for twenty-five years, which in light of available computerized technology was shameful, he felt.

He persuaded the Department of Justice to host a conference at Sam Houston State University, and VICAP was born. The FBI was assigned to run it out of Quantico, and in 1985 Brooks become its first director. The BSU then came under the auspices of the FBI's National Center for the Analysis of Violent Crime (NCAVC), and was eventually renamed the Behavioral Analysis Unit, with an Investigative Support Unit offering the Criminal Investigative Analysis Program (CIA).

Around the same time, a case in Narborough, England, precipitated one of the most dramatic contributions to law enforcement since the onset of fingerprinting. In 1983 and 1986, two fifteen-year-old girls were raped and murdered along similar village pathways. Semen specimens showed the killer's blood type to be A. While a kitchen porter capitulated to pressure and confessed to the second incident, he denied involvement in the first one, and there was no compelling evidence to tie him to either crime.

Not far away, in Leicester, geneticist Alec Jeffreys had mapped human genetic profiles via markers in specific regions of the DNA. He had also discovered the profile's consistency across different types of body cells, and since each "map" was unique for each person, aside from those

for identical twins, he named his discovery DNA finger-
printing. He used a process called restriction fragment
length polymorphism (RFLP).

Hearing about this discovery, the Narborough police
approached Jeffreys for help, so he put the semen samples
through RFLP. But while there was no match to the man
who had confessed, indicating that he had made false
statements, the samples matched each other. Determined
to solve these crimes, detectives asked every man in the
area with type-A blood to submit to testing. Thousands
of men were cleared, but the police learned that a man
named Colin Pitchfork had tried to trick them with a
substitute. They interrogated him, getting a confession,
but this time they also had a match via genetic finger-
printing to the semen samples. In 1987 he became the
first person to be convicted with this kind of biological
evidence.

The case made headlines around the world, and investigators paid attention. So did defense attorneys. It
seemed that a potentially foolproof method for solving
many crimes was at hand. The rush was on to apply DNA
technology to more crimes, but defense attorneys challenged it, citing contamination during evidence handling.
The courts grew cautious, so scientists submitted the
process to increased testing and tighter regulations.

Also during the 1980s, Dr. Robert Hare and his colleagues studied the potential for using brain imaging in
the detection of deception. In experiments, they examined how the brain reacted to contexts from which it
would have acquired and stored knowledge, and they pre-

sented their findings to the Society for Psychophysiological Research in 1988. While they went on to pursue brain imaging in psychopaths rather than detection deception, others exposed to these ideas looked into creating mechanisms that would detect brain potentials specific to guilty knowledge in a crime.

The Trend Moves

In Alabama, Jerry Marcus, a black man, offered investigators a lengthy treatise about serial killers like himself, after confessing to seven murders of women between 1970 and 1986. He described his own sick mentality and violent compulsions, as well as his method of charming victims into feeling safe. He thought that people should be aware of shy personalities, for they could hide dangerous souls. Residents of Oregon City, Oregon, learned this around the same time with the seven sexually assaulted female victims of Dayton Leroy Rogers, and then Philadelphia became a hotbed of serial crimes.

Between 1985 and 1989, the City of Brotherly Love experienced three separate series of murders. The "Frankford Slasher" stabbed seven people to death, even as the police learned from an escaping victim about Gary Heidnik, who was holding females prisoner in his house on North Marshall Street. One had died from hanging in chains for several days and Heidnik had electrocuted the other. When police invaded, they found three more nearly-dead women chained in a filthy basement. Heidnik had used them as sex slaves and was planning to add more. After his arrest, he admitted to eating pieces of one victim and feeding some to his captives. Understandably, he offered an insanity defense, but the jury convicted him and gave him a death sentence.

Then, on a sweltering August day in 1987, Harrison "Marty" Graham was evicted from his north Philadelphia apartment for obnoxious odors. He left, but the smell grew worse, so the police went in. They discovered the decomposing corpses of six women, with remains from a seventh. Graham tried to claim that the bodies were there when he moved in, but then confessed to strangling them all during sex—and he had used the same filthy bed for each one. Despite his insanity plea, a judge convicted him in every case.

Then Leonard Christopher, a black man, was arrested and convicted of the Frankford Slasher murders, even as an eighth woman was being similarly murdered, making his conviction controversial. One set of witnesses had seen a white man with some of the victims, but others stood by their identification of Christopher: He had worked in the fish market where the seventh woman was found dead, had inconsistencies in his story, was seen with the victim and a knife, and had spots of blood on his clothing.

Richmond experienced a similar spree with the "Southside Slayer," who committed four rape-murders of women in their beds. In an early use of DNA in a U.S. case (and the first in Virginia), Timothy Spencer was linked to all four cases, as well as one in 1984 for which another man had been convicted. This man became one of the first people in the U.S. to be exonerated with DNA evidence and freed.

Trace evidence analysis assisted in the capture and conviction of a sadistic killer in Wilmington, Delaware. Three prostitutes had been tortured and bludgeoned, and on their battered bodies, investigators found blue carpet fiber from a car or van. A female officer posed as a prostitute in an area where streetwalkers plied their trade, checking out the vehicles of men slowing down to proposition the women. As she talked with the driver of a blue van, she ran her fingernails over the carpeting on the inside of the door, collecting several fibers before she stepped away. They resembled the fibers on the bodies, and the police were able to identify Steve Pennell as the brutal offender, with John Douglas getting a signature analysis from his profile admitted into court.

Angels of Death

While physicians and nurses who enjoyed deciding when their vulnerable patients should die was nothing new, the number of such cases during the eighties was alarming. In Texas, Genene Jones seemed to enjoy the distress of infants whom she had injected with muscle relaxant, and especially loved holding their corpses or transporting them to the morgue. A hospital dismissed her, but when she began to work as a nurse in a private practice, her crimes came to light and a grand jury considered evidence in forty-seven suspicious deaths. With little firm evidence in most of the cases, Jones was convicted of only one murder and one case of causing harm to a child.

In a hospital in Albany, Georgia, after a number of suspicious deaths between October 1985 and February 1986, the police charged nurse Terri Rachals with killing six people with potassium chloride. Given how circumstantial the evidence was, Rachals was eventually sentenced only on aggravated assault. Bobbie Sue Terrell claimed Munchausen syndrome, aggravated by schizophrenia, in the cases of four victims at nursing homes where she worked in Florida. She actually mutilated herself and told police she suspected a serial killer in a St. Petersburg home. In 1988 she pled guilty to reduced charges of second-degree murder and received a sixty-five-year prison term.

The problem with investigating health-care workers accused in these crimes is that they generally knew what medicines the body would absorb. But the males often confessed, in part because the confession itself felt powerful to them. Between 1970 and 1987, when he was arrested, Donald Harvey got away with multiple murders. In 1985, when he was caught with a pistol and forced to resign, he was reading a biography of serial killer Charles Sobhraj. He found another job and resumed killing patients by smothering them or injecting them with such substances as arsenic, cyanide, and petroleum-based cleansers. He chose some victims by occult means, as he chanted over fingernails or hair that he'd placed on a homemade altar. Harvey also poisoned people outside the hospital, including a neighbor and a lover's parents.

It was the death of a patient named John Powell that finally brought him down. During his autopsy, the physician detected high levels of cyanide. Harvey was arrested, but he pleaded not guilty by reason of insanity. Then he confessed to killing thirty-three people, then fifty-two, then more than eighty. He claimed that most of them were mercy killings. In 1987, he entered guilty pleas in various murders in Ohio and Kentucky, until his final official count settled at thirty-nine, along with a number of murder attempts. That gave him the U.S. serial killing record to date.

Operating around the same time, at Good Samaritan Hospital on Long Island in New York, was Richard Angelo, twenty-six. Unlike Harvey, he said that he wanted to save people. "I wanted to create a situation," he confessed, "where I would cause the patient to have some respiratory distress or some problem, and through my intervention or suggested intervention or whatever, come out looking like I knew what I was doing. I had no confidence in myself. I felt very inadequate." He didn't prove very good at "saving" those patients: It's estimated that he managed to kill ten before a patient finally caught him. Nicknamed Long Island's "Angel of Death," Angelo was charged with multiple counts of second-degree murder, or murder with depraved indifference. He claimed a form of temporary insanity at the time of each death, and two psychologists testified that he suffered from multiple personality disorder. The jury convicted Angelo of two counts of second-degree murder, one count of second-degree manslaughter, one count of criminally negligent homicide, and six counts of assault. He was sentenced to sixty-one years to life.

But these nurses were compassionate in comparison to their counterparts in Walker, Michigan. In 1987, Gwendolyn Gail Graham, twenty-three, and Catherine May Wood, twenty-four, were working at the Alpine Manor Nursing Home and became lovers. As they practiced sexual asphyxia to achieve greater orgasms, Graham raised the subject of murder. Soon they were playing "the murder game," picking patients to kill whose initials, when taken all together, would spell out the word "murder." Wood would stand watch while Graham suffocated someone, and then they would wash down the corpse together, sometimes keeping items of the victims to remind them of their atrocities. But when Graham pressured Wood to kill, too, the game fell apart. Wood eventually turned herself and Graham in. For her cooperation, she was sentenced on second-degree murder and conspiracy, drawing consecutive terms of twenty to forty years, while Graham got life on five counts of murder and one of conspiracy, with no possibility of parole.

Babysitters, too, became killers. In Florida, Christine Falling killed three children and claimed that a voice from television had urged her to "kill the baby." In New Zealand, Lise Jane Turner killed three babies, two of them her own, as well as attempting to murder two others. Like Jeanne Weber many years before, Turner offered to watch these children for their grateful mothers and would then attack them. Usually they were found bleeding from the nose and mouth. She was convicted in the three deaths and received life in prison. Debra Sue Tuggle, a rare black female serial killer, ended the lives of four children, hers and her fiancé's, by drowning and suffocation.

Then there were the mothers. Martha Ann Johnson punished her husband by rolling her massive weight on four of her children, killing them. In New York, over a period of fourteen years, Mary Beth Tinning had given birth to eight children and adopted a ninth. All of them died, ostensibly from SIDS—sudden infant death syndrome—but after she was arrested in 1986 Tinning admitted that she had killed several of her children. Acquaintances said that she appeared to like the attention that came with sympathy. She was found guilty in only one death, convicted of second-degree murder, and given twenty years to life.

Then there was the gentle soul in Sacramento, California, named Dorothy Puente. She was quick to "help" those down on their luck, and during the 1980s, this fifty-nine-year-old woman opened her home to welfare and social security recipients. She offered low rent and hot meals, but the turnover was high. Yet the government checks kept getting cashed. Then a social worker looked into the care of a client who was reported missing. She heard about the bad smells coming from Puente's house, so she notified police. Upon investigating, the police dug up the home's lawns and gardens and soon discovered the odor's source: seven bodies covered in lime and plastic, one of which had been beheaded and dismembered. Autopsies later confirmed that the men had died from drug overdoses. Two more bodies were found elsewhere. When arrested, Puente reportedly said, "Did you know I used to be a very good person once?"

It turned out that Puente had a history: She had forged signatures on over sixty checks and had served prison time for theft and fraud. She had been released despite being considered a danger to the elderly. Puente was tried for nine murders but convicted of only three because one male juror refused to believe she had killed that many people. She got life in prison.

Booming Business

In the same year that the Berlin Wall came down, ending the Cold War and joining East and West Germany again, U.S. planes shot down two Libyan fighters over international waters, and George Bush replaced Ronald Reagan as president. People in Beijing demonstrated for democracy and thousands were killed in Tiananmen Square. Oliver North was convicted on three counts in the Iran-Contra Affair (later overturned), Gorbachev became Soviet president, and a Romanian uprising overthrew the communist government.

Serial killers both young and old made their mark as well. Craig Price, fifteen, was arrested in Rhode Island for the triple-stabbing homicide of a woman and her two children, and was then traced to a murder two years earlier, making him thirteen when he got his start. In Rochester, New York, Arthur Shawcross was convicted in the murders of ten women (he pled to an eleventh), and Daniel Lee Corwin was picked up in Texas after raping and attempting to murder a university student. She identified him, and under the new serial murder law, with his confessions to psychiatrists of three other murders, Corwin was the first man to be convicted of "serial murder" and was sentenced to death.

In Chillicothe, Missouri, farmers Ray and Faye Copeland, seventy-five and sixty-nine, respectively, were arrested for killing drifters. The remains of five men were dug up and a ledger was discovered that listed the names of transients who had worked for them; some names were ominously marked with an X. While it was first believed that the murders were Ray's work, Faye wrote a note to her husband to "remain cool," and the handwriting matched that in the ledgers. In addition, Faye had made a patchwork quilt from strips of material identified as clothing from the victims. She was prosecuted for five counts of first-degree murder, found guilty, and sentenced to die. Then Ray was tried, found guilty, and also sentenced to die. They were the oldest couple ever condemned in the United States, but Faye's sentence was commuted to life.

A decade that had started with Satanic crimes also ended with them. Adolfo de Jesus Constanzo was the High Priest and Sara Maria Aldrete his High Priestess. Their murderous behavior was uncovered after twenty-one-year-old college student Mark Kilroy turned up missing. A student at the University of Texas, he had gone with three classmates to Motamoros, Mexico, just over the border, and then disappeared. His family instigated a search and received a tip about a drug raid on Rancho Santa Elena. Apparently a blond man from the States was seen bound and gagged in a van at the ranch. A search turned up an altar in a shed, along with bloodstains, human hair, and something else organic that was later identified as part of a human brain. A severed goat's head indicated that the people there had been involved in a religious cult, which turned out to be a Satanic form of Santeria. They performed human sacrifices to prevent police investigations, and Mark Kilroy's headless torso was discovered in a mass grave containing the decapitated and mutilated bodies of fourteen other men and boys.

All of these people had been killed on the orders of the cult leaders, Constanzo and Aldrete, who had fled before the raid. They had insisted that prior to any major drug deal, they needed the heart and brain of a human victim to boil and consume. Many hapless victims had served that purpose. These two elders were traced to Mexico City in 1989, but Constanzo had ordered his cult members to shoot him while he was locked in an embrace with his lover, and they had obeyed. Aldrete fled but was caught. Though she denied having any part in the human sacrifices, she was indicted. She got six years for her association in the crimes, and in another trial was convicted of multiple murders and received a sentence of sixty-two years.

During the 1980s, coverage of serial killers became its

own industry, inspiring groupies, wanna-bes, and entrepreneurs who created trading cards and sold serial killer memorabilia. Some people even wrote books or participated in documentaries denouncing their fathers as serial killers, albeit without actual evidence. One brother-sister team used unsolved cases in newspapers to support their belief that their father had murdered seventy people. In a "wound culture," where people openly displayed their past damage on talk shows, serial killers were the superstars, as both perpetrators and sufferers. They were the ultimate traumatized children, and many were willing to play this to the hilt. While child abuse was evident in many cases, it did not characterize all of them, but details were made up or exaggerated into "poor me" tales for the public. For television cameras, these killers spoke about their lack of self-esteem, their abuse, and their unrestrained compulsions to erase the lives of others in order to feel alive themselves. Crime analysts thought they were trying to level things out by making others as powerless as they felt.

Newspapers noted how the rash of killings seemed rooted in the critical tensions of unspoken social values—what widespread public behavior truly indicated rather than society's stated ideals. Instead of family values, the culture clearly glorified violence. Those who solved the crimes, covered them, wrote about them, or fictionalized them became celebrities-by-proxy. Whoever had a story about knowing Ted Bundy or John Wayne Gacy got on some television talk show. Eyewitnesses embellished and audience fascination increased with each gory detail.

Serial killers became a pervasive theme on television and in novels, and newspapers prepared for the next grisly offender. "Slasher films" like *Halloween* and *Friday the 13th* provided cultural icons, and just as killers felt enlivened by murder, their audience thrived on reading about them or watching them on television. There were interesting parallels between so-called ordinary people and these offenders, in a manner similar to how gangsters and outlaws had become heroes to people who lived vicariously through their show of boldness and effrontery. Serial killers imbibed the attention, and the media was pleased to give it.

Given a decade of diverse and gruesome violence, as would soon be captured in the controversial best-seller *American Psycho,* reporters believed they had seen it all . . . but they hadn't. Though Thomas Harris's 1988 novel *The Silence of the Lambs,* which featured a cannibalistic serial killer, had seemed surreal as America went into the final decade of the century, in truth it presaged things to come.

CHAPTER FOURTEEN

Still Surprising Us

Decade of Discovery

During President George Bush's tenure, Iraqi dictator Saddam Hussein invaded neighboring Kuwait, prompting a firm response from the UN, with the United States leading the charge in the 1991 Persian Gulf War. It proved popular with Americans as they witnessed exciting high-tech military might forcing Hussein to capitulate. (At least one veteran, Andrew Urdiales in Chicago, went on to become a serial killer.) But Hussein was not forced from power, an oversight that would precipitate another war in a more perilous time. In 1992 U.S. troops invaded Haiti to help overthrow a dictatorship there. Unrest in the States took the form of racial rioting in south-central Los Angeles after four police officers were acquitted in the brutal beating of an African-American, Rodney King. Then a genocide decimated Rwanda and in 1996, U.S.

troops went to Bosnia. The 1990s revealed the global community in a stressful state.

Morality was reassessed as postmodern ideas trickled from academic circles to the masses. A reliance on absolutes, dissolved by political scandals, yielded to a cynical reaction that truth was a protean concept. Yet even as people sought moral footing, the economy recovered from the eighties' overindulgence and surpassed most predictions.

In wealthy countries, widespread computer sales and satellite communications contributed to a stable and lucrative market, and the World Wide Web was born (with more than a hundred million participants by the end of that decade). But contrary to the youth culture's "Celestine prophecies," it wasn't "all good." Violence framed entertainment and children prepared to start killing their classmates—a phenomenon that would reach its pinnacle by the decade's end.

Early in the decade, serial killing was reported in many more places, such as Norway, Sweden, Costa Rica, Spain, Poland, Holland, Mexico, Belize, Venezuela, Greece, and Pakistan. It seemed that the global economy and the way the increasingly popular Internet could inform the international community within hours of any event created shared conditions—notably, stress—for the emergence of serial crimes. Brazil had multiple reports, as did South Africa, Japan, Italy, Canada, Australia, and Russia, but Britain weighed in with more than a dozen serial killers. Even China had several, and Singapore announced its first such arrest with "Tourist from Hell" John Martin Scripps (a British citizen), who was convicted and hanged for butchering a man from South Africa.

The highest victim toll of any one case occurred outside the U.S. In six years, drifter Luis Alfredo Garavito killed at least 140 young boys in Colombia and Ecuador. He won their trust by parading as a priest or teacher, only to rape, mutilate, and behead them. When more than two dozen sets of remains were found, the investigation spotlighted Garavito, already arrested for child murder. He had recorded each of his murders in a journal, and under intense grilling he confessed to them all.

When Pakistani police dismissed a criminal complaint filed by Javed Iqbal against two boys who had beaten him, he plotted revenge. In 1999, the thirty-seven-year-old merchant enticed poor children to his residence for food and offered them a place to sleep. Once they were vulnerable, he asphyxiated them with cyanide. Then he dissolved the bodies in acid and dumped the liquid paste into a sewer. He too kept a detailed journal of every murder, and even tallied the exact cost of each one. Once he had killed his allotted number, one hundred, he turned himself in. In explanation, he said, "I wanted one hundred mothers to cry for their children." Iqbal was sentenced to be strangled in front of the families of his victims and cut into pieces that would be dissolved in acid. Instead, he committed suicide in his cell in October 2001.

One reason that serial killers were getting caught with greater frequency was that forensic science had become a high-tech arena, with more exacting ways to analyze evidence. Fiber analysis pieced together three murders of young girls in Virginia in 1996, because examiners could use a high-powered microscope to measure the precise diameter and color, shine a beam of infrared light to get the absorption spectrum, use polarized light to find refractive indices, or turn to chromatography to separate dye compounds into specific chemicals.

With the emerging science of DNA, a 1989 case in New York had significant repercussions. The lab had made a technical error with the analysis, invalidating the DNA results. Aware of the potential for mistakes, the courts then ruled that DNA could be used only to *exclude* suspects, not to make claims that a suspect's DNA was a match to biological evidence from a scene. Scientists raced to improve their methods, and ultimately technology that could demonstrate the chance that a sample originated with a specific defendant would show statistical odds so overwhelming that the courts finally allowed increased use of DNA testimony. In 1992, the National Research Council Committee of the National Academy of Sciences affirmed the use of DNA but recommended tight regulations over collection and analysis. Such improvements limited defense challenges to human error during evidence collection or during the application of new techniques.

DNA testing helped to pin twelve murders on Lorenzo Gilyard in Kansas City, Missouri. It also exonerated a man imprisoned eight years for attacking his pregnant wife by linking that 1978 crime to serial killer Gerald Parker, who had invaded the couple's home.

Monsters

During the 1990s, claims about Satanism were infrequent, although killers such as Joshua Rudiger in San Francisco, Brazil's Marcelo Costa de Andrade, and Robert Gadek in Indonesia were dubbed "criminal vampires" because they sometimes drank the blood of their victims. Heriberto Seda showed up in New York City as another "Zodiac" killer, inspired by author Aleister Crowley and signing his letters to news agencies as "Faust." He succeeded for several years before he was arrested for an assault on his sister. He confessed to a number of murders, was convicted, and received a sentence of eighty years. There were more arrests of health-care killers and more men vying to be the world's most notorious serial murderer. Incidents of prostitute murders such as the six killed in Florida by Tamiami strangler Rory Conde, were frequent (Minnesota reportedly had thirty-four attributed to the "Twin Cities Killer"), as were child murders (by mothers as well as strangers) and attacks on elderly victims. With so many cases, it became easier to categorize this type of killer into such types as lust killers; rape-murderers; gay killers like Juan Cordoba and Herb Baumeister; delusional killers such as Long Island murderer Joel Rifken and "Railway Killer" Angel Maturino Resendez; those motivated primarily by gain, such as the Tene Bimbo Gypsy clan who victimized elderly men; and episodic killers who moved from one situation to another via erasure of witnesses or people considered to be burdens. Criminologists set to work devising and analyzing data, watching as predictable patterns developed, and preparing for media commentary. While many cases acquired infamy only in local areas, some did stand out.

Since the end of the seventies, the U.S. had been acknowledged as the country that produced the most serial killers—overestimated at 75 percent (it was likely around 60 to 65 percent at best) and historical case analysis was forgotten as experts studied the social conditions that made this type of murderer so prevalent on American soil. But they received a surprise when a dismantled U.S.S.R. admitted to the capture of a man wanted for nearly a decade for the murder and mutilation of over fifty women and children. In this case, behavioral analysis played a crucial role.

On girls and women, this killer would gouge the breasts and destroy the vagina, uterus, and bladder or abdomen. On boys, he would mutilate the penis, scrotum, and anus, and once even chewed out a tongue. A few victims were stabbed through the eyes. His signature was clear, but the Russian investigators' technology was archaic, making it difficult to run a proper investigation. They were able to determine that the killer had AB blood, which helped to eliminate suspects, but were forbidden from publicizing the murders to get public assistance. When they applied for funding and manpower, government officials insisted that serial killers were a "bourgeois phenomenon." (They were reluctant to admit to Gennadiy Mikasevich, who had killed thirty-three; to Vladimir Ionosyan, with his five murders in Moscow; or to Ivan the Ripper, with his eleven.)

Trying with scant resources to narrow leads, and influenced by the FBI's BSU, chief investigator Viktor Burakov asked psychiatrists to draw up a profile. Dr. Alexandr Bukhanovsky said that the killer was a sexual deviate, twenty-five to fifty years old, around five feet ten, and suffered from sexual inadequacy, explaining that he brutalized the corpses to enhance his arousal.

The U.S.S.R.'s disintegration eased political control of the investigation, and Andrei Chikatilo was nabbed at a train station picking up children. Searching his bag, detectives found Vaseline, a rope, and a knife. But Chikatilo had type-A blood, and for that reason, they had released him earlier when he'd been a suspect. This time, however, they were certain they had the right man. All they needed was a confession, but Chikatilo offered nothing. When his release appeared imminent, they brought in Dr. Bukhanovsky. The psychiatrist recognized in Chikatilo the type of man he had described in his profile: ordinary, solitary, nonthreatening. Painstakingly, he read his report to Chikatilo, who then broke down and confessed to fifty-six murders, although there was corroboration for only fifty-three: thirty-one females and twenty-two males. He received sexual gratification, he admitted, from murder, mutilation, and cannibalism.

The blood-type discrepancy was most likely due to improper procedures or contaminated crime labs. Placed into a cage for the trial, Chikatilo was found legally sane and sentenced to die.

From the mid-1980s to the end of the century, twenty-nine such offenders were caught around the country. Dr. Bukhanovsky studied the brains of these killers, finding structural abnormalities in the frontal lobes. One of the most devilish of these offenders was a man who invaded homes to slaughter whole families with a shotgun.

Called "The Terminator," Anatoly Onoprienko terrorized the Ukraine, murdering a dozen women before he turned his rage into more wholesale slaughter. Then, after taking what he could, he burned the home. Sometimes he scattered photographs of the family, as if the very idea of kinship enraged him—perhaps because he'd been an orphan. In addition, he killed people at random—a police officer, men sitting in a car, people who merely looked at him as he fled a crime scene. His cousin alerted police, who found possessions from the victims in Onoprienko's girlfriend's home. Like Chikatilo, Onoprienko claimed to have killed more than fifty people, and he too thought the authorities ought to study him. He said that "voices from above" had ordered him to kill. But the authorities had the same opinion of him as of his murderous countryman, who had been executed before Onoprienko's arrest.

Russian investigators also had to contend with Ilshat Kuzikov, suffering from schizophrenia, who was arrested for three murders. In his apartment were severed human limbs, bones, and buckets full of flesh that he had marinated for later consumption—reportedly with onions. Sergei Shipin, also a cannibal, confessed to eleven murders; a man in Novokuznetsk admitted to nineteen; and in Sebastopol, a cannibal killer had butchered three people for consumption.

The U.S., too, had its heinous cases. In Gainesville, Florida, during the summer of 1990, there were five gruesome rape-murders in quick succession. The first crime scene involved two freshmen at the University of Florida who had been repeatedly stabbed, mutilated, and posed for shocking effect. That same night, investigators found a missing eighteen-year-old in her bedroom: Her head was propped on a bookshelf and her nude, mutilated body bent over onto the edge of the bed. Two days later, a mile away, a male and female student were found dead in their apartment. As with the others, entry to the apartment had been forced with a pry tool.

An FBI profiler indicated that the perpetrator had probably watched each apartment from the nearby woods. The police found a campsite, and there they discovered a black bag with a screwdriver, money taken during a bank robbery, duct tape, a cassette recorder, and clothes. But when the screwdriver failed to match the pry marks from the scenes, these items were forgotten . . . until Danny Rolling was arrested for robbing a store. They listened to the cassette in the recorder, which began, "This is Danny Rolling." He sang a song about being insane and signed off with "something I gotta do." Confronted, Rolling confessed but blamed an alter ego, Gemini—inspired by a movie, *The Exorcist III.*

In this 1990 film, based on *The Exorcist,* a demon that had variously possessed the child Regan and a priest has migrated into a wandering lunatic, who is locked up. But fifteen years later, murders begin with the same MO and the police are confronted with the sadistic Gemini Killer. His favorite method is to paralyze his victims with succinlycholine, which leaves them alert and aware of their torture. Gemini is the "thing" inside the killer, using the man's body to perform his gory deeds.

Rolling did not get a pass on this lame attempt at a multiple personality defense. He was convicted and sentenced to die, and while going through appeals wrote a book about his crimes. He was not alone in being inspired by this movie.

Fiction and Facts

During the early 1990s, the world learned about serial killers in a more accessible venue. Novelist Thomas Harris had attended meetings at the FBI's Behavioral Science Unit and then wrote *Red Dragon* and *The Silence of the Lambs*. In 1991 the latter was made into an internationally acclaimed film. In the story, agent-in-training Clarice Starling is sent to meet with imprisoned serial killer and cannibal Dr. Hannibal Lecter to learn about the mind of "Buffalo Bill," a murderer who is holding a woman hostage. This killer was based on a combination of the MOs of Ted Bundy, Gary Heidnik, and Ed Gein.

Not long afterward, several of the first-generation profilers retired from the FBI and penned books. They were touted by publishers as contemporary versions of Sherlock Holmes. Thanks in large part to these media events, profiling evolved from its place as just one among many crime investigation tools into the "ultimate" weapon. In fiction, serial killers were redesigned to become worthy adversaries to these super-sleuths, and the public was increasingly fed inaccurate information.

In the meantime, police officers faced other surprises, and the early part of the decade featured a unique incident in the lore of serial killers. It started in December 1989 when an abandoned car was found not far from Daytona Beach, Florida, with bloody seats. The car belonged to Richard Mallory, known to pick up prostitutes. Mallory's corpse was found in the woods, shot four times in the chest with a .22-caliber gun.

In May 1991, a truck was found along a Florida highway, registered to David Spears. His naked corpse was discovered sixty miles away, shot with a .22. While no fingerprints were found in the car, there was a strand of blond hair. Five days later, another male corpse was found, also shot with a .22. Then someone spotted two women removing the license plates from a silver Sunbird that had been stolen from a missing missionary. Composite sketches were distributed, and more male corpses were found. Finally, several people identified a pair of lesbians, Tyria Moore and "Lee," aka Aileen Wuornos, who was soon arrested in a biker bar, the Last Resort. Police pressured Moore to tell what she knew, and used a key found in Wuornos's possession to enter a storage space, where they located items missing from some of the victims.

Moore agreed to get Wuornos to talk on tape. On January 16, 1991, Wuornos went to the police and confessed that she had killed seven men. She said that she had wrestled with Mallory before she shot him and claimed self-defense. Psychologist Elizabeth McMahon supported her, explaining that Wuornos's background had made her paranoid about men: Her mother had abandoned her as an infant and her schizophrenic father had been imprisoned for rape. Wuornos had lived with her maternal grandparents. When a friend of her grandfather's impregnated her, she was forced to give up the baby and live on the streets, so to survive she turned tricks. In Florida, she acquired a gun. Since her first victim, Mallory, had served ten years in a psychiatric institute for sexual offenses, Dr. McMahon believed that his allegedly brutal behavior had triggered the spree.

The prosecutor used Tyria Moore as his star witness. She said she had known about the murders but had never heard a word about self-defense. Wuornos was convicted of murder and given the death penalty six times. Thereafter, she was dubbed the first female serial killer. While not the first by a long shot, or the worst, and not even the first to use a gun (contrary to claims by criminologists), she became *the* predatory female psychopath. Later she gave an interview recanting her testimony that she had killed in self-defense.

While Wuornos commanded media attention for her uniqueness, there was much less fanfare for former nurse Dana Sue Gray in California. Like Wuornos, she murdered strangers, killing three elderly women, whom she strangled and bludgeoned. It was a rare series of murders for a woman, exhibiting direct physical contact and excessive force. She also admitted to being excited by the violence, but there was nothing in her background indicative of abuse or deprivation. She merely appeared to enjoy the feeling of domination although she also took the victims' credit cards and indulged in spending sprees.

Around the same time as the Wuornos series, a killer in Austin, Texas, left an alarming signature. Between 1990 and 1991, three prostitutes turned up murdered, and their eyes had been cut out so skillfully that the eyelids had not been nicked. On a tip from a woman who'd gotten away, Charles Albright, fifty-seven and married, was arrested. In his home were a number of dolls. A hair and fiber analysis on debris from his vacuum cleaner, a blanket, and the victims identified him—resulting in the first murder conviction in Texas based on such an analysis. Highly intelligent and friendly, Albright was fluent in several languages, coached baseball, and had taught biology. He could also paint and play musical instruments. Yet he had a brutal side and a criminal record, as well as an obsession with eyes, which he maintained even in prison by drawing eyes and hanging them around his cell.

In Claremont, California, Cleophus Prince, too, left a signature, in the form of picquerism, or the gaining of sexual satisfaction by substitute penetration. Entering homes and stabbing six women to death with multiple punctures, he seemed always to group the wounds in circles on several areas of the chest, especially the left breast.

Then the killer who would be dubbed "The Real Hannibal Lecter" was arrested in July 1991 in Milwaukee.

Inside his apartment, police came upon a scene that they'd heard about only in *Psycho,* but this killer's favorite movie, like Danny Rolling's, was *The Exorcist III.* Acting on a complaint by a handcuffed victim, the police had gone into Jeffrey Dahmer's apartment. A look inside his refrigerator revealed human heads, intestines, hearts, and kidneys. Around the apartment they found skulls, bones, rotting body parts, bloodstained soup kettles, and complete skeletons. There were three torsos in the tub. A collection of Polaroid snapshots showed mutilated bodies, and what was going on became clear with the discovery of chloroform, electric saws, a barrel of acid, and formaldehyde. The soft-spoken Dahmer was killing men, then cutting off body pieces and preserving them or dissolving them in acid. In all, investigators were able to find the remains of eleven different men. Dahmer quietly confessed to six more.

It seemed that serial killing with primitive accoutrements had made no shifts in appetite since Ancient Rome or medieval times. Dahmer's case, along with those of many of the Russian killers, demonstrated that some predators still consumed human flesh and still eroticized the godlike hubris of absorbing another's life. Dahmer became the new symbol of evil. Like Ted Bundy, Dennis Nilsen, and killers from earlier decades, he'd lived among his potential victims, suspected by no one. The serial killer was the new vampire.

Dahmer's first murder occurred when he was eighteen. He lured an attractive hitchhiker named Steve Hicks to his home with the promise of getting high. When Hicks decided to leave, Dahmer smashed his head with a barbell and strangled him. "I didn't know how else to keep him there," he said to FBI profiler Robert Ressler. He discovered during the incident that the captivity of another human being aroused him, and while cutting the body into pieces for disposal, he'd masturbated over it.

Later he moved in with his grandmother, but the compulsion gripped him again. Attending the funeral of a young man, he made plans to go to the cemetery at night and dig up the body, but thwarted in that, he began to pick up men in bars. After drugging and strangling them, he'd have sex with the corpses and then dismember them. While living with his grandmother, he killed and cut up four people in her basement. Getting his own apartment facilitated the murders and allowed him to keep body parts. In an effort to create zombielike slaves, he drilled holes into the heads of his unconscious victims and injected acid or boiling water. He also tried to preserve their faces as masks, and designed an altar made of skulls.

Lionel Dahmer, Jeffrey's father, was overcome upon learning that the sons of seventeen other fathers had been treated thus by *his* son, so he wrote a memoir to explore the cause. He was unaware that his son had a substance abuse problem, but he did notice that Jeffrey often seemed vacant—"enclosed"—as if thinking about nothing. Was he born this way, Lionel Dahmer wondered, or did he lose or acquire something along the way? Was his proclivity terrible to him, or was he indifferent?

These questions were on everyone's minds as the research on antisocial personality disorder and psychopathy became more urgent and spread to such populations as females, children, and ethnic groups. In *Without Conscience,* Robert Hare wrote about the high percentage of psychopaths among us. They were not easy to spot and since many used a chameleonic persona, they might get away with secret crimes for quite a while. Their drive was based on the need for power and control. They viewed the world in terms of "givers" and "takers," feeling justified about being takers. According to some of Hare's neurological studies, they apparently failed to process emotions the way ordinary people did, potentially undermining their bonds with others and their ability to develop empathy and remorse—the typical hindrances to aggression.

Researcher Adrian Raine, from the University of Southern California and long interested in the neurological correlates of psychopathic behavior, found brain deficits in several areas that appeared to contribute to violence—specifically the limbic system (the emotional center) and the prefrontal cortex. Psychopaths, he found, were impulsive, fearless, less responsive than others to aversive stimulation, and less able to make appropriate decisions about aggression toward others. They also tended to seek out sensation-stimulating activities. Predatory murderers were lacking in affect and were much more likely to attack strangers than were those whose violence was reactive.

Many people believed that if anyone deserved to use the insanity defense, it was a man like Dahmer, but the jury found him to be sane, and he was convicted.

Within a month of Dahmer's arrest, after killing a ten-year-old child, Donald Leroy Evans, thirty-four, a self-described white supremacist, confessed to more than sixty murders in several different states since 1977. Police were wary of such a string of confessions after the Henry Lee Lucas fiasco, but hoped to close many unsolved cases. They didn't. Evans was convicted in only two murders and later recanted his extravagant confession.

Strangely enough, sometimes killers who tried to confess were ignored. Cross-country trucker Keith Jesperson had strangled a number of women, but to his surprise, someone else claimed credit for the first one, in 1989. Laverne Pavlinac had reported her boyfriend, John Sosnovske, to the police as the killer. He denied being involved, but Pavlinac insisted he had boasted about it. Sosnovske was arrested, and a jury gave Pavlinac ten years for being an accomplice. At no point did she recant. Sosnovske then pled no contest in exchange for a life sentence.

Jesperson decided (as he asserts in the autobiography he later penned) that he wanted credit for his murders, so he left messages signed with smiley faces in truck stops and sent a letter to the Portland, Oregon, newspaper. Finally identified in 1995, he confessed to six murders, including that of the young woman for whose death Pavlinac and Sosnovske were serving time, so they were released. It turned out that Pavlinac habitually reported Sosnovske to police whenever they had a serious quarrel. Jesperson went on to admit to more than 160 murders, but recanted and then accepted responsibility for a crime that he could not have done, so the authorities settled on eight victims for the "Happy Face Killer." He was sentenced in only four.

Then there was Glen Rogers, the "Cross-Country Killer." Not only did he confess to seventy murders from California to Florida and then recant, but he was also implicated in the murders of Nicole Brown Simpson and Ronald Goldman. The attorneys for O. J. Simpson, who went through the "trial of the century" in 1995, posed Rogers as a likely suspect. Yet while Simpson was acquitted in a controversial verdict that threw glaring light on faulty evidence handling, Rogers was never arrested for the double murder. Still, he proved a strong suspect in five other murders. From prison, he offered strands of his hair and beard to prison groupies who clamored to see him, and was sentenced to death in Florida for murdering a woman there.

Dangerous Decade

Bill Clinton became U.S. president in '93, despite numerous accusations from women of sexual misconduct (a source of material for a later impeachment hearing in a scandal with White House intern Monica Lewinsky). He had to deal at once with the botched Bureau of Alcohol, Tobacco, Firearms, and Explosives (BATF) raid on the Branch Davidian compound in Waco, Texas, which turned into a siege and ended with the deaths of more than eighty people, including children. At the end of that year, the U.S. experienced a terrorist attack when a bomb exploded at the World Trade Center, killing six and injuring more than a thousand.

In response to the incident at Waco and on its anniversary, Timothy McVeigh, twenty-seven, drove a Ryder rental truck into Oklahoma City on August 19, 1995. He parked outside of the seven-story Alfred P. Murrah government building and walked away. At 9:02 A.M., a 4,000-pound bomb exploded, killing 168 people, including children in a day-care center, and injuring more than 500. The threat of domestic terrorism alarmed the American people.

Forensic science was increasingly involved in these investigations, and at the Body Farm, Dr. Bill Bass analyzed a series of murders for a time-since-death analysis. Just east of Knoxville, Tennessee, on October 20, 1992, a hunter found the bound body of a decomposing prostitute. Police suspected a brutal john known for bringing women to this area: Thomas Dee Huskey, thirty-two, who had a prior arrest for rape (for which he was convicted in 2004). The streetwalkers knew him as the "Zoo Man" for his propensity to take women behind the zoo for sex.

Then three more victims were found in the same vicinity, so police interrogated Huskey. He confessed on tape to all four murders, but then his voice became aggressive and he indicated that he was now "Kyle," another personality, and that *he* had committed the murders. Then came "Philip Daxx," who had a British accent. So it was no surprise when Huskey's attorney entered a plea of not guilty by reason of insanity. The case came to trial in 1999, with a defense of multiple personality disorder (now called dissociative identity disorder to shed the stigma). The question before the jury was whether his case was genuine or he was malingering, and one expert said that the alters were based on characters from a daytime soap opera, *Days of Our Lives*. A jailhouse snitch testified that Huskey had read *Sybil*. After much deliberation, the jury was unable to arrive at a decision, and the judge declared a mistrial. Later, in 2002, due to Huskey's having been denied a lawyer during the course of his confession, it would be ruled inadmissible. The case is awaiting a second trial.

Chameleons

Some serial killers were not only handsome and charming but had also learned how to remain under the investigative radar. Even when they were suspected, it was difficult to believe the extent and nature of their crimes. As they were studied, experts wised up, but even so, the very clever ones still managed murder sprees.

When several murdered women were found in Austria, strangled with their underwear, a retired detective suggested that law enforcement learn the whereabouts of convicted murderer Jack Unterweger. He had been sent to prison, but not long before the victims turned up, he'd been paroled. Having learned to read and write in prison, he'd become a best-selling novelist and playwright, inspiring the Vienna literati to pressure for his release. Once out, he'd been hired to cover crimes such as murder, and began to castigate police for not solving this series of crimes. But he was always in the right place at the right time. In fact, in Los Angeles, he had asked police to show him where prostitutes could be found so he could write about them for an Austrian magazine. Three then turned up dead, strangled in the same fashion as eight female victims in Czechoslovakia and Austria.

A VICAP analysis at Quantico assisted the Austrian task force in linking the eleven murders, and Unterweger was caught and tried. Despite his protests of innocence, he was convicted. Since he had insisted he would not spend another day in prison, while the guards were not looking he hanged himself.

Like Unterweger, Karla Homolka and Paul Bernardo seemed above suspicion. Known as "Ken and Barbie" around the Toronto, Canada, area where they lived, they killed three times. As they jetted off on their honeymoon, authorities were pulling the dismembered remains of their second victim from a lake, encased in eight separate cement bricks. Homolka was a seemingly average middle-class girl who just wanted a boyfriend, but Bernardo was a sexual sadist who had raped more than a dozen women. Nevertheless, Homolka became a coequal with him in violence. She offered her fifteen-year-old sister to him, comatose, as a Christmas gift, but overdosed the girl with the tranquilizer, causing young Tammy to drown in her own vomit. They passed it off as an accident, and within a month Karla was dressing in Tammy's clothes so Bernardo could reenact raping the child.

Then Bernardo brought home Leslie Mahaffy, four-

teen, whom he raped on videotape, strangled, and dismembered. Following her, he and Homolka grabbed
schoolgirl Kristen French while she was walking home.
Weeks later she was found murdered, her long brown hair
hacked off. Before killing her, they had kept her captive
for a few days for their pleasure. As the police closed in,
Homolka negotiated a short prison term in exchange for
details about Bernardo's involvement, and he was charged
with forty-two criminal counts. Convicted on all of them,
he went to prison for life. (Years later, he was suggested as
the perpetrator in a fourth murder.) Karla was released in
2005.

By that time, some experts indicated that around 20
percent of all serial killers were male-female teams, including the nice couple next door, Fred and Rosemary
West, who were sexual sadists with more than twelve victims between them. Fred had killed three times before
meeting Rosemary, including his first wife, and he
and Rosemary had tortured young girls, including their
sixteen-year-old daughter. To elude detection, they had
buried the remains in their home and garden, placing the
beds of their living children over graves in the cellar. After
his arrest, Fred said he had killed more than twenty
women.

Fred tried to exonerate his wife, but a young woman
who had escaped their sexual tortures testified that Rosemary was a fiend as well, and a scientific analysis of the
exhumed remains of Fred's daughter from a prior relationship proved that Rosemary was a killer in her own
right. Fred committed suicide in 1995, leaving Rosemary

to go it alone. She denied everything, but the jury convicted her in ten of the murders.

Profiling Overseas

In 1992, as the practice of apartheid was abolished, Africa reported a number of serial murderers operating in quick succession, many of them claiming to have multiple personalities. Between 1994 and 1996 alone, seven serial killers were arrested, and most of the reported seventy-five murders were around Johannesburg. As in Russia, the dismantling of a political system seemed either to spark more such killing or to allow it to be uncovered more readily.

A police officer-turned-security guard in East London, South Africa, began to shoot people whom he claimed had been "resisting arrest." He was thought to have killed thirty-nine out of a hundred targeted people over three years. Once apartheid had dissolved, authorities reexamined Louis van Schoor's behavior, and he was found guilty of seven of the murders and sentenced to twenty years.

Many killers in South Africa acquired savage monikers: the "Cape Town Strangler," who tortured and killed at least twenty prostitutes; "Donnybrook Serial Killer" Christopher Mhlengwa Zikode, who murdered eighteen people and attempted another eleven killings over two years; "Kranskop Rapist-Killer" Samuel Bongani Mfeka, who confessed to raping and strangling six women; and

Sipho Agmatir Thwala, who was charged with being the "Phoenix Strangler" and convicted of the murders of sixteen women. David Mmbengwa, the "Lover's Lane Murderer," believed he was on a divine mission each time he murdered a couple making love. He was charged with eight murders, while the "Station Strangler," suspected of sodomizing and strangling twenty-one boys at train stations, turned out to be Norman Avzal Simon, who could speak seven languages. Multiple killers in that area also murdered people to grab their body parts for a lucrative black market among witch doctors. Many of the victims were children, and all had their necks from the shoulders to the chin removed.

Others were arrested as well, including one crossdresser, but the most surprising case involved two different killers working at the same time. Between July and October 1994, fifteen bodies of females in their twenties were found in South Africa, near the Pretoria-Johannesburg suburb of Cleveland. All had been raped and strangled. "Cleveland Strangler" David Selepe was identified as the offender and jailed, but when fifteen more bodies turned up the next year in Atteridgeville, it seemed that the real killer was still at large. Seven months later, another cache of bodies was discovered near Boksburg with the same MO but dumped closer together, and these three groups of victims were dubbed the ABC killings after the areas in which they'd been found.

FBI profiler Robert Ressler said that the killer had returned to the bodies and there was evidence of escalation and increasing expertise. Ressler deduced that the

offender was familiar with the areas, had done surveillance, and had grown arrogant. He was also luring victims
rather than attacking them by surprise. He was probably
black, owned a vehicle, appeared to be well-off, was young,
and had a strong sex drive. Ressler believed he would contact the police or newspapers, and soon an anonymous
caller claimed credit and said that he'd once been falsely
accused of rape, and going to prison had ruined him. The
police arrested thirty-one-year-old youth counselor Moses
Sithole. They believed he'd been in cahoots with Selepe,
but he proved to have acted alone and was in fact responsible for several of the murders linked to Selepe. By the
end of the decade, at least thirty serial killers had been
identified in South Africa, with several still on the loose.

Ressler was also involved in a series of killings in Britain that proved to be unfortunate artifacts of the media
machine. Colin Ireland was among those men who fanta-
sized about being a serial killer and then decided to act on
it, rather than being driven to it by compulsion; he just
wanted to be thus identified. Bullied as a boy, he started
with a series of juvenile crimes. Then he studied murder
and prepared a murder kit, selecting victims he believed
would be off society's radar and therefore easy targets:
men who would willingly accept bondage for kinky sexual
escapades. He posed the corpse of his first victim, a forty-
five-year-old man, and waited for the news. But it didn't
come, so Ireland telephoned a newspaper to "leak" the
story. Two months later, he killed another man and found
himself forced to call again. With the third victim he
anonymously told the police he had left two clues.

Ressler profiled the three crime scenes. Then a fourth victim turned up, his cat strangled and left with its mouth on his penis. The killer made several calls, claiming he was losing control. He'd inadvertently left a fingerprint, but managed a fifth victim and another phone call, in which he admitted that he read a lot of books about serial killers and knew that he could now be classified as one, so he was going to stop. But his fingerprint identified him and he finally confessed, receiving five life sentences.

From the mid-1980s until 1996, Marc Dutroux developed an international child pornography ring in Charleroi, Belgium—although he himself had three children. He supported them and his second wife by kidnapping young girls and selling them into prostitution across Europe. In 1989, he was convicted in the rape of five young girls, but was granted early release after three years. He continued to abduct girls and keep them imprisoned in secret dungeons in empty houses that he owned. When police raided one of those homes in 1996, they found three hundred pornographic videos of children and a concrete dungeon containing two girls, ages twelve and fourteen. They had been grabbed off the streets, thrown into the dungeon, and forced to pose for films. But other girls had died under this treatment: When Dutroux had been incarcerated for a month for car theft, they had starved to death, and he had later buried them in his backyard, along with the body of an accomplice, who was buried alive. Two other girls were found under concrete near another of his houses. Dutroux was convicted of rape, kidnapping, and murder, and sentenced to life in prison.

Italy experienced several killing sprees near the end of the decade, one involving elderly women, another security guards and people in washrooms on trains, while a Portuguese killer called the "Lisbon Ripper" was linked to the strangulation murders of five prostitutes in the Lisbon area and seven in five other European countries. "Jack the Butcher" raped, murdered, and mutilated a number of young girls in Belize City, Belize.

An Australian predator, Ivan Milat, murdered seven hitchhikers in the Belanglo State Forest in New South Wales. Like Robert Hansen in Alaska, he would allow them a head start into the forest and then hunt them down and kill them. Known as the "Backpack Murderer," he shot some, stabbed some, and decapitated one with a sword. But even as some of these killers were getting caught, many murders believed to be linked in a series went unsolved as well, especially in countries where the investigation system was lacking in training and resources.

At least ten prostitutes were slain by the same killer in Spokane and Tacoma, Washington, and authorities in North Dakota linked four more to that series. Robert Lee Yates was arrested for a 1997 murder in Spokane and then admitted to ten other murders, though not the ones in North Dakota. More than two dozen strangulation murders committed between 1991 and 1996 were tentatively linked in the New Orleans area, mostly involving black women and transsexuals with histories of drug abuse and prostitution. All were found nude and dumped in swamps or remote roadsides and bayous. Often such investigations, once cold, offered little hope of resolution, but with greater technology, some of them eventually yielded. In Illinois the mother of one killer (the third in a string of three killers in Chicago) actually helped him to hide a body.

Difficult to Categorize

Also in the States, the FBI had long been after a man who did his killing by mail. He was dubbed the "Unabomber." Between 1978 and 1995, this person had constructed and mailed lethal bombs that killed three people and injured twenty-three others. Finally, after police learned that the style of the Unabomber's manifesto, printed in the *New York Times,* resembled the ramblings of a man named Theodore Kaczynski, he was arrested in Sacramento, California, in April 1996. He tried to defend himself, despite being diagnosed with paranoid schizophrenia, but finally he pled guilty to thirteen of the crimes.

Andrew Cunanan gripped the nation's attention between April and July 1997, inspiring a publicized debate among criminologists over the distinction between spree and serial killers. Cunanan killed two people he knew in Minnesota, moved on to Chicago shortly thereafter to kill a businessman, and then murdered a cemetery worker in New Jersey for his truck. Cunanan ended his spree in South Beach, Florida, with the fatal shooting of fashion designer Gianni Versace, before killing himself on a houseboat. This cluster of killings had taken place over six weeks, with an obvious "cooling off" period, yet were all related to the same psychological momentum from start to finish. Cunanan's case would continue to be a source of disagreement.

There was an epidemic, too, of children who took guns to school to kill teachers and classmates. While not an example of serial killing, this burst of incidents of multiple murder by children was clearly a cultural event. Between 1979 and 1999, there were thirty-one separate incidents, but the majority—and the most dramatic—occurred in the last half of the 1990s.

By 1996, the country had taken note of the phenomenon when student Barry Loukaitis of Moses Lake, Washington, went into a classroom dressed as an Old West gunslinger and shot four people, killing three. He was convicted of murder and assault. A month later in Georgia, another boy killed a teacher in the hallway, and the following year saw four separate school shootings around America. One boy in Mississippi, Luke Woodham, said that demons had told him to kill, but it was more likely a reaction to a girlfriend's breaking up with him. He killed her, as well as his mother and one of the girl's friends. His insanity defense was rejected and he was convicted of murder and aggravated assault. Michael Carneal shot into a prayer group in Kentucky, killing three girls, and later pled guilty but mentally ill. Then, in 1998, eleven-year-old Andrew Golden joined his buddy Mitchell Johnson, thirteen, in shooting female teachers and students as they fled a school in Jonesboro, Arkansas. Of fifteen people hit, five died. Four were children. Both boys were too young to be waived to an adult court and were ordered to be confined to a juvenile facility until they were twenty-one.

That same year, Andrew Wurst, fourteen, took a pistol to a school dance in Pennsylvania and killed a popular teacher. He went to prison. Less than a month later, on May 21, fifteen-year-old Kipland Kinkel murdered his parents, booby-trapped his home with bombs, and went to school to shoot his classmates and commit suicide. He killed two and wounded seven before being arrested. Contemplating an insanity defense, he pled guilty to four counts of murder and other charges and received life in prison. Things settled down for a while, but on April 20, 1999, at Columbine High School in Littleton, Colorado, Eric Harris and Dylan Klebold went to school to use the arsenal of bombs and guns they had collected over the previous year to get back at people who had bullied them. That morning they ran through the school with guns and bombs they'd hidden under their trench coats. They hoped to blow up the school and kill as many people as possible, and in the end they did claim thirty-four victims, of whom thirteen died, before the two boys took their own lives there in the building.

While the incidents that followed Columbine were not as dramatic, several copycat wanna-bes attempted to "out-Columbine Columbine" but were caught before they could do any damage. A few of them were girls, one of them thirteen. Criminologists and sociologists set about looking for factors to blame, from violent videos to parental neglect, but the incidents seemed to have run their course, with only sporadic violence taking place in schools thereafter, including a massacre in Red Lake, Minnesota, on March 25, 2005, when sixteen-year-old Jeff Weise killed nine people and then shot himself.

And while he was not a school killer, in 1997 a fourteen-year-old boy in Kobe, Japan, killed and mutilated four children for sexual gratification, placing the head of one on the school gate.

"Care" Givers

The decade of the nineties seemed to either inspire or uncover more health-care serial killers (now known as HCSKs). Beverly Allit, convicted in four deaths in England, claimed to suffer from Munchausen Syndrome by Proxy, a disorder in which people harm others in order to gain attention. Nurse Joseph Dewey Akin, thirty-five, who worked at Cooper Green Hospital in Birmingham, Alabama, was tried in 1992 for one murder but was suspected in more than a hundred deaths in twenty different facilities. He pled guilty.

Three years later, the employment of male nurse Orville Lynn Majors at Vermillion County Hospital in Indiana coincided with a rise in the death toll there. It was a small facility with fifty-six beds, but the deaths reached 101. After Majors's license was suspended, the death rate returned to normal. A $1.5 million investigation revealed that Majors sometimes took his own initiative in "treating" patients. Investigators exhumed fifteen bodies to examine tissues, and found that at least six deaths were consistent with the administration of epinephrine and potassium chloride. On October 17, 1999, Majors was convicted in all six deaths.

Even a respiratory therapist got into the act. At the Glendale Adventist Medical Center near the Ventura Freeway in southern California, coworkers of Efren Saldivar whispered about his "magical syringe." Saldivar had become a hospital therapist reportedly because he liked the uniform, but he did not like it when the job became burdensome. In 1998, he confessed to murdering fifty patients for "humanitarian reasons." Twenty bodies were exhumed and the remains yielded the drug Pavulon. When Saldivar was arrested in 2001, he admitted that he often killed just to lighten the workload during shifts that were understaffed. After sixty victims, he'd lost count. "You don't plan it," he said to the investigators. "After that, you don't think about it for the rest of the day, or ever." He pleaded guilty to six provable murders and received a life sentence.

In China around that time, Hu Wanlin, who practiced medicine illegally and claimed to perform miracles, was suspected in at least 150 deaths, while Ahmad Suraji, an Indonesian sorcerer, was arrested after an investigation turned up the bodies of several missing women on his sugarcane plantation. Police officers found twenty-six skeletons of females believed to be the remains of some of Suraji's victims. They were mainly prostitutes who had wanted the sorcerer to make them more beautiful. Suraji confessed to forty-two murders, saying that he had actually planned to kill even more—seventy-two in all. He stated that in 1986 his late father, from whom he believed he had inherited his supernatural powers, had contacted him in a dream and ordered him to do so as part of a black magic ritual. He admitted that after strangling the women, he drank their saliva. On April 28, 1998, a judge found Suraji guilty of the murders and ordered him put to death.

Doctors, too, came under scrutiny. Dr. Michael Swango moved around to several hospitals in America, experimenting on patients. He had once told colleagues a fantasy of his that involved a school bus smashing into a trailer truck loaded with gasoline, sending it up in flames. He imagined burning children hurled out the windows and landing on the road, poles, and fences. His colleagues were horrified. To keep moving on to other facilities, Swango faked some of his credentials, adopted aliases, and misrepresented his past employment history. When the FBI finally stopped "Double-O" Swango, (nicknamed thus by colleagues for "licensed to kill"), he'd been operating for almost two decades and was suspected in over thirty deaths. Arraigned on July 17, 2000, he pled guilty to fatally poisoning three patients in 1993 at a New York hospital, and was convicted of a murder in Ohio. He received a life sentence without the possibility of parole.

Yet as shocking as that was, trusted and affable physician Dr. Harold Shipman, who began killing his elderly patients in England in 1974, was estimated to have been responsible for a whopping 250 deaths. Most were female between the ages of forty-nine and eighty-one, and he'd pat their hands and say soothing words as he overdosed them. Yet evidence made it clear that he actually despised them and had disparaging labels for them, such as FTPBI: "Failed to Put Brain In." He claimed he was engaged in mercy killing, but it was discovered that he had faked one will to become its beneficiary and had removed the jewelry from many of his victims. When the investigation closed in 2005 and the results were publicized, people in Britain were stunned to learn the full extent of his atrocities. Sentenced to life, Shipman committed suicide in prison.

A shift in American consciousness about sudden infant death syndrome (SIDs) caught another killer. In 1963, *Life* magazine had done a story on Philadelphia's Marie Noe, "the unluckiest mother alive," who had lost ten children shortly after birth to SIDs. Few people then could believe that a woman might not welcome the joys of motherhood and might instead dispatch her babies, one by one. In 1999, she confessed that she had killed eight of them. "We just weren't meant to have children," Noe stated to a reporter, while her husband added, "The Lord needed angels." She received twenty years' probation, the first five under house arrest, and the requirement to undergo psychiatric analysis to determine why she had committed these crimes. (Japan had had a similar case the previous decade, when a woman killed nine of her children over a span of ten years.)

In Brussels, Belgium, a father-daughter team was arrested in 1997 for multiple counts of murder. Pastor and renowned humanitarian Andras Pandy had raped and brutalized his forty-four-year-old daughter, Agnes, since she was thirteen. Out of fear, she'd helped him to kill six people and get rid of their bodies before she finally turned him in. She said that Pandy's first two wives and four of his children and stepchildren had been killed, but the body parts and sets of teeth pulled from the basement and refrigerators on one of his properties were tested for DNA and proved to belong to other people. In the end, authorities suspected Pandy in the deaths of thirteen people. Some had been shot, Agnes reported, and some bludgeoned to death with a sledgehammer. Then she and Pandy hacked the corpses into pieces and wrapped them in plastic. Some were dumped outside their home, while others were immersed in an acidic drain cleaner that could dissolve meat and bones.

Pandy claimed that his missing relatives were still alive and that he contacted them "through angels." At the conclusion of his trial, he was convicted on six counts of first-degree murder and three counts of rape, getting life in prison, while Agnes got twenty-one years for her participation.

In 1999, in Snowtown, Australia, twelve bodies were found in plastic barrels in an abandoned bank vault and buried behind a house in town, the victims of a team of serial killers. John Bunting and Robert Wagner were eventually found guilty, Bunting of eleven murders and Wagner of ten, and sentenced to life without parole. The judge, Justice Brian Martin, reportedly believed they were beyond rehabilitation.

Serial Killer Culture

Several communities protested art exhibits that featured paintings by executed killer John Wayne Gacy, who had amassed over $100,000 from his prison-based artwork. His subjects ranged from Elvis Presley to fellow killer Jeffrey Dahmer. Arthur Shawcross, the killer of eleven women in Rochester, New York, also offered pictures in an exhibit, including a pencil sketch of the deceased Princess Diana, while "Happy Face Killer" Keith Jesperson and "Night Stalker" Richard Ramirez sold or gave away their art as well.

In literature, Gerard Schaefer's *Killer Fiction: Tales of an Accused Serial Killer* was believed to disguise actual crimes that went beyond the two murders for which he'd been convicted. He insisted that he was not "the characters in my fiction," but there was little doubt that the fifty pages of writing and the many erotic drawings he produced before he was arrested for a double rape-homicide, featuring detailed half-clad females strung up by the neck, arose from his sadistic fantasies. At one time he'd claim eighty victims, another time over a hundred, and other times he denied killing anyone, but the truth went with him when he was murdered in prison.

In a documentary by Julian P. Hobbes, *Collectors,* Texas killer Elmer Wayne Henley indicated that art is an act of appreciating nature, which "proves to me there's a God." Louisiana mortician Rick Stanton, one of the "collectors," had made a name for himself through his encouragement of incarcerated serial killers to produce pieces that he could sell. He developed three successful "Death Row Art Shows" for such exhibitors as Henley and Henry Lee Lucas, and had a mailing list of several hundred interested buyers. He acquired pieces from Ottis Toole and Charles Manson, and his business partner, Tobias Allen, developed a serial killer board game, which was banned in Canada. Other morbid entrepreneurs bought and sold items that killers had owned, such as Ted Bundy's Volkswagen. Prison groupies, too, became much more prominent, and one of them, Sondra London, helped killers such as Danny Rolling publish accounts of their crimes.

Strides of Science

In 1998, the same year in which Wayne Adam Ford brought a severed breast to the police in California to turn himself in for four murders, the FBI established CODIS, the Combined DNA Indexing System. The following year it had acquired more than sixty-five million fingerprints for AFIS, the Automated Fingerprint Identification System. As the century and millennium turned, the FBI and the BATF merged their firearms databases to create the National Integrated Ballistics Network. Having comprehensive collections made things easier for those with access to them, but even with improving technology, not everyone took advantage. VICAP was not operating at its expected efficiency, because the report forms were long and complex and few jurisdictions were sending information, let alone checking the system. Yet many cold cases that were once believed lost causes were getting solved. "Cold hits" entered the terminology as fingerprints from years earlier and DNA from cases with preserved biological evidence were entered into systems and found to match the fingerprints or DNA of convicted felons. It was a heady time for law enforcement and a victory for forensic science.

A recent development was the brain-fingerprint, although similar tools had been in the works in Robert Hare's lab in Canada since the 1980s. Psychiatrist Lawrence Farwell developed this technology in his brain research laboratory in Fairfield, Iowa, claming that it was 99.9 percent accurate. Since the brain is central to all human activities, he said, it records all experiences. A crime scene would then be stored in the brain of the offender and a brainprint would offer measurable evidence. The suspect's electrical activity was monitored via a headband with sensors, while the subject was exposed to "prod" words or images that were both relevant and irrelevant to the crime. If his brain activity showed recognition of the relevant stimuli—a distinct spike called a MERMER (memory and encoding related multifaceted electroencephalographic response)—that meant he had a record of the crime stored in his brain. Innocent people, the scientist claimed, would display no such response. If the suspect offered an alibi for the time of the crime, scenes from the crime scenario could be analyzed as well to elicit MERMERs.

One flaw was that if the person was at the crime scene but did not commit the crime, there was no way to make that distinction; he or she might also recognize some part of the scene, or the victim. The best images were designed to trigger the memories of those with very specific knowledge about a crime. And indeed, this technology was instrumental in obtaining a confession from Missouri serial killer James B. Grinder in 1999. When confronted with the possibility of a death sentence after the brainprint indicated he was at the scene of a 1984 rape-murder, he confessed to it, adding it to three other murders that he had already admitted to.

Then, in the fall of 2000, a television series called *CSI: Crime Scene Investigation* aired. It purported to show the work of people who processed crime scenes and evidence, and was destined to become the number one program on television. The masses paid attention and it was syndicated around the world, giving more people the chance to see how science solved some of the most brutal crimes imaginable. Still, many of the myths about serial killers derived from sparse data produced in the 1970s and 1980s—such as the idea that serial killers always had a specific victim type and MO, and that they actively indulged in baiting the authorities—were promoted as fact, continuing to miseducate the public. The next decade would see little correction, but law enforcement investigators, faced with some of the greatest challenges in the history of the world to date, would work to update their data and turn technology to their side.

CHAPTER FIFTEEN

The Future

Terror

On September 11, 2001, Islamic fundamentalist Osama bin Laden sent teams of fanatic disciples to crash planes into strategic areas in the U.S. They hit the Pentagon and the World Trade Center's Twin Towers, bringing them down, killing thousands, and shocking the country. Another plane, destined for an unknown target, crashed into a field in Pennsylvania. The quick assessment was a packaged presentation of nineteen terrorists trained for suicide missions, though some people saw a more complex agenda at work. But there was little time to contemplate international conspiracies, as letters laced with anthrax posed more immediate questions about American security. Despite resistance from other nations, President George W. Bush took the U.S. into a second war against Saddam Hussein, this time capturing him but allowing bin Laden to escape. Bush antagonized the world community, yet even as Americans hoped for peace most supported the war. Many purchased aggressive video games for their children and promoted movies that reached unprecedented levels of violence into box-office hits. The American economy, already weakening along with that of once-strong Japan and many European countries, went into a serious tailspin. The stock market hit astonishing lows.

Given these conditions of global strain, dissonance, and aggression, it's no surprise that serial killers continued to proliferate. In their own small arena, they exercised their chosen means of power and control. Even as other murder rates declined, repetitive killers popped up in all the usual places, as well as in Brazil, Korea, China, India, Iran, Yemen, Switzerland, Denmark, and the Bahamas. In Vietnam in 2001, a forty-eight-year-old woman who had foiled the police twice finally admitted to poisoning thirteen people. The World Wide Web even came into play, when Andy Shonkri, nineteen, was sentenced to a month in prison for spreading false Internet rumors about a serial killer in Cairo.

In Belgium, when Michel Fourniret's wife learned how Marc Dutroux's wife had gone to prison for covering up his murders, she told police about her husband's ten victims in France and Belgium (she would later add more). He admitted to eight while he awaited the results of a French investigation, and as of mid-2005 a trial is still pending. In the first half of the decade, stranger killings continued the pace set during the 1990s. This may have been symptomatic of stress on an international scale, with the chances of an outright Armageddon seeming a genuine possibility.

Mass media kept up with the most unique cases, such as Spain's "playing card killer," Alfredo Galen, although the presence of a serial killer inspired less attention than it had two decades earlier. But there were instances when the media played a role. In an ironic twist, an acquaintance of James "Whitey" Bulger, believed responsible for nineteen murders, spotted him in *Hannibal,* the sequel to *The Silence of the Lambs.* In the film, Hannibal Lecter's photo is placed on the FBI's Most Wanted site alongside photos of actual criminals (including Bulger). Police soon learned from this viewer that Bulger had been in London in September 2002.

Nurses continued to kill as Lucy de Berk was sentenced to life in The Hague for the murder of four patients (she was suspected in thirteen deaths). Kristen Gilbert was convicted of killing three patients in a veterans' hospital in Massachusetts because she reportedly got a thrill from emergencies. A thirty-four-year-old Swiss man, Roger Andermatt, was arrested for the murder of twenty-four patients in Swiss nursing homes between 1995 and 2001. He claimed to have killed out of pity, although he admitted that he "felt totally overworked by the volume of care they had to provide to their patients." There were similar cases in France and Germany. Then, in New Jersey in 2004, nurse Charles Cullen was caught having administered digoxin to two patients who had died. At his hearing, he admitted that over the past sixteen years, in ten different health-care institutions in two states, he had taken the lives of between thirty and forty patients. The facts of several of the actual cases contradicted his stated motive of mercy. Even his voluntary confession suggested that the murders may have been a means of empowerment for him during periods of depression, and his actions inspired immediate evaluations of the U.S. health-care industry. In exchange for life in prison, he cooperated with authorities in both states by naming at least thirty of his actual and intended victims.

Persistence Pays

In Seattle, Gary Leon Ridgway was identified as the infamous Green River Killer from the 1980s, whom many criminologists had believed would never be caught. DNA linked him to several victims and, as the trial approached, he pled guilty, showing authorities more and more graves until his toll reached forty-eight. Ridgway said that in the midst of his spree, he'd sent an anonymous letter to a newspaper in 1984. It was the letter that profiler John Douglas had evaluated as amateurish and without connection to the murders, so profiling, once so highly touted, came in for a beating in the press. Nevertheless, investigators had finally received their payoff—but the same success seemed unlikely in Ciudad Juarez, Mexico.

In November 2001, eight women were found murdered and dumped in cotton fields. These killings appeared to be part of a decade-long wave of kidnappings and murders that had reportedly claimed nearly two hundred victims. Since 1993, fifty bodies had turned up and dozens of men interrogated, but the murders continued. Many victims were young women who worked in assembly plants that supplied the U.S. When a women's group from Mexico City brought media attention to the incidents in 1998, authorities contacted Robert Ressler, who'd by now retired as an FBI profiler, to train their task force in the psychology of serial killers. Ressler concluded that not all of the murders were linked by similarities. "They were talking in excess of a hundred women at the time," he recalled, "and saying that someone was running amuck and had killed them all. When we sorted the cases out, we ended up with seventy-six homicides of concern. Some suspects were clearly family members and some were gang members. I also believed that some of the murders were done by people—possibly a team—coming over the border from El Paso."

Ressler suggested a surveillance of the buses that let young female workers off at night, and five bus drivers were arrested for thirteen of the murders and disappearances. Later, bus drivers Victor Uribe and Gustavo Gonzalez confessed that they would get intoxicated and then, when they spotted a vulnerable woman, would force her into their van to rape and kill her.

Back in the U.S., another series of murders was subjected to a unique high-tech crime analysis. Along the rural East Coast during the early 1990s, the remains of five middle-aged men had been dumped along roadways in Pennsylvania, New Jersey, and New York. They had been murdered, dismembered, and wrapped tightly in several layers of plastic bags. From the method of cutting, wrapping, and disposal, it seemed to be the work of a single perpetrator, dubbed the "Last Call Killer." The case went cold until a technique for getting fingerprints off plastic bags was developed. Vacuum metal deposition (VMD) involved an expensive process that coated evidence with gold and zinc to develop the latent prints into near–picture quality by absorbing the oils from the prints and bonding the zinc and gold. New Jersey investigators sent gloves believed to have belonged to the Last Call Killer, found on a body, and two dozen of the bags that had been collected from the bodies for analysis. Scientists in Toronto lifted some prints, which the New Jersey police ran through AFIS, getting hits on sixteen prints with Richard Rogers, a fifty-year-old registered nurse from Staten Island, New York.

This man had once bludgeoned an acquaintance to death, wrapped the body in a tent, and dumped it on the side of a road. Charged with manslaughter, he'd claimed self-defense and was acquitted. But the MO in all these crimes was too similar to be coincidental. On May 27, 2001, Rogers was charged with the murder and dismemberment of two of the victims found in New Jersey. As of this writing, he remains a suspect in the other three killings, but the fingerprint analysis is being challenged.

The longest and most involved serial killer investigation in Canadian history began in 2002 when Robert Pickton, the "Pig Farmer," was linked to the disappearance of sixty-nine women, mostly drug addicts or prostitutes who came to Piggy Palace, a bar on his pig farm. In

2002, the authorities indicated that they had used DNA to identify the microscopic remains of eighteen Vancouver area women. They suspected that Pickton had been putting them through a wood chipper to make food for his pigs. In March 2004, authorities announced that he may have fed some remains to associates, and by the end of that year, with the aid of more than a hundred forensic anthropologists, the remains of thirty women had been found, although three remained unidentified. Pickton's trial is pending. As Canadians await the results, they have learned about another series of murders around Edmonton.

While criminologists and profilers espoused the belief that serial killers are too compulsive to stop their crimes, both the Green River Killer and Robert Yates in Seattle had done so, and then another serial killer who had not been caught during the 1970s emerged again after twenty-five years of silence. In March 2004, the *Wichita Eagle* newsroom in Kansas received a letter from "Bill Thomas Killman"—BTK (Bind, Torture, Kill)—that contained three photographs of a woman who was clearly dead. She had been posed in a variety of ways, and a photocopy of her driver's license was included. It had belonged to Vicki Wegerle, a woman who had been murdered in 1986 and not officially linked to BTK. Then, late in 2004, a package was found in a park that contained a partial manuscript entitled "The BTK Story," as well as the driver's license of one of the 1977 victims (BTK had reported the murder to police dispatchers). He also used an eroticized symbol formed from the letters BTK that he had included in his 1970s communications (and that was kept out of media stories by the police). So after a quarter of a century, this predator had resurfaced. That meant that unless he had moved or been in prison or an institution, he had stopped killing for a long period of time. The police believed they knew his age and some of his interests, but despite more than five thousand tips, they continued to have difficulty identifying him.

Then, early in 2005, BTK sent a computer disk that was traced to a Lutheran church. The pastor offered the names of people who had access to the computer, and a DNA sample from the daughter of a man on the list sent them to Dennis Rader, an active church member, a good family man, a security specialist, and a seemingly stable citizen. He was arrested and charged with the eight BTK murders, as well as two others, and investigators set to work in nearby jurisdictions to determine if more murder charges might be added.

If Rader is convicted of the BTK murders, he adds new dimension to the typical ideas about serial killers offered by criminologists and law enforcement. While not unique for being a family man with a stable job while also killing people, that he had communicated so often early in his murder career and then let decades go by before communicating again was unprecedented. Analysts went over and over the details in an attempt to understand his motives and psychological makeup. Criminal profiling came in for another round of attacks, although most of the criticism was aimed at the new breed of television commentators posing as profilers, many of whom had no credentials for such analysis and access to nothing more than news reports for drawing their conclusions.

Such cold cases were being solved, however, and one in Washington State revealed that John Dwight Canaday, fifty-nine, already serving life sentences for two 1969 murders, had a third one to his credit. In 1968, he had gone randomly knocking on doors. Sixteen-year-old Sandra Bowman, five months pregnant, had answered, and Canaday had bound her and stabbed her fifty-seven times. Canaday's DNA profile was on record from his other convictions, and a state forensic scientist matched it to sperm found on this murder victim. Canaday attributed his murders to a bitter divorce that had angered him.

In another long-standing case, in a legal quirk, Eugene Coral Watts was scheduled for early release from prison in Texas and nearly became the first confessed serial killer to be freed. But then a witness came forward in an unsolved Michigan murder, and in 2004 Watts was tried there for the murder of Helen Dutcher. A jury convicted him, so he failed to make history after all.

The Internet

John Robinson started his criminal career committing white-collar crimes and went on to use his knowledge of technology to lure victims over the Internet. He is considered the first serial killer to do so. Born in Chicago to a blue-collar family, he'd been an Eagle Scout and had attended a seminary to become a priest. Yet he developed

into a forger, thief, embezzler, and liar. He was also suspected in the disappearances of three women. While in
jail for a petty crime, he learned computer technology,
with its potential for swindling unwitting people. He also
became romantically involved with a married woman,
Beverly Bonner, who worked in the prison library. When
he was released in 1993, she went with him and was never
heard from again. A mother and daughter also fell into his
net, and he collected the daughter's disability checks to
the tune of more than $150,000.

Robinson then found women via the Internet, where
he would enter bondage-oriented chat rooms as "Slave-
master." He soon had women signing slave contracts that
granted him total control. In 1997, he developed a relationship with a student at Purdue University named Izabela Lewicka, who was interested in the sexual world
of sadomasochism. At Robinson's behest, she went to
Kansas City, Missouri, and filed for a marriage license
before she disappeared. Then he started an on-line relationship with Suzette Trouten and, in the typical pattern,
no one heard from her again.

Prompted by tips from her friends and family, the authorities began to watch Robinson, and in April 2000 a
psychologist named Vickie Neufeld moved to Kansas City
to pursue a relationship with the man. She ended up filing
a complaint with the police, and after they questioned her
for several hours, they arrested Robinson on charges of
sexual assault and theft. Linking him via items in his possession to the missing women, they had a forensic computer expert go through his files and e-mail. Warrants

were obtained for Robinson's storage units and for property at La Cygne, Kansas. There, cadaver dogs led the investigators to two eighty-five gallon drums by the side of a pole barn. The drums proved to contain human remains, which dental records linked to Suzette Trouten and Izabela Lewicka. In Robinson's storage units, they found three more barrels, which contained the remains of Beverly Bonner, Sheila Faith, and her daughter Debbie.

In Kansas, a jury found Robinson guilty just before Halloween in 2002 and sentenced him to death. For the Missouri charges, he pled guilty in exchange for admitting to five murders, including two for which authorities did not have bodies. He was fifty-nine, making him one of the oldest serial killers ever convicted. Then, in 2004, Kansas overturned an old law that gave prosecutors an advantage in death penalty cases, and Robinson's sentence was commuted to life.

Thanks to improvements in DNA databases and to better education in computer forensics for police officers, in St. Louis in 2001 police linked six murders of prostitutes with DNA from semen and entered the profile into CODIS (Combined DNA Indexing System), but obtained no matches.

Then Bill Smith, a reporter for the *St. Louis Post-Dispatch,* received a letter with an Internet-generated map that led him to "Victim number 17"—and skeletal remains. The map's sender had removed the borders that would identify its origin, so investigators enlisted the members of Illinois State Police Cyber Crime Unit, who recognized the design as an Expedia.com illustration. Expedia's computer logs contained the IP addresses of computers that had visited its Web site, and the police found an address for Maury Travis, a convicted felon. They visited him with a search warrant and found evidence in his home of possible torture and murder. Travis wanted to see the victim photos, which revealed that he knew they had been murdered. When the police confronted him, he cursed the Internet and then agreed to show them another body dump site. In jail, he requested a can of soda, from which the detectives extracted a sample of his saliva for DNA analysis. It matched the semen collected from two of the victims. They also got a match from tread marks across one victim's legs to Travis's car. They believed they could pin a dozen homicides on him, but before the investigation was complete, he committed suicide in jail.

Serial to Spree

For three weeks, from October 2, 2002, until they were caught in their car during the early morning of October 24, John Allen Muhammad, forty-one, and Lee Boyd Malvo, seventeen, randomly shot at people from Maryland to Virginia at least fourteen times. They hit thirteen people, killing nine. There was no link among victims or a clear victim type, so the police, under Chief Charles Moose, had a difficult time trying to find and stop the two men. They set up a hotline, asking for the FBI's assistance, and by October 18 they had received nearly sixty thousand calls. The Rapid Start computer program had gone through 15,293 solid leads and cleared more than 60 percent of them. Yet that left more than 7,000 still to pursue.

Where there had been snipers before, even in teams, none had held the country in such a terrorized mode, especially along the I-95 corridor. Three agents from the FBI offered a profile on October 9, based on probabilities from past cases. They had little to go on behaviorally, so they relied on archival data to develop their ten-page report. That meant that there was an 80 percent chance that the UNSUB was a lone male with no solid relationships, had military experience and a collection of guns, and was angry, egotistical, and familiar with the killing territory. He would be unstable and frustrated by inconveniences, feel underappreciated for his talents, be hypersensitive to criticism, and experience a lack of empathy. His victims were targets of opportunity. It was likely that his normal behavior or routine had noticeably changed, such as becoming more withdrawn than usual or keeping his vehicle hidden. People who knew him would realize this.

It soon seemed clear that these shootings involved two killers, and they began to leave communications. One was a tarot card at the scene of the shooting of a thirteen-year-old boy at school. Handwriting on the card expressed the sentiment, "I am God." Then, at another shooting, a note was pinned inside a bag to a tree. It was a garbled message requiring a ransom of $10 million to stop the shooting.

Via ballistics and circumstantial analysis, the task force

traced the snipers to an unsolved murder in Montgomery County, Alabama, on Sept 21. Two women had been shot and one had died. The suspect had dropped a copy of a firearms magazine, offering a fingerprint. AFIS provided an identity: John Allen Williams, who had served in the National Guard and the army and had a badge for outstanding marksmanship. He'd had a bitter custody dispute with his first wife and had a restraining order filed against him by his second wife. One lived in Maryland and the other in Baton Rouge—another area where someone had been shot by a sniper. Williams, aka Muhammad, had a companion, an adolescent named Lee Boyd Malvo, a Jamaican national, and was known to have purchased a blue Chevrolet Caprice.

On October 24, the suspects were run to ground as they slept at a roadside rest area. They were removed from the Caprice, along with a Bushmaster XM-15 E2S assault rifle that proved to be the murder weapon. The Caprice had been modified for long-distance shooting, with a porthole drilled into the trunk lid to accommodate the gun muzzle and scope. When their spate of killings came to an end, it appeared that within a matter of months, they had turned from serial shooters to spree killers. That is a unique combination, and as a result, the art of profiling, which had failed on some key points, incurred even more disfavor.

This method also took a hit in the case of a Baton Rouge, Louisiana, serial killer who had murdered five women. Contrary to the FBI's predictions that the perpetrator would be awkward around women, the killer,

Derrick Todd Lee, turned out to be confident and personable, and to have a family and a job. (Contrary to media reports, the profile did not predict that he would be white.) Yet, while the Baton Rouge killer's profile was mistaken on some points, it was correct on such items as the killer's age, controlling behavior, physical strength, tight finances, and nonthreatening style. But the media failed to take note, and earlier failures of the profiling method in places like Chicago and Canada were now magnified.

Clearly, both the good guys and the bad guys were going through cycles of social opinion, from heroes to fall guys, from monsters to antiheroes. They seemed to represent parts of ourselves about which we were ambivalent—but it was an ambivalence easily camouflaged with uninformed social commentary. That is, they were among the many social narratives designed to form and inform our culture. The "truth" was decided by the media and a public willing to accept its analyses.

A review of outstanding investigations indicates that currently more than two dozen suspected serial killers are operating around the world in places like Peru, South Africa, England, Canada, Ireland, Belgium, and the United States. In February 2005, the FBI admitted to reporters that it was engaged in sixteen potential serial killer investigations (During the summer, the FBI would organize an international conference of experts, the result of which was to change its original definition of a serial killer to something simple: two murders in two separate incidents.). In China, a predator who hunted women dressed in red was publicized in newspapers, as was a truck driver who murdered fourteen prostitutes and a man who killed boys he lured from Internet cafes. Costa Rica's "Psychopath" has claimed at least nineteen victims, the "Highway Maniac" of Argentina has half a dozen, and Italy has investigated twenty gay murders over the past decade. Not only has serial killing continued to be a staple of crime—albeit a comparatively rare one—but more countries, especially those in which stability has eroded, are reporting it. Multiple murders by a single offender appear to be related to specific forms of pressure associated with modes of power in a given society. Serial killers share a common attitude about victims-as-objects, but the way they exploit victims to acquire and sustain a sense of power is influenced by their cultural context. A study by Kaori Aki comparing 82 Japanese to 402 American serial killers indicated that Americans were more likely to be sexually motivated while Japanese offenders tended to kill for financial gain and were more likely to have accomplices and to choose male victims. Historically, culture has also played a role: Peter Stubbe attacked people as a dreaded werewolf, Erzsebet Báthory as an indulged aristocrat, Jeffrey Dahmer as a secretive loner too nondescript to be noticed.

Our monsters derive from covert social values, exacerbated by social tensions, that encourage violence as power and control, and there are always people who move easily into such roles—committing the same violence repeatedly as it continues to satisfy a personal need. A review of how such killers have behaved throughout history indicates that they represent part of the human condition that emerges under pressure and in times of social dissonance. What people are told and what they sense is true about society's values may be so at odds that there appears to be no foundation. People with low impulse control and poor coping skills may internalize the stress of this disparity and play it out in aggression.

Based on historical patterns, global destabilization and its concomitant pressures will likely increase the number and diversity of serial predators. But it's not just about environmental factors. Neurological research, too, supports the notion that culture affects just how such killers act out. While they may not necessarily be born predators, they may have physiological conditions that yield to certain influences and support the predatory path.

Feedback Loop

Debra Niehoff, a neuroscientist and the author of *The Biology of Violence,* sought to understand in her review of significant literature on the subject the interplay of genes and the environment in the development of violent behavior. In her opinion, each modifies the other in such a way that an individual may uniquely mentally process a situation toward a violent resolution. Thus any given factor may have different effects on different people, and these effects can be modified positively or negatively over the course of a lifetime. That is, some people with a brain abnormality may become violent, others may not, and others with no such disorder may turn to violence. The same can be said about the contribution to violence of childhood trauma, childhood abuse, substance abuse, violent role models, violent video games, pornography, and other factors. What each person does to sort out and manage his or her situation depends on a unique interplay of external and internal factors.

A person's brain, Niehoff says, tracks experiences through chemical codes and makes habitual associations with the past. Every experience involves dedicated chemicals that influence and control emotions, moods, and reactions, so that our feelings derive from the sum of many diverse chemical and physiological states. Each new interaction gets handled via a specific neurochemical profile, which has been influenced by attitudes that derive from our array of encounters and experiences; in other words, those attitudes have influenced our brain chemistry. After every interaction, the neurochemical profile gets updated, either confirmed or altered. If we're paranoid, for example, we will process a new situation suspiciously, and how it turns out may continue the tendency toward caution or relax it. The brain adjusts along with the attitudes.

With some people, the ability to properly evaluate a situation becomes impaired and may trigger aggression. While most violence occurs under some type of provocation, certain people initiate it for pleasure and erotic stimulation. (We'll see why in a minute.) Yet even for them, such behaviors become part of a cumulative exchange between their experiences and their nervous systems. It all gets coded into the body's neurochemistry as a physio-emotional record. The more they succeed and feel the high, the more likely it is that they will return to this behavior, especially if impulse control or empathy for others is lacking.

As mentioned, Dr. Adrian Raine found brain deficits in violent individuals—specifically in the limbic system (emotional center) and the prefrontal cortex. These deficits may influence certain people to be impulsive, fearless, less responsive to aversive stimulation, and less able to make appropriate decisions about aggression toward others. In addition to this research, we have information about excitement, reward, and fascination that also indicates how experiences are perceived and acted on.

The behavioral machinery of the brain involves neurotransmitters, which choreograph the body's information processing system. Serotonin is implicated in moods, for example. When we're confronted by novelty, dopamine and norepinephrine levels surge, triggering the brain's reward system. Thus, we approach with anticipation those behaviors and situations that may feel good, and dopamine in particular provides an edgy high that spurs us to seek the experience again. It helps us to notice particular stimuli. Thanks to this neurotransmitter, we have a biological investment in life's twists, an appetite for what's still around the bend.

The "salience theory" about dopamine's function indicates that it's quite involved in helping us to focus. That is, when something important happens, the release of dopamine assists us in being alert to new material and to make sense of it. So novelty stimulates the brain into action. Dopamine is involved in the thrill of being alive and may be implicated in the sense of enlargement beyond ourselves that follows activities that make us learn, grow, and feel in control.

Yet the brain also adapts to keep balance. Dopamine keeps track of whether we actually get what we anticipate getting; the levels of it increase or decrease accordingly. When dopamine levels diminish, the person seeks more stimulation and new avenues of reward. In addition, research indicates that those people with fewer dopamine receptors in the brain seek more stimulation and may thus be vulnerable to addiction or compulsive pleasure-seeking. Add in the neurochemical feedback loop from Niehoff's theory, and you have the notion that the reward expectation threshold may be subject to influence from physiology and adjustment by experience. Whatever our latest results are in terms of anticipation and reality, that's what will influence how we look to our future experiences. If we get a lot, we anticipate a lot and thus want a lot.

If the prefrontal cortex fails to function as an inhibitory agent, increased desire and reduced control may lead to our seeking what the neurons reward—that which fascinates and interests us. For those who grow fascinated with certain types of violence—and who have that fascination repeatedly rewarded in fantasies and activities—it feels better to act out on than to inhibit the impulse, and they grow bolder in pursuit of it. If they succeed at getting it, they anticipate getting it again.

Yet it's not quite that straightforward. Other bodily processes affect the dopamine surge as well. Comfort hormones such as oxytocin may diminish dopamine's effect, so that new stimuli are required to reproduce the high. Elevated testosterone levels also increase dopamine production, and adrenaline can kick in during risky situations. The longer reward is delayed, the more the brain produces these hormones, and frustration can actually have a facilitating effect.

In the brains of adolescents, which are as malleable as the brains of infants, neural pathways strengthen for those behaviors that the person is engaging in more often, while other pathways weaken. In other words, certain rewarding behaviors can become habitual, and if begun during adolescence, can become firmly entrenched in the neurochemical profile.

To make this specific to the development of a predatory serial killer, I propose an environmental-physiological feedback mechanism akin to Niehoff's neurochemical profile adjustment. I call it the spiral of erotic enthrallment. Let's take someone like Jeffrey Dahmer. As a boy he found dead animals fascinating. His brain responded with pleasure, rewarding his interest in roadkill. When he grew bored, he sought more stimulation, which for him was associated with dead things. No doubt, these actual experiences informed his fantasies. Then one day, while bored (low dopamine level), he picked up a hitchhiker. This excited him (elevated dopamine). When the man decided to leave, Dahmer killed him and now had a human body at his disposal (novel, and thus stimulating and neurologically rewarding). Even if initially shocked by his action, he was also fascinated and aroused. The act of killing and handling the corpse stimulated him and ensured that erotic enthrallment with the dead would continue. Dahmer felt a vital, godlike rush, but eventually the dopamine level would decrease, making him feel empty and bored again. He would need to reexperience the high, so eventually the cycle would repeat, further strengthening the erotic charge. Yet he would also seek even greater stimulation for a higher high (craving and expectation of more), so he would (and did) do more things to bodies, taking greater (more exciting) risks, or escalating the episodes closer together. Much like the normal person who feels affirmed or not in processing each new situation, serial predators develop a neurochemical profile that includes and even demands violence.

So erotic enthrallment with harm to others for one's own gratification starts with environmental opportunities and associations and becomes stronger via acts that stimulate the brain's reward mechanisms. In other words, when what's dangerous and forbidden appears to become magical, larger than life, and transcendent, it's likely to be performed and repeated by those who make the association and feel the physiological reward response, for their neural reward system processes these forbidden behaviors in a way that ensures repetition. And possibly the experiences of their childhood (abuse, violence in the home, unresolved anger, etc.) will influence the manner in which they seek out and carry through on their opportunities.

Now let's add the influence of a particular historico-cultural context. In medieval France, for example, when the witch-finders hunted down "werewolves" as Satan's spawn, the excitement of this form of the forbidden could cause a mentally unstable person to begin to find wolflike behavior enthralling, particularly when viewed as super-natural and powerful. Or the anticipatory focus of a bud-ding killer in Germany as the country's resources declined and imperial Nazis came into power—can we really be surprised that so many in a cluster were cannibals? Or in the U.S., as restrictions relax on depictions of sex and violence, encouraging much more exposure, those with less impulse control may well act out what the culture affirms.

But some serial killers act from anger rather than erotic enthrallment, so let's add what we know about the brain and revenge. When we act aggressively to punish others for a wrong we believe they have done, we feel satisfac-tion. Researchers have found that this activates the dorsal striatum, which is also implicated in enjoyment. People who show greater activation in this area—a stronger flow of cerebral blood and higher oxygen consumption—are more willing to accept greater costs to themselves in order to mete out punishment. Whatever the cost, the satisfac-tion they derive encourages the act and adds increased levels of dopamine to the sense of anticipation. However, the prefrontal cortex helps weigh satisfaction against cost. Thus, as long as the prefrontal cortex is operating appropriately, they can still make rational decisions. But if their ability to weigh gain against cost is disturbed, so might their decision-making and subsequent behavior be.

In conjunction with the neurological reward system that influences the neurochemical profile in the processing of one's world, we can see how serial killers develop—whether by lust, anger, or personal failings—and maintain their violent cycles.

Perspective

Whether aggressively psychotic, psychopathic, or just generally antisocial, the development of these behaviors results from a cumulative exchange between experience and the nervous system. It's all coded into the body's neurochemistry as an emotional record. Whenever these behaviors succeed, it affirms and updates the brain chemistry, thus increasing the probability of returning to these same behaviors.

Over the past two decades, serial killers have spread into more cultures around the world, especially as nations have grown more interconnected and global tensions have heightened. Serial killers may mirror with more intensity things that the normal human beings around them do on a lesser scale. Social narratives, especially those that affirm compartmentalized morality, will play out in diverse ways in different people, but the parallels will nevertheless be apparent to those who look. As the world grows more complicated, with sophisticated philosophies erasing moral foundations, people will sense the instability and pursue things that offer a feeling of security and self-satisfaction.

Yet when we reach for the empty high of drugs, sex, money, status, and other social lures, we're akin to killers who chase their own transcendent acts but in the process empty themselves rather than achieve inner fulfillment. While they may achieve a transient sense of vitality, the effect wears off and demands to be sought again and again. We, like such predators, seek more intensity as a way to connect with vitality. Thus, Bundy's and Dahmer's and Wuornos's experiences are not set entirely apart from ours.

It's our accommodation of evil (getting used to serial killers, for example) and our blindness to how it arises from within us that allows it to proliferate. From within our own needs, we create a world that supports the serial narrative, the drive to repeat the focus and anticipation that feels so good. Since serial killers amalgamate our covert social practices and reveal something about us in their behavior, there's little question that in our current social-cultural frame, we will see more cases, more diversity in these cases (blacks, women, adolescents), and greater geographical spread. In other words, the more self-indulgent and self-centered we become as a world community—which will only increase global power struggles—the more escalation we will likely witness in the serial killer phenomenon.

Selected Bibliography

Acocella, Joan. "The Politics of Hysteria," *The New Yorker,* April 6, 1998.

Ahmed, S. H. "Addiction as Compulsive Reward Prediction." *Science,* 306, December 10, 2004.

Aki, Kaori. "Serial Killers: A Cross-Cultural Study Between Japan and the United States," master's thesis, California State University, Fresno, CA, 2003.

Allen, Matthew. *Essay on the Classification of the Insane.* London: John Taylor, 1837.

Bass, Bill, with Jon Jefferson. *Death's Acre: Inside the Legendary Forensic Lab Where the Dead Do Tell Tales.* New York: Putnam, 2003.

Blundel, Nigel. *Encyclopedia of Serial Killers.* London: JG Press, 1996.

Brady, Ian. *The Gates of Janus: Serial Killing and Its Analysis by the "Moors Murderer."* Los Angeles: Feral House, 2001.

Brussel, James. *Casebook of a Crime Psychiatrist.* New York: Grove Press, 1968.

Bugliosi, Vincent, with Curt Gentry. *Helter Skelter.* New York: Bantam, 1995.

Bullock, Alan, ed. *World History: Civilization from its Beginnings.* Garden City, NY: Doubleday & Company, Inc., 1962.

Campbell, John H., and Don DeNevi, eds. *Profilers: Leading Investigators Take You Inside the Criminal Mind.* Amherst, NY: Prometheus Books, 2004.

Carlo, Philip. *The Night Stalker: The Life and Crimes of Richard Ramirez.* New York: Kensington, 1996.

Carlson, Oliver. *James Gordon Bennett: The Man Who Made the News.* New York: Duell, Sloan, and Pearce, 1942.

Cartel, Michael. *Disguise of Sanity: Serial Mass Murderers.* Toluca Lake, CA: Pepperbox Books, 1985.

Cheney, Margaret. *Why—The Serial Killer in America.* Saratoga, CA: R & E Publishers, 1992 (originally *The Co-ed Killer.* New York: Walker Publishing, 1976).

Cleckley, Hervey. *The Mask of Sanity,* 5th edition. St. Louis: Mosby, 1976.

Colaizzi, Janet. *Homicidal Insanity, 1800–1985.* Tuscaloosa, AL: University of Alabama Press, 1989.

Cullen, Robert. *The Killer Department: Detective Viktor Burakov's Eight-Year Hunt for the Most Savage Serial Killer in Russian History.* New York: Pantheon Books, 1993.

Damio, Ward. *Urge to Kill.* New York: Pinnacle, 1974.

Davies, Norman. *Europe: A History.* New York: Harper, 1996.

DeNevi, Don, and John H. Campbell. *Into the Minds of Madmen: How the FBI Behavioral Science Unit Revolutionized Crime Investigation.* Amherst, NY: Prometheus Books, 2004.

De River, J. Paul. *The Sexual Criminal.* Springfield, IL: Charles C. Thomas, 1949.

Diagnostic and Statistical Manual of Mental Disorders–IV. Washington, D.C.: American Psychiatric Association, 1994.

Douglas, John, and Mark Olshaker. *Mindhunter: Inside the FBI's Elite Serial Crime Unit.* New York: Scribner, 1995.

—*Unabomber.* New York: Pocket, 1996.

—*Journey into Darkness.* New York: Scribner, 1997.

—*Anatomy of Motive.* New York: Scribner, 1999.

—*The Cases That Haunt Us.* New York: Scribner, 2000.

Douglas, John, Ann W. Burgess, Allan G. Burgess, and Robert K. Ressler. *Crime Classification Manual.* San Francisco: Jossey-Bass, 1992.

Douglas, John E., and Corinne Munn. "Modus Operandi and the Signature Aspects of Violent Crime," *Crime Classification Manual.* New York: Lexington Books, 1992.

Egger, Steven A. *The Need to Kill: Inside the World of the Serial Killer.* Upper Saddle River, NJ: Prentice Hall, 2003.

—*The Killers Among Us.* Upper Saddle River, NJ: Prentice Hall, 1998.

Everitt, David. *Human Monsters.* Chicago: Contemporary Books, 1993.

Fido, Martin. *The Chronicle of Crime.* London: Carlton Books, 1999.

—*A History of British Serial Killing.* London: Carlton Books, 2001.

Fisher, Joseph C. *Killer Among Us: Public Reactions to Serial Murder.* Westport, CT: Praeger, 1997.

Fletcher, Jaye S. *Deadly Thrills.* New York: Onyx, 1995.

Fox, James Alan and Jack Levin. *The Will to Kill: Making Sense of Senseless Murder,* 2nd edition. Boston: Allyn and Bacon, 2005.

—*Extreme Killing.* Thousand Oaks, CA: Sage, 2005.

Frasier, David K. *Murder Cases of the Twentieth Century.* Jefferson, NC: McFarland & Company, 1996.

Friedman, Lawrence M. *Crime and Punishment in American History.* New York: Basic, 1993.

Gaskins, Donald, and Wilton Earle. *Final Truth: The Autobiography of a Serial Killer.* Atlanta: Adept, 1992.

Geberth, Vernon J. *Practical Homicide Investigation,* 3rd edition. Boca Raton, FL: CRC Press, 1996.

Gerber, Samuel M., and Richard Safterstein, eds. *More Chemistry and Crime.* Washington, D.C.: American Chemical Society, 1997.

Gerdes, Louise, ed. *Serial Killers.* San Diego: Greenhaven Press, 2000.

Giannangelo, Stephen J. *The Psychopathology of Serial Murder: A Theory of Violence.* Westport, CT: Praeger, 1996.

Godwin, Maurice. *Hunting Serial Predators.* Boca Raton, FL: CRC Press, 2000.

Gollmar, Robert. *Edward Gein: America's Most Bizarre Murderer.* New York: Pinnacle, 1981.

The Green River Killer. Bellevue, WA: *King County Journal,* 2003.

Grun, Bernard. *The Timetables of History,* 3rd edition. New York: Simon & Schuster, 1991.

Halberstam, David. *The Fifties.* New York: Villard, 1993.

Hare, R. D. *The Psychopathy Checklist—Revised,* 2nd ed. Toronto, Ontario: Multi-Health Systems, 2003.

—*Psychopathy: Theory and Practice.* New York: Wiley & Sons, 1970.

—"Psychopaths and Their Nature: Implications for the Mental Health and Criminal Justice Systems." T. Millon, E. Simonsen, M. Biket-Smith, and R. D. Davis, eds. *Psychopathy: Antisocial, Criminal and Violent Behavior,* (188–212). New York: Guilford Press, 1998.

—*Without Conscience: The Disturbing World of the Psychopaths Among Us.* New York: Guilford Press (first published in 1993 by Simon & Schuster), 1999.

Hare, R., A. Forth, S. Hart, and T. Harpur. "Event-Related Brain Potentials and Deception of Detection," *Society for Psychophysiological Research.* San Francisco: October 1988.

Hare, R. D., S. D. Hart, and T. J. Harpur. "Psychopathy and the DSM-IV Criteria for Antisocial Personality Disorder," *Journal of Abnormal Psychology,* (100, 391–398), 1991.

Harris, G. T., T. A. Skilling, and M. E. Rice. "The Construct of Psychopathy," in M. Tonry and N. Morris, eds., *Crime and Justice: An Annual Review of Research.* Chicago: University of Chicago Press, 2001.

Hazelwood, Robert R., and Stephen Michaud. *Dark Dreams: Sexual Violence, Homicide, and the Criminal Mind.* New York: St. Martin's Press, 2001.

Helmer, William, with Rich Mattox. *Public Enemies: America's Criminal Past.* New York: Checkmark, 1998.

Hoffmann, Eric van. *A Venom in the Blood.* New York: Donald I. Fine, 1990.

Holdel, Steve. *Black Dahlia Avenger.* New York: Arcade, 2003.

Holmes, Ronald M., and Stephen T. Holmes. *Profiling Violent Crimes,* 3rd ed. Thousand Oaks, CA: Sage, 2002.

—*Murder in America.* Thousand Oaks, CA: Sage, 2001.

Holmes, Ronald, and D. Kim Rossmo. "Geography, Profiling, and Predatory Criminals," in R. Holmes and S. Holmes, *Profiling Violent Crimes.* Thousand Oaks, CA: Sage, 1996.

Horn, David G. *The Criminal Body: Lombroso and the Anatomy of Deviance.* New York: Routledge, 2003.

Houck, Max M. *Trace Evidence Analysis.* New York: Elsevier, 2004.

Howard, Amanda, and Martin Smith. *Rivers of Blood: Serial Killers and Their Victims.* Boca Raton, FL: Upublish, 2004.

Innes, Brian. *Bodies of Evidence.* Pleasantville, NY: Reader's Digest Press, 2000.

—*Profile of a Criminal Mind.* Pleasantville, NY: Reader's Digest Press, 2003.

Iverson, Kenneth. *Demon Doctors: Physicians as Serial Killers.* Tucson, AZ: Galen Press, 2002.

James, Earl. *Catching Serial Killers.* Lansing, MI: International Forensic Services, 1991.

James, Stuart H., and Jon J. Nordby. *Forensic Science: An Introduction to Scientific and Investigative Techniques.* Boca Raton, FL: CRC Press, 2003.

Jeffers, H. Paul. *Who Killed Precious?* New York: St. Martin's, 1991.

Jenkins, Philip. *Using Murder: The Social Construction of Serial Homicide.* New York: Aldine de Gruyter, 1994.

Johnson, Steven. *Mind Wide Open: Your Brain and the Neuroscience of Everyday Life.* New York: Scribner, 2004.

Jones, David A. *History of Criminology: A Philosophical Perspective.* Westport, CT: Greenwood Press, 1986.

Jones, Prudence, and Nigel Pennick. *A History of Pagan Europe.* New York: Barnes & Noble, 1995.

Jones, Richard Glyn, ed. *The Mammoth Book of Women Who Kill.* New York: Carroll & Graf, 2002.

Kelleher, Michael D., and C. L. Kelleher. *Murder Most Rare: The Female Serial Killer.* New York: Dell, 1998.

Kennedy, Ludovic. *Ten Rillington Place*. New York: Simon & Schuster, 1961.

Keppel, Robert D. "Investigation of the Serial Offender: Linking Cases Through Modus Operandi and Signature," in *Serial Offenders: Current Thoughts, Recent Findings*. Louis B. Schlesinger, ed. Boca Raton, FL: CRC Press, 2000.

—*The Riverman: Ted Bundy and I Hunt for the Green River Killer*. With William J. Birnes. New York: Pocket, 1995.

—*Signature Killers*. New York: Pocket, 1997.

—*The Psychology of Serial Killer Investigations*. With William J. Birnes. San Diego: Academic Press, 2003.

Kidder, Tracy. *The Road to Yuba City*. New York: Doubleday, 1974.

Kiehl, K. A., R. D. Hare, J. J. McDonald, and J. Brink. "Semantic and Affective Processing in Psychopaths: An Event-Related Potential (ERP) Study," *Psychophysiology*, (36, 765–774), 1999.

King, Brian, ed. *Lustmord: The Writings and Artifacts of Murderers*. Burbank, California: Bloat Books, 1996.

Krafft-Ebing, Richard von. *Psychopathia Sexualis with Especial Reference to the Antipathic Sexual Instinct: A Medico-Forensic Study*, revised edition. Philadelphia: Physicians and Surgeons, 1928.

Lane, Brian, and Wilfred Gregg. *The Encyclopedia of Serial Killers*. New York: Ballantine, 1992.

Larson, Erik. *The Devil in the White City*. New York: Crown, 2003.

Lee, Henry C., and Frank Tirnady. *Blood Evidence: How DNA Revolutionized the Way We Solve Crimes*. Cambridge, MA: Perseus, 2003.

Leon, Vicki. *Outrageous Women of Ancient Times*. New York: John Wiley & Sons, 1998.

Lester, David. *Serial Killers: The Insatiable Passion*. Philadelphia: Charles Press, 1995.

Lewis, Dorothy O. *Guilty by Reason of Insanity*. New York: Ballantine, 1998.

Leyton, Elliott. *Hunting Humans: The Rise of the Modern Multiple Murderer*. Toronto, Ontario: McLelland and Stewart, Ltd., 1986.

Linedecker, Clifford. *Babyface Killers*. New York: St. Martin's Press, 1999.

Lourie, Richard. *Hunting the Devil: The Pursuit, Capture and Confession of the Most Savage Serial Killer in History*. New York: HarperCollins, 1993.

Lunde, Donald T. *Murder and Madness*. San Francisco: San Francisco Book Co., 1976.

MacDonell, Herbert L. *Bloodstain Patterns*. Corning, NY: Laboratory of Forensic Science, 1993.

Martingale, Moira. *Cannibal Killers*. New York: Carroll & Graf, 1993.

Masters, Brian. *Killing for Company*. New York: Dell, 1993.

Masters, R. E. L., and Eduard Lea. *Perverse Crimes in History*. New York: Julian Press, 1963.

McConnell, Virginia. *Sympathy for the Devil: The Emmanuel Baptist Murders of Old San Francisco*. Westport, CT: Praeger, 2001.

McCrary, Gregg, with Katherine Ramsland. *The Unknown Darkness: Profiling the Predators Among Us*. New York: Morrow, 2003.

—"Are Criminal Profiles a Reliable Way to Find Serial Killers?" *Congressional Quarterly,* Oct 31, 2003.

McNally, Richard. *Remembering Trauma*. Cambridge, MA: Harvard University Press, 2003.

Mendoza, Antonio. *Killers on the Loose*. London: Virgin, 2001.

Michaud, Stephen, and Hugh Aynesworth. *The Only Living Witness: A True Account of Homicidal Insanity*. New York: New American Library, 1983.

Michaud, Stephen G., and Roy Hazelwood. *The Evil That Men Do*. New York: St. Martin's Press, 1998.

Miller, Hugh. *Proclaimed in Blood: True Crimes Solved by Forensic Scientists*. London: Headline, 1995.

—*What the Corpse Revealed: Murder and the Science of Forensic Detection*. New York: St. Martin's Press, 1998.

Millon, Theodore. *Masters of the Mind: Exploring the Story of Mental Illness from Ancient Times to the New Millennium*. New York: John Wiley & Sons, 2004.

Morrison, Helen. *My Life Among Serial Killers*. New York: William Morrow, 2004.

Newton, Michael. *The Encyclopedia of Serial Killers*. New York: Facts on File, 2001.

—*Still at Large*. Port Townsend, WA: Loompanics Unlimited, 1999.

Nickell, Joe, and John Fischer. *Crime Science: Methods of Forensic Detection*. Lexington, KY: University Press of Kentucky, 1999.

Niehoff, Debra. *The Biology of Violence*. New York: Free Press, 1999.

Nietzsche, Friedrich. *The Will to Power*. 1889. W. Kaufmann and R. Hollingdale, trans., New York: Vintage, 1968.

Nordby, Jon. *Dead Reckoning: The Art of Forensic Detection*. Boca Raton, FL: CRC Press, 2000.

Norris, Joel. *Serial Killers*. New York: Doubleday, 1988.

Olsen, Jack. *"I": The Creation of a Serial Killer*. New York: St. Martin's Press, 2002.

—*The Man with the Candy*. New York: Simon & Schuster, 1974.

Owen, David. *Hidden Evidence: Forty True Crimes and How Forensic Science Helped Solve Them*. Buffalo: Firefly Books, 2000.

Parry, Leonard. *Some Famous Medical Trials*. New York: Charles Scribner's Sons, 1928.

Penrose, Valentine, and Alexandre Trocchi. *The Bloody Countess*. London: Calder, 1970.

Perry, Marvin. *A History of the World*. Lawrenceville, NJ: Houghton Mifflin Co., 1985.

Pistorius, Micki. *Catch Me a Killer*. Sandton, South Africa: Penguin, 2000.

Platt, Richard. *The Ultimate Guide to Forensic Science*. London: DK Publishing, 2003.

Putnam, James. "A Unique Murder Case with Applications to the Law," *American Journal of Insanity*. LXXII, No. 4, 1916.

Raine, Adrian and Jose Sanmartin, eds. *Violence and Psychopathy*. New York: Kluwer Academic, 2001.

Ramsland, Katherine. *The Criminal Mind: A Writer's Guide to Forensic Psychology*. Cincinnati: Writer's Digest Books, 2002.

—*The Forensic Science of C.S.I.* New York: Berkley Boulevard, 2001.

—*The Science of Cold Case Files*. New York: Berkley, 2004.

—*Inside the Minds of Mass Murderers: Why They Kill*. Westport, CT: Praeger, 2005.

Ressler, Robert K., and Tom Schachtman. *I Have Lived in the Monster*. New York: St. Martin's Press, 1997.

—*Whoever Fights Monsters*. New York: St. Martin's Press, 1992.

Rolling, Danny, and Sondra London. *The Making of a Serial Killer*. Portland, OR: Feral House, 1996.

Rossmo, D. K. "Geographic Profiling," in *Offender Profiling: Theory, Practice and Research*. Janet L. Jackson and Debra Bekerian, eds. New York: John Wiley & Sons, 1999.

Rule, Ann. *Green River, Running Red*. New York: Free Press, 2004.

—*The Stranger Beside Me*. New York: W. W. Norton, 1980.

—*The I-5 Killer*. New York: Signet, 1989.

—*The Want Ad Killer*. New York: Signet, 1995.

Rumbelow, Donald. *Jack the Ripper: The Complete Casebook*. New York: Contemporary Books, 1988.

Russell, Sue. *Lethal Intent*. New York: Kensington, 2002.

Ryzuk, Mary. *The Gainesville Ripper*. New York: St. Martin's Press, 1994.

Saferstein, Richard. *Criminalistics: An Introduction to Forensic Science*, 7th edition. Englewood Cliffs, NJ: Prentice Hall, 2000.

Schechter, Harold. *The A to Z Encyclopedia of Serial Killers*. New York: Pocket, 1996.

—*Depraved: The Shocking True Story of America's First Serial Killer*. New York: Pocket, 1994.

—*The Serial Killer Files*. New York: Ballantine, 2003.

Schwartz, Anne E. *The Man Who Could Not Kill Enough*. New York: Carol Publishing Group, 1992.

Schwartz, Ted. *The Hillside Strangler*. New York: Signet, 1989.

Scott, Gini Graham. *Homicide: 100 Years of Murder in America*. Los Angeles: Lowell House, 1998.

Sellin, Lawrence. "Outside View: FBI Behind the Anthrax Curve," *Insight on the News*, March 15, 2004.

Seltzer, Mark. *Serial Killers: Death and Life in America's Wound Culture*. London: Routledge, 1998.

Shepherd, Slyvia. *The Mistress of Murder Hill*. www.1stbook.com, 2001.

Sifakis, Car. *The Encyclopedia of American Crime*. New York: Facts on File, 1982.

Simpson, Phillip L. *Psycho Paths: Tracking the Serial Killer Through Contemporary American Film and Fiction*. Carbondale, IL: Southern Illinois University Press, 2000.

Snyder Sachs, Jessica. *Corpse: Nature, Forensics and the Struggle to Pinpoint Time of Death*. Cambridge, MA: Perseus, 2001.

Sparrow, Gerald. *Women Who Murder*. New York: Tower, 1970.

Starrs, James E., with K. Ramsland. *A Voice for the Dead*. New York: Putnam, 2005.

Stewart, James B. *Blind Eye: How the Medical Establishment Let a Doctor Get Away with Murder*. New York: Simon & Schuster, 1999.

Summers, Montague. *The Werewolf*. Secaucus, NJ: Citadel, 1966.

Symons, Julian. *A Pictorial History of Crime: 1840 to the Present*. New York: Bonanza Books, 1966.

Tatar, Maria. *Lustmord: Sexual Murder in Weimar Germany*. Princeton, NJ: Princeton University Press, 1995.

Thorwald, Jurgen. *The Century of the Detective*. New York: Harcourt, Brace & World, 1964.

—*Crime and Science*. New York: Harcourt, Brace & World, 1966.

Tithecott, Richard. *Of Men and Monsters*. Madison, WI: University of Wisconsin Press, 1997.

Tobler, P. N. and C. D. Fiorillo. "Adaptive Coding of Reward Value by Dopamine Neurons." *Science*, 307, March 11, 2005.

Trestrail, John Harris. *Criminal Poisoning*. Totowa, NJ: Humana Press, 2000.

Tullet, Tom. *Strictly Murder: Famous Cases of Scotland Yard's Murder Squad*. New York: St. Martin's Press, 1979.

Vidocq, Francois Eugene. *Memoirs of Vidocq: Master of Crime*. Edinburgh: AK Press, 2003.

Vorpagel, Russell. *Profiles in Murder*. Cambridge, MA: Perseus, 1998.

Vronsky, Peter. *Serial Killers: The Method and Madness of Monsters*. New York: Berkley, 2004.

Wambaugh, Joseph. *The Blooding: The True Story of the Narborough Village Murders*. New York: William Morrow & Co., 1989.

Ward, Bernie. *Bobbie Joe: In the Mind of a Monster*. Boca Raton, FL: Cool Hand Communications, 1995.

Williamson, S. E., T. J. Harpur, and R. D. Hare. "Abnormal Processing of Affective Words by Psychopaths," *Psychophysiology*, (28, 260–273), 1991.

Wilson, Colin. *Murder in the 1940s*. New York: Carroll & Graf, 1993.

Wilson, Colin, and D. Seaman. *The Serial Killers: A Study in the Psychology of Violence*. London: Virgin Publishing, 1992.

Wilson, Duff. "Profiler Can't Recall Why He Said Letter Wasn't from Green River Killer." Seattletimes.com, November 26, 2003.

Wiltz, Sue, with Maurice Godwin. *Slave Master*. New York: Pinnacle, 2004.

Winerman, Lea. "Criminal Profiling: The Reality Behind the Myth," APA publication, 2004.

Winwar, Francis. *The Saint and the Devil*. New York: Harper & Brothers, 1948.

Yochelson, Samuel. *The Criminal Personality*. New York: Jason Aronson, no date.

Index